BETWEEN FORTUNE

AND

PROVIDENCE

*Astrology and the Universe in Dante's
Divine Comedy*

Joseph Crane

The Wessex Astrologer

Published in 2012 by
The Wessex Astrologer Ltd
4A Woodside Road
Bournemouth
BH5 2AZ
England

www.wessexastrologer.com

Copyright Joseph Crane 2011

Joseph Crane asserts the right to be recognised as the author of this work

ISBN 9781902405766

A catalogue record of this book is available at The British Library

Cover design by Tania at Creative Byte, Poole, Dorset

All rights reserved. No part of this work may be used or reproduced in any manner without written permission. A reviewer may quote brief passages.

Contents

Preface		v
Introduction		xiii
Part 1:	Our Redemptive World	1
	The *Inferno*: World Without Light	3
	Purgatorio: Light and Shadow	28
Part 2:	*Paradiso* - Empire of Light	87
	Our Planetary Journey	89
	Beyond the Planets: Time into Timelessness	133
Part 3:	Astrology: Art and Nature	169
	Stars in Heaven, Diviners in Hell	171
	Celestial Nature, Philosophers, and Astrology	225
	Appendix 1: The Divine Comedy as Poetry	257
	Appendix 2: An Astrological Chart for Dante	265
	Bibliography	276
	Index	282

Dante Alighieri

Dedicated to my mother, Dorothy Monesi Crane, and my aunt, Mary Kathryn Crane (1931-2011)

Preface

Dante's *Divine Comedy* tells of a journey of alienation and redemption cast as a guided tour through the Christian afterlife. Composed of over 14,000 lines of rhymed verse, the poem is organized into one hundred 'cantos' that make up three books called *cantica* or canticles, *Inferno*, *Purgatorio*, and *Paradiso*, referring to Hell, Purgatory, and Paradise respectively. The original meaning of the word 'comedy' was a story with a happy outcome rather than the modern implication of humor: this is 'comedy' as opposed to 'tragedy.' The poem's journey is arduous but concludes on a note of personal and universal reconciliation.

Through this tour of an imagined afterlife we ponder qualities of evil and goodness, free will and responsibility, the purification of sin, the nature and means of Heaven's purposes on Earth, and finally we are presented with a poetic vision of eternity. Regardless of the reader's spiritual focus, the *Divine Comedy* is one of literature's most spiritually uplifting creations. It is also a great work of psychological and moral insight, especially into the redemptive journey itself. Even if the particulars are different, Dante's broad critique of his contemporary politics and culture is in some way as relevant to our times as it was to his own. The *Divine Comedy* provides many moments of drama, strong character depiction and a visionary agenda.

Along with its poetry and narrative is a wealth of astronomical and astrological depiction and symbolism that provides much of the *Divine Comedy's* environment. From a 'higher' point of view they reveal a world whose structures descend from the supernatural to the natural, from a divine origin through the stars and planets to the particularities of our lives. From the perspective of the *Divine Comedy's* ascent, the Heavens allow us to see the narrow field of our ordinary concerns, and mark the journey toward a larger vision and greater ability to make a difference in the world.

The poem is also a study of the relationship between fortune and providence. We begin with fortune: all of us are concerned with its vicissitudes and usually it's personal: is the Wheel of Fortune going up or down and how quickly? Often in misfortune we ask ourselves: why is this happening to me? When will all this end? What can I do to make it different? In its own sphere this is perfectly valid.

A more mature approach would be to ask how we can acknowledge and grow from the circumstances that occur in our lives. Perhaps we have caused the difficulties we now experience, but even if they seem to come arbitrarily, they can wake us up into making important changes in our lives. We may find in our problems a summons from the universe, a 'wake-up call' of some kind, and then we may even call our difficulties 'providential' and be grateful for them – usually long afterwards, however.

We may take an even wider view, for perhaps what happens is not about us after all but what the larger world needs from us. In Dante's Christian view, this would be providence or the divine governance of the universe. The word is from the Latin word for 'foreknowledge' and the Greek is *pronoia*.

Fortune is not just about what happens to us personally. As we do, Dante also stands within a particular cultural and historical era. We have the same questions about our age as he had about his own. What has brought humanity into its current confusion and corruption? Why are the most ambitious and covetous of us rewarded in life and the rest of us become their victims? Why is it that, to quote W.B. Yeats, "the best lack all conviction/while the worst are full of passionate intensity"? Is there a way out of this, perhaps an opportunity to change the world? Although the modern reader may be daunted by the amount of local and world history contained within the *Divine Comedy*, one may also find Dante's critique of his age to be applicable and even helpful to understanding our own.[*]

We all live and act on the larger stage of culture and history, giving us greater responsibility than to ourselves alone. How do we attain that larger mind that allows us to think and act for a greater benefit without lapsing into dogmatism or self-righteousness? In Dante's view it is to think of ourselves and our actions in coordination with the providential, as transitory moving aspects of eternity.

---

[*] A historical essay accompanies this volume that can be downloaded. For information go to www.astrologyinstitute.com

This idea of providence finds full expression in the monotheistic world religions, by which a supreme deity has an ongoing involvement in the larger world and in each individual's life. We also find ideas of providence in the ancient world, from the Olympian religion to the philosophical pieties of stoicism. We find this in Babylonian and Egyptian systems that helped foster the origins of Western Astrology. Although not as fully developed, modern astrology includes a notion of providence, usually referred to not as a particular deity but as the 'Universe' or 'Higher Self'.

The underlying issue is of no small importance: what is the meaning or purpose of the ever-changing circumstances of our lives and our worlds? Dante's universe is purposeful and intentional; compared with the vast mind of eternity our ordinary notions of purpose and intention are shallow at best. With its roots in ancient cosmology and the Judeo-Christian heritage, this portrait of a universe governed by divine intent has pervaded Western culture, directly and indirectly, to the present day. This includes the hidden assumptions of many modern astrologers.

This differs greatly from our all-too conventional modern approach: everything is tied together through cause and effect and ripples of chance without intention and purpose. This can become close to nihilism and it has its many modern admirers, particularly in the scientific community. This viewpoint would be considered heretical from Dante's Christian context. It also creates an intellectual environment that most astrologers find destructive to their work.

Between Dante's universe of intention and modern materialistic nihilism is what is usually called a 'systems approach.' In this view smaller and simpler structures coalesce and differentiate to form larger structures. As systems grow more toward greater inclusiveness and complexity, intention and meaning happen along the way. This kind of conceptualizing is attractive to many modern thinkers (and astrologers) but requires much further development. Perhaps we should look backward into the richness of previous traditional formulations and allow ourselves to be challenged and stimulated by them. The past can broaden and deepen our modern understanding.

The *Divine Comedy*'s narrative approaches these issues of meaning and intent through the character of Dante who is the poet himself recast as a younger man. This younger Dante – the pilgrim (as opposed to the older man writing the *Divine Comedy*) – is not Everyman, for that would be too abstract; instead, as commentator Charles Singleton notes, Dante is "Whichever Man".[1] He can stand for me and you and humanity in general simultaneously – not as an abstract entity but just like us, embodied as a singular irreproducible person.

The narrative begins with the younger Dante, a spiritual and moral slacker on the cusp of personal disaster and in dire need of divine intervention. Dante the Poet has placed the narrative about 10 – 15 years earlier in his life – when he was beginning a successful political career in Florence. The poet writing later knows that within two years of the narrative of the *Divine Comedy*, he will be unjustly banished from his native city, never to return. His lifelong ties to community will be cut: he is to leave his family and loved ones, the place and city of his ancestors, and be fated to live off the generosity of others. Our pilgrim is the hopeful and successful young Dante, whose upcoming calamity provides much of the poem's dramatic force and, ironically, its relevance to our own lives. In the *Divine Comedy's* narrative, the 'wake-up call' of Dante's exile was preceded by his journey through the Christian afterlife. In real life, what Dante learned from the calamity of his exile would become the *Divine Comedy*.

Now we begin to explore stars and planets and the wheels of Heaven and its relevance to the poem.

In the *Divine Comedy* both personal and universal factors are intertwined with the heavens. According to an astrologer's understanding, stars and planets move rhythmically and regularly within our seemingly random ups and downs and help explain our lives' conditions and how they continually change. The stars and planets are also higher images that beckon up toward a greater perspective.

For Dante, the stars and planets are the instruments of Heaven by which Divine Purpose manifests in our individual and collective lives. In the *Divine Comedy*, the stars and planets guide us on the journey and are also the means by which we take our places in a larger universe. Dante, who clearly disliked and mistrusted career astrologers like me and perhaps like you, nevertheless viewed the universe in an astrological way.

I first address some legitimate concerns you may have about the medieval poet and his Christian work. Then I take up the poem's opening scene and its symbolic depiction of the pilgrim's spiritual crisis.

Part One and Part Two review the narrative and characters of the poem and its astronomical and astrological backdrop. Part One is the journey down through Hell and then up, culminating in the reunion of Dante and his long-lost love Beatrice at the top of Purgatory's Mountain.

Through the *Inferno* and the early cantos of the *Purgatorio*, we are narrowly concerned with the ups and downs of personal and cultural fortune. Noting the earthly and rugged terrain of Hell, we see that the poet used the elemental and physical qualities of astrology's planets – especially the malefics Mars and Saturn – to help organize Hell. On Purgatory's Mountain we will also contemplate the Seven Cardinal Sins and their relationships to astrology's seven visible planets; in this realm we consider astrology's planets in a psychological manner.

Part Two is the journey through Heaven toward the vision of God and a fleeting understanding of how the universe works. Paradise is eternally day and is constructed from astrology's stars and planets and the realms above. In Paradise the worldly elements become increasing quantities of light, and the planetary symbolism becomes a description of the best human qualities. As we continue through the planets, fortune becomes reconciled with providence, and in the Sphere of Mars Dante hears the prophecy about his future and Heaven's intent for him in his lifetime. We leave the sphere of the planets and, from the upper reaches of Paradise we, along with pilgrim and guide, look downwards onto the small Earth itself: we take on the viewpoint of providence.

In Paradise, we gradually make the transition from being in time to timelessness. Signaled by the image of the stars vanishing at daybreak, the stars and planets disappear altogether and what appears is the Highest Heaven, beyond time and space. At the very end of the *Divine Comedy* we briefly glimpse the changing universe and the structure of divinity. In the end, both fortune and providence have become temporal aspects of eternity.

Part Three begins with a survey of the art of astrology in the *Divine Comedy*. You will see that Dante's lucky stars contribute to the narrative of the poem, yet *Inferno* 20 places astrologers in Hell along with diviners and practitioners of magic. We will view the sad track and the people of the fourth Malebolge or "Evil Pit".

The discussion of astrology in *Inferno* 20 opens up wider fields of inquiry. If diviners and magicians are in Hell, we need to discuss Dante's and our understanding of divination and magic. Additionally, what is the place in the *Divine Comedy* for the related but more religiously tinged concepts of prophecy and miracle? Part Three concludes with discussion of nature and super-nature and the place of astrology.*

The art of astrology also stands between fortune and providence. Astrology provides a means to find fortune's content and its timing. It may also help disclose one's life purpose – the realm of providence – and help us appreciate the universe and our own lives as purposeful.

If Parts One and Two represent the upward journey from Earth to the Heavens, Part Three explores life and form moving downward from Heaven to Earth. As we note the complexities of astrological signification and causation within the *Divine Comedy*, we will explore parallel ways in which modern astrologers conceive the relationship between astrology and nature. Part Three concludes with a brief exploration of influences of Christian Neoplatonism and Aristotle on the *Divine Comedy*; we will also see that modern astrology contains the same influences.

This present work does not dwell on Dante's poetic form. I assuage my guilt by providing the original Italian in translation when appropriate. Appendix 1 considers two passages from the *Purgatorio*, looking at their poetic style and comparing different versions of them in English. This includes the famous moment of Venus' appearance in the predawn sky when the pilgrims step out of Hell. Appendix 1 gives us a chance to compare different translation styles and to glimpse the poem in a different way.

Appendix 2 looks at possibilities for Dante's astrological chart. In Dante's works there are some tantalizing clues that he had a sense of his own astrological chart. Could we use these clues to arrive at a plausible chart for him? As an astrologer how could I not attempt such a project? A proposed astrological natal chart should reflect the character of Dante, account for his lucky stars that gave him his gifts, and give symbolic indications for major events in his life. This is the subject of Appendix 2.

Let me conclude with a word about my most important sources. There is a wealth of commentarial literature on Dante and his great poem.

---

* I add the words "super-nature" to distinguish the traditional concept of nature from a purely materialistic expression of nature we often find in the modern sciences.

There are many contributions in English that are directly relevant to this book.

I begin with Edward Moore's 1903 essay that is specifically concerned with the astronomy of the poem. This was a very good beginning, for Moore's essay goes into great detail about many of the difficult astronomical allusions in the *Paradiso*. Yet Moore's essay does not place its astronomical allusions within the poem's thematic context nor does it concern itself with astrology.

Alison Cornish's *Reading Dante's Stars* (2000) picks up where Moore left off. I have gained much from her contextual style of rendering the poem's astronomy and her many fine interpretations of Dante's astronomical verse.

A series of essays by John Freccero have been published in book form as *Dante: The Poetics of Conversion* (1986). Freccero's work has shown me the philosophical and spiritual possibilities embedded within the poem's astronomical imagery.

There are some essays about Dante's astrology in English: Richard Kay's *Dante's Christian Astrology* (1994) is a good source of information on the abundant astrological imagery found in the *Paradiso*. Kay also presents the astrological sources that the poet himself probably used.

A recent version of *Paradiso* (2010) by Durling and Martinez specifically addresses the astrology of Dante's poem in an understanding and sympathetic way. I highly recommend this last book to the interested reader who wants to learn more about astrology in Dante's works.

For translations, texts, and textual commentary of the *Divine Comedy*, there is much to choose from. For versions that provide the Italian alongside the English and include detailed commentaries, I have used recent works by the Hollanders (2000, 2003, and 2007) and Durling/Martinez (1996, 2003, and 2010). An older commentary on the *Paradiso* by Charles Singleton (1973) has also been particularly helpful. All have been inseparable from me during this project and I am grateful for their companionship.

And then were those who helped me bring this work to life. Many people read and commented on parts of the text and gave helpful feedback, especially Michael Fagan, Diane Horton, Liz Rozan, and Sarah Fuhro and my sisters Annie, Mary, and Judy Crane. Lucy Gedrites went through the text thoroughly and commented on matters great and small.

Patrizia Nava helped check the Italian and Jeffrey Jackson helped with a final read-through. I also want to thank Professor Ronald Martinez of Brown University for his encouragement and a helpful perspective. Most thanks to my fiancée Penny Burke, who never imagined she would learn so much about fourteenth century Italian poetry. She helped with every stage of this project and forced me into realms of clarity hitherto unexplored by me.

As children raise their parents, developing and writing *Between Fortune and Providence* has also helped raise me. I am especially grateful to Margaret Cahill of The Wessex Astrologer for her unflagging confidence in a project that, like any spiritual journey, has had momentary epiphanies, many dark nights, and finally some understanding.

Notes

1. Singleton, C. (1958), p.5.

Introductions

To My Friends who are Astrologers

My aspiration is for astrologers and astrology students to be inspired to read the *Divine Comedy* and make it their own. In that way they can further their own understanding of the cultural and historical context of their work. As astrologers increase their appreciation of what they do, they will become better understood and appreciated by the culture at large. This work is a small attempt in that direction.

But first I need to address several concerns that many modern astrologers may have about Dante and his great poem. Dante is a medieval Catholic, an ardent believer in 'conventional religion' and particularly in an institution that has been unfriendly to astrology for centuries. The poet also puts magicians and diviners – including the renowned astrologers Michael Scot and Guido Bonatti – in Hell. Their eternal destiny is to walk around a large circle with their heads twisted backwards. Often their punishment is what astrologers have heard about the *Divine Comedy*; they surmise with reason that the poem contains a blanket condemnation of astrology on religious grounds in the style of Augustine or modern Christian fundamentalism.

Dante was a poet and the *Divine Comedy* is a work of *fiction*; what can an astrologer possibly learn from a work of fiction? Finally, although there is much medieval astronomy that has some resemblance to astrology, there are no particular astrological interpretative techniques used in the poem. Why, then, would a busy astrologer bother with this long and complicated work of literature?

We can address the first concern by drawing a distinction between religion that is divisive and spirituality that contains essential truth. Many modern astrologers are interested in spirituality and applying astrology's symbol systems to this area, and in my view there is no better resource than Dante's *Divine Comedy*. I write this confidently, having explored different versions of astrology influenced by different spiritual approaches. I expect that the poem's riches will provide inspiration and challenges to many spiritually-inclined astrologers.

When I was a new astrologer, I was strongly drawn to the work of twentieth-century astrologer Dane Rudhyar. On a trolley ride through Boston I was reading some of Rudhyar's speculations on what he called "galacticity" from his *The Galactic Dimension of Astrology*.

> "The galactic center is not occupied by an enormous mass of matter like a super-Sun, but could be better compared to the hub of a wheel. At the galactic core the cosmic force which in our physical world of dark planets we call gravitational – or its galactic analogue – must be condensed and or concentrated. At this core, which may be what recently astronomers have thought of as a "white hole", spirit may surge outward from a higher dimension or possibly another universe."[1]

Suddenly I was no longer reading a description of a symbolic galactic core but a modern recasting of Dante's final vision of Paradise. The galactic center was like the center of a wheel that seemed lifted out of the last cantos of the *Paradiso*. For the medieval poet, the center was not a higher dimension but God himself beyond space and time. (We will see there are other interesting connections between the fourteenth century poet and the twentieth century astrologer.)

I went back to the version of the *Divine Comedy* I had read years before and also found newer translations and more complete commentaries. I found that the poem contained far greater riches than I had previously recognized. In contrast to its profundity, I began to find modern astrology's spiritual dimensions rather thin. I wanted something richer and more provocative for my own understanding and my work with clients.

The *Divine Comedy* abounds with psychological and spiritual truths that are meaningful to people from different traditions. I suggest that you approach Dante's orthodoxy sympathetically, for if you don't, you will miss much. Because the poet lived during the culmination of a thousand years of theology and the flowering of the Scholastic movement in philosophy, his personal understanding was interwoven with a conceptual approach that is systematic and profound. While you may not agree with all of his conclusions, the thoughtfulness and completeness of this universe can help us develop our own understanding.

All religious traditions have similar teachings about how people grow spiritually and what obstacles they face along the way. The pilgrim's upward journey can reveal motifs that are universal. In our promise and in our confusion, we are much the same everywhere and over the course of history. We can then ask ourselves, "Is the final goal of a spiritual journey the same or different among different traditions?" At the end of Part Two, when encountering *Paradiso* 33 and the vision of God and the universe, you may consider different ways to answer this.

Part Three discusses freedom and free will, necessity and contingency, and the order of nature and super-nature. They all relate to astrology as we understand and practice it. The medieval poet will give modern astrologers much to think about.

Why would an astrologer be interested in a medieval poem, a *fiction* about a Christian afterlife? For many this is not an issue, but for some it will be. I counter with a Jewish proverb you may know:

Question: *What is truer than truth?* Answer: *A story.*

Anybody who has attempted to teach philosophy knows that students will personally and intelligently relate to movies like *Bladerunner* or *The Matrix*, when these same students are completely lost when presented with the same philosophical questions in a classroom setting. Much of the most important knowledge and wisdom we impart and receive are from our activity of telling each other stories. Stories allow us to relate to situations in an intensely personal and meaningful way. The *Divine Comedy* is one such work that discloses truth through means of imagination and literary artifice.

Prominent astrologer and author Liz Greene says this in another way when discussing astrology itself.

> "As the cultural context of science changes in the post-modern era, the sharp distinction between astrology as science and astrology as art, allegory, philosophy, poetic metaphor, symbolic language or stellar religion becomes increasingly meaningless."[2]

Miraculously, Dante's great poem gives us all the features that Ms. Greene mentions, blurring the boundary between 'fiction' and 'nonfiction' perhaps into something greater than either.

Sadly, not all of my astrology readers have affinity for or even sympathy with poetry. I can only hope that this distant encounter with a great poet from the past can open up new possibilities for you.

Another objection concerns the lack of specific astrological technique in the poem. However, I argue that a modern astrologer is in a unique position to read this poem with understanding.

Much of the *Divine Comedy*'s depictions of planets, stars, the zodiac, and the celestial sphere will be of great interest to the modern astrologer. Purgatory tells time using the horizon, the path of the Sun or Moon, and Paradise utilizes the celestial sphere, even dwells on it. The structure of Paradise is the medieval cosmology that astrologers also know well. Instead of using the as-yet unknown outer planets to account for the transpersonal dimension of life, Dante offers our familiar visible planets in sanctified form. We also see that the poet's depictions of rivers, rocks and ledges, and the random patterning of the earth's physical features are contrasted to and are connected with the orderly movements of the Heavens. Dante's poetic world is both hierarchical and integrated.

Importantly, all three regions of the afterlife comprise sets of circles that correspond to groupings or sequences of astrology's planets. In Hell the planets are elemental and show us benefics out of control and malefics fully expressive of their own ill natures. In Purgatory planets are more oblique but are rendered psychologically within correlations between Seven Planets and Seven Cardinal Sins.

In the *Purgatorio*, the canticle that is the closest to our modern concerns and with a geographical and stellar environment similar to our own, there is much that will be familiar to a modern astrologer. Much of its content will be on astronomical and astrological expressions of the processes of spiritual transformation.

In Heaven the planetary natures are obvious and at their highest levels of manifestation. At last in Paradise we go beyond even the planets and finally we depart from the stars themselves. For here we approach the timeless and the vision of God himself.

Now I address the eternal ill-fortune of Michael Scot and Guido Bonatti and how it reflects Dante's assessment of astrology. Did the poet condemn astrologers? Well, yes. Both these men are in Hell and there is much to explain about that. You may also have heard that high up in Heaven, astride the stars of Gemini, Dante gives praise to those stellar bodies that brought about his talent. How does Dante reconcile these two views?

It is not enough to produce evidence from the poem that Dante 'believed' in things that would appear astrological to a modern person. How do we know this is not just poetic artifice? We know this from Dante's earlier writings and because the *Divine Comedy never* uses poetic artifice for its own sake.

What kind of astrology would Dante 'believe' in and what does this mean in the context of his view of reality – earthly and ultimate? How does the poet's sense of astrology square with divination, magic and science, or theology and metaphysics, or fortune and providence?

Part Three will go into these issues in detail. Although the *Divine Comedy* was written during a flowering of medieval astrology, its depiction of astrology is closer to a modern viewpoint and modern life – yet it remains rooted in basic human concerns that were his and are also our own.

The Modern Reader's Journey

There are broader concerns I now need to address. Conforming to the prejudices of his time, Dante's attitude toward other religions lacks tolerance. Mohammad's place is in Hell among the eternally mutilated inciters of discord. Nor does Dante seem bothered by some of the excesses of the crusades against Islam or against the 'heretics' of his previous two centuries. Dante's discussions of God's 'justice' and the destiny of the Jews tell us much about the conventional attitudes of his time. See *Paradiso* 6.92-93, and 7.43-51.

On the other hand, Dante's attitudes toward homosexuality seem more modern and 'enlightened' than his medieval contemporaries. Although we see 'sodomites' running a hot track in *Inferno* Cantos 15 and 16, homosexuals in *Purgatorio* 26 receive more sympathetic treatment.

Those influenced by modern feminist thinking may also have trouble with the poem. Dante's avowed love for Beatrice, with whom he had hardly spoken in real life, can feel like one more example of male romantic projection: love based on a man's one-sided longing without reference to the real woman. Yet his love for this particular woman becomes his connection to the divine and his portal to salvation: she becomes not only muse but a personal incarnation of divinity.

Dante's political and economic ideas may seem a bit strange to us. His ideal of a universal (Roman) empire and universal (Catholic) church may strike us as totalitarian, yet the re-establishment of a universal empire is a theme throughout European history and cannot be confined to Dante or his time. When we look at Italy and Europe of the thirteenth and early fourteenth centuries we may also sympathize with the poet's desire to see an end to the conflict and institutional decay of his time.

The *Divine Comedy* betrays extensive hostility to what we might call free market capitalism, much of which the poet would consider usury and culturally sanctioned avarice. Writing this after so many recent worldwide financial upheavals, I suspect people will have less trouble with his criticisms than they might have had earlier.

Let's take on the subject of the regions of the afterlife as depicted in the *Divine Comedy*. We will encounter some of our modern stereotypes. You will miss much by thinking that the *Divine Comedy* is just Christian allegory replete with standard caricatures of sinners and saints. Throughout the work we find inhabitants of the afterlife to be sharply drawn as people with mixed qualities like us. Throughout the work one finds a strong and profound engagement with *this* world and the complex people who inhabit it.

Readers who take this journey with Dante and Virgil will find that the *Divine Comedy*'s Hell and its inhabitants are fascinating, provocative and not always unsympathetically drawn. At the same time the *Inferno* is a systematic presentation of human frailty and evil: their origins and developments, their seductions and many unhappy outcomes. The *Inferno* also shows different imitative responses to the banality and – toward the bottom of Hell – the naked intensity of evil. Instead of being a quaint artifact of a strange medieval imagination, Dante's *Inferno* is an insightful psychological and moral document that easily applies to modern culture. As for its form, Dante's Hell is like a funnel spiraling down toward the center of the earth that contains people who are eternally condemned for their sins.

Emerging from Hell we arrive at the southern ocean directly across from Jerusalem and the mountain of Purgatory, the setting for the second canticle. In Purgatory souls become cleansed of their sins and God's grace descends. In the first cantos of the *Purgatorio*, we will see many souls who are still waiting to take this part of the journey.

Different religions have different labels for purification, variously called confession, atonement, reflection, taking a fearless moral inventory. All these versions of purification have ingredients of honesty and a willingness to surrender or give away our limiting tendencies. The *Purgatorio* articulates this universal process. On the way up toward Heaven, we see humility and willingness which in turn allow the grace of healing divinity to come downwards. We also find much spiritual laziness '*acedia*' that keeps them (and us) from moving forward.

Dante's Paradise differs greatly from our modern caricatures of Heaven. Its citizens are blissful, experiencing the fulfillment of all human loves and longings. Dante crafts some of his most sublime poetry to describe this. In the *Paradiso* there is eloquence, philosophical and theological dialogue and great concern about the affairs back on Earth, that "small place (or 'threshing floor') that drives us insane," to paraphrase lines from the end of *Paradiso* Canto 22. Dante's Paradise is at the summit of the world but is not removed from the world.

When does this whole thing happen?

We begin our specific examination of the *Divine Comedy* by considering the time of the journey through the afterlife. Attempting to establish the date of the poem's journey tells us much about the poem itself.

The *Divine Comedy* begins sometime during the morning of Good Friday, the day of the death of Christ. On Good Friday, Dante realizes he is "lost in a dark wood" of spiritual wandering. He meets Virgil and they begin their descent into Hell. Dante and his guide Virgil climb out of Hell onto the island of Purgatory's mountain at sunrise on Easter Sunday. The symbolism of the timing is rich: Dante emerges from Hell – like Christ had emerged from Hell on a different mission – and came from the dead on Easter Sunday.

Dante symbolically brings together the personal and universal redemptive processes. Easter is after the spring equinox, a time of renewal. Easter is on a Sunday – the day allocated to the Sun. We also know it's at the time of a *waning* Moon – the overcoming of the Moon by the Sun after the Full Moon, symbolizing the victory of light over the power of darkness.

The Sun is the symbol of clarity, the correct path, and the rhythmic order of the cosmos. The Sun's symbolism takes us all the way to the Sphere of the Sun in Paradise, wherein reside those who in life manifested aspects of divine wisdom. To the poet, the Moon is a darker force and represents more regressive tendencies. Easter's multifaceted ascendance of the Sun over the Moon sets up the interaction between the two lights that we will see throughout the *Commedia*.

We also know that the activity of the *Divine Comedy* is set for 1300, when Dante was thirty five. It was also the year of a papal jubilee, at which time pilgrims to Rome could receive special dispensation for their previous sins. These are the planetary configurations for that Good Friday morning when the pilgrim discovers he has lost the true path.

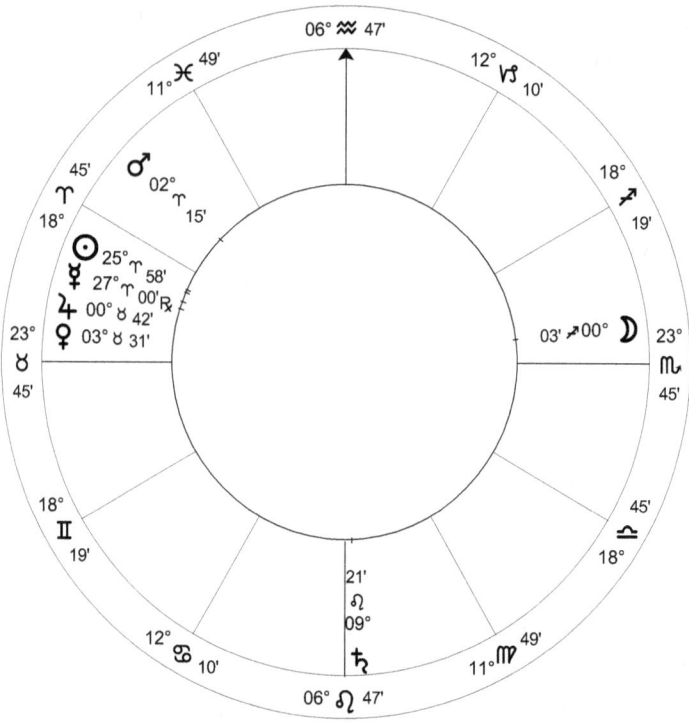

'Lost in the Woods', April 8 1300, 7.00 am LMT -2:20:56
Jerusalem, Israel.

Note that the Sun's position at 25 Aries 58 seems a bit late for April 8. This is the date from the 'old style' Julian calendar that gradually brought the spring equinox back in time. In Dante's time the vernal equinox would have occurred on March 12, not March 20, an eight day difference. Europe gradually changed to the more accurate Gregorian calendar late in the sixteenth century. Dante and his educated contemporaries were well aware of this discrepancy between their Julian calendar and the vernal equinox.

The greater difficulty with the year 1300 is with the celebrated rising of Venus at the beginning of *Purgatorio* Canto 1. According to *Purgatorio's* opening lines, Venus is in Pisces rising ahead of the Sun in Aries. Venus hides the stars of Pisces that surround her. In 1300 it is the Sun that would hide Venus. Although Venus in 1300 would be in the *constellation* Pisces and could conceal its stars, as Dante says in *Purgatorio* 1.21, Venus could not have appeared before the Sun in 1300 because that year's Venus was eight degrees *behind* the Sun.

For centuries scholars have known that Venus was a morning star in Pisces not in 1300, *but in the following year 1301.* Over a century ago, somebody discovered an almanac used in Dante's time, the *Almanach of Prophacius Judaeus*. Interestingly, the version that Dante probably used begins in 1300 but gives Venus' position for 1301.[3]

In this Almanac, Venus' position for 1301 was 20° Pisces which places this planet at the beginning of the *constellation* Pisces, far enough ahead of the Sun to be visible in the morning sky, and indeed the planet could cover over the stars of that faint constellation. The strong symbolic presence of Venus in Pisces presenting the beginning moment of the spiritual climb may override the question of Dante's almanac source. It is possible that Dante may have gotten his facts wrong – but at this pivotal moment in the *Divine Comedy* it's hard to imagine Venus not being in the zodiacal sign Pisces. It is Venus' place of exaltation in astrology and the sign of the Fish would remind Christian readers of Christ.

Now onto the Moon's position in the 1300 chart. At the end of *Inferno* 20 we learn from Virgil that the Moon had been full when Dante was lost in the dark woods. Although during the morning of Good Friday 1300 the Moon could be rising, the Full Moon would have been a few days earlier when the Moon was in Libra. This would be troublesome until we look at *Inferno* 20 more closely, for we discover that *all* the facts provided in that canto are subject to doubt.

A Full Moon, especially to somebody lost and confused, could have an imposing and threatening presence. During the remainder of the poem's narrative the Moon will begin to wane and less than two weeks later will sink into the Sun's rays. There is some important symbolism here: being lost in the dark wood, as Dante says at the very beginning of the poem, was the point from where things would become much better for him. (*Inferno* 1:8-9). In this way Dante's trials and tribulations mirror Christianity's Holy Week and mankind's redemption.

As with Venus, the Full Moon's symbolism may outweigh its position on April 8, 1300. In those days the Moon's position was very difficult to determine from almanacs alone – the Moon's motion is too irregular and too fast for measurements of his day to be reliably accurate. It would have been extremely easy to get the facts wrong. That is the easy answer.

Another possibility intrigues me. I move to the opening sequence of *Purgatorio* 9, an ambiguous and controversial passage that we will discuss in depth later. In one interpretation of this passage, the Moon is rising in the East with the stars of Scorpio forming gems about her forehead. This poses a solution to the Moon's position, for in 1301 the Moon was in the tropical sign Scorpio but would those be the stars of the constellation Scorpio? If we stay with the Moon's 1300 position, the *constellation* Scorpio would rise ahead of the Moon: if the Moon is a face, the stars of Scorpio are like a garland of pearls around her.

Throughout the *Divine Comedy* Dante appears to fuse constellations of the zodiac with the tropical signs, although their positions were apart by 15°. Was he naïve? Was he taking 'poetic license,' a desire to fudge some technical matters to communicate with his less-educated medieval audience?

The poet of the *Divine Comedy* is never naïve. Dante was knowledgeable about the precession of the equinox although the calculations during his time were different than ours: the precessional rate is 1° every 72 years although, following Ptolemy and many others, he thought the precessional rate was 1° every one hundred years. In his previous *Da Vita Nuova* or the *New Life*, he casts the time of Beatrice's birth to precessional factors.* In his later *Convivio*, Dante mentions

---

* "Nine times already since my birth had the heaven of light returned to the self-same point almost, as concerns its own revolution, when first the glorious Lady of my mind was made manifest to mine eyes… She had already been in this life for so short as that, within her time, the starry heaven had moved towards the Eastern quarter one of the twelve parts of a degree; so that she appeared to me at the beginning of her ninth year almost and I saw her almost at the end of my ninth year." (*The New Life*, trans. Rossetti. p.3)

precessional motion possibly being the motion of the ninth sphere of heaven, the *Primum Mobile*.

During Dante's lifetime and for centuries before and afterwards, the ordinary person would have had a clearer sense of the positions and movements of the constellations than specific planetary positions and movements. The constellation Scorpio would be quite dominant in the spring evening sky and the Moon's position following this constellation could be familiar to all – whether the Moon was 'really' there at that time in 1300. For these reasons we'll use the planetary position of April 1300 to render the time and space of the *Divine Comedy*'s journey.

The Prologue Scene or "You Can't Get There from Here"

The pilgrim's journey is necessitated by a spiritual crisis that many of us have experienced in our lives. Dante's first tercet may be the most frequently cited three lines in the history of poetry.* Its opening tercet describes the existential situation of the pilgrim at the beginning of the *Divine Comedy*. Out of respect for the importance of this verse, I will first provide the Italian by itself.

> "Nel mezzo del cammin di nostra vita
> mi ritrovai per una selva oscura,
> ché la diritta via era smarrita." (Inferno I.1-3)

Here is what this says: in the middle (*mezzo*) of our life's journey (*di nostra vita*), I found myself (*ritrovai*) in a dark forest (*selva oscura*), for the right way (*la diritta via*) was lost.

This opening brings together the personal and the universal: the story begins in the middle of *our* life. Like the pilgrim Dante, we find ourselves lost, suddenly not knowing where we are. We were distracted or simply numb and now we cannot figure out where we are, where the wrong turn was, or how we get back onto the right road. This has happened for most of us sometime in life, perhaps many times.

Immediately a solution presents itself to the pilgrim. He – the character of the poem whom I will call "the pilgrim" – has reached the foot of a hill at the edge of this fearful valley. He looks up and sees

---

* The only possible exception may be a haiku about a pond and a frog written by the seventeenth-century Japanese poet Basho.

that the Sun, the planet that can show the right way, is shining on the hill. Now he can get his bearings and find his way out of the darkness. His body is weary and he struggles toward the top to find his way out. Alluding to a will that is too weak to accomplish what it sets out to do, the pilgrim's "firm foot" drags along below.* A leopard appears and blocks his path.

Then, at the beginning of the poem, we get the *Divine Comedy*'s first astronomical reference; although placed at its beginning these lines already anticipate the poem's solution. The pilgrim sees the Sun rising, accompanied by the stars of spring. This gives him hope.

This is the morning sky with *the Sun in Aries surrounded by planets in Aries*. This was thought of as the configuration of the Heavens at the creation of the world and also in the 'holy week' of Passover and Easter. We will encounter the sacred symbolism of Aries again and again in the *Divine Comedy*; these lines evoke the first sign of the zodiac to express the created universe and an auspicious time to make a beginning.

But Dante fails to move toward the Sun. The moment may be perfect but the means are not at hand to arrive at a successful outcome. What has happened? Although the leopard does not now intimidate Dante once he saw the Sun and planets in Aries, a raging hungry lion then blocks the path and drives him back in fear. Then a she-wolf, all skin and bones, appears and Dante retreats and despairs.

What do these three beasts represent? Nobody is quite sure and there are many ideas about this. Some have suggested that they allude to the insignias of three families of Florence. This ambiguity may be in keeping with the dreamlike nature of the opening of the first canto.

These three animals are mentioned elsewhere in the poem. The leopard is referred to in *Inferno* 16.106-108 as a possible symbol for fraud. An uncertain consensus has built up over the years that the leopard is lust, the lion pride, and the she-wolf avarice.[4] During his journey through Purgatory, Dante identifies his character with lust and pride (along with anger) and symbolically purifies himself of them. He presents avarice

---

* See Freccero, "*The Firm Foot on the Journey without a Guide*" (1985). " Ever since Adam's sin, man's ability to see the good has outstanded his ability to do it on his own, for in the life without sanctifying grace, the middle ground of which St. Paul was so painfully aware, only one foot takes the forward step." p.44.

as more a problem of his society and culture than for himself. Perhaps they are not sins particularly belonging to the pilgrim but are symbols of the inclinations toward sin that we all have, those habitual patterns over which we tend to attain only temporary victories without major transformation.[5]

Although Dante's motive to get back on track is correct and the time is excellent, he cannot find his way to the right path by himself. He needs help from the outside – or from Above. According to Dante's Christian belief, one requires God's grace in addition to our efforts to rise above ourselves.

Dante, despairing, sees a person nearby and begs him for help. The man soon identifies himself a historical figure, the Roman poet Virgil whom Dante considered an inspiration and literary ancestor. Dante's character of Virgil, an inhabitant of the region of Hell set aside for "virtuous pagans", will escort him through much of the afterlife. The Heavens sent Virgil knowing that Dante needed an intervention.

Why Virgil? The historical Roman poet was renowned for his epic poetry in ancient Rome. He seems rather out of place guiding Dante through a Christian afterlife. It is like Isaac Newton showing you a space ship or Thomas Jefferson showing you the Internet. Yet the writer of the *Divine Comedy* was foremost a poet and therefore chose the poet Virgil, an artistic poetic model and comrade. In the *Inferno* but especially in the *Purgatorio*, it is through Virgil that we will meet other poets and converse with them. In the *Purgatorio*, poetry and other art forms become an important topic of conversation. If the *Divine Comedy* were a writing of speculative philosophy perhaps Aristotle would have been his guide.

Virgil wrote two works that figure prominently in the *Divine Comedy*. The shorter poem, the Fourth *Eclogue*, was thought to foretell the birth of Christ; this poem makes a strong appearance in the *Purgatorio*.

Dante was a sophisticated and attentive reader of Virgil's epic *Aeneid* and the great Roman epic permeates the poem. The *Aeneid*'s historical perspective is foundational to Dante's entire poem. Both works deal with history as divinely providential and Dante the pilgrim becomes like the epic's hero Aeneas. The action of the *Aeneid* culminates in the founding of Rome; Dante's poem takes place during a time of crisis in European history in which a new beginning and a new Rome is sought. As Aeneas and many others had a hard task to fulfill divine prophecy and establish

Rome, Dante and his readers have a similarly hard task, in conformity with prophecy, to correct and renew Christian Europe.

Dante's character Virgil is a wonderful literary creation. If one thinks of the first guide solely as symbol for "reason unaided by faith", one misses the completeness of Dante's depiction of him: Virgil is fatherly and wise, occasionally gullible and insecure, and, as we reach the upper reaches of Purgatory, increasingly out of his depth.

The pilgrim's personal situation is dire and he needs a crash course in reality on his way to becoming whole and right. Previously he thought he could get out of the dark wood on his own: this was an error of pride and of underestimating the depth of his difficulty. Instead he must first go through Hell where people suffer a "second death", through Purgatory where people suffer but with hope for salvation to come, and finally to Heaven where those who are saved reside. The character Dante, and we by implication, must undergo a long and difficult journey – the end of which is the fulfillment of all of our longings.

Notes
1. Rudhyar, D. *The Galactic Dimension of Astrology* (1975) New York: Aurora Press, p.156.
2. Liz Greene, "Is Astrology a Divinatory System?", *Culture and Cosmos*, Vol. 12 no. 1, Spring/Summer, p.25.
3. Moore, Edward. "The Almanac of Jacob ben Machir ben Tibbon" (Latin: Profacius) c.1300. *Modern Language Review* Vol.3, No.4 (July 1908) pp.376-378.
4. Hollander (2000) pp.16-17.
5. Freccero, John (1985) p.46.

Part One

Our Redemptive World

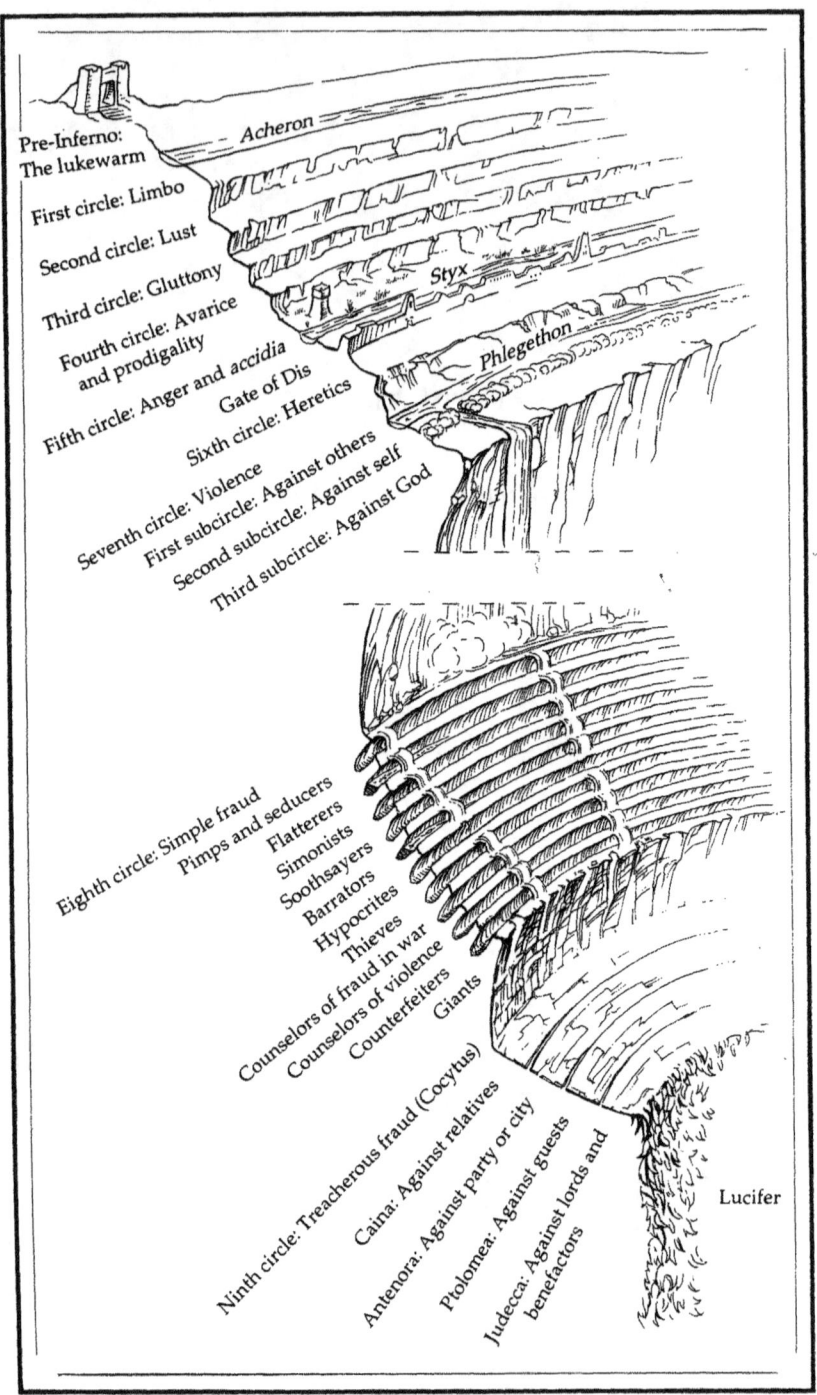

The Structure of Dante's Inferno
The Divine Comedy of Dante Alighieri: Volume 1: Inferno: Inferno Vol 1 by Dante Alighieri, Ronald L. Martinez, Robert M. Durling and Robert Turner (1996). Illustration p.xvi. Reproduced by permission of Oxford University Press, Inc.

The *Inferno*: World without Light

Dante and Virgil begin their journey through Hell at sunset – the best time to enter the realms of darkness. While the approaching night calls other creatures to their rest, Dante prepares himself as if for battle.

At the beginning of the Canto 3, they have reached the threshold of Hell. The gate has an inscription above which announces that this place was created by divine justice, its Maker defined as absolute power, wisdom, and love that is the doctrine of the Christian Trinity. The last line of the inscription is well known and I have heard it several times as I've entered different places of employment. "Abandon all hope, ye who enter here" is the popular rendering.

What follows is the world and its worst features; our world, Dante's world, they may as well be one and the same in this realm.

After passing through the gates, Dante and Virgil meet the first group of souls before actually entering Hell. These souls are usually called 'trimmers' – they are those who could not choose between good and evil and neither Heaven nor Hell can accept them. They wander around futilely, lamenting, being bitten by insects, and following a blank flag.

Similar to the traditions of ancient epic, souls condemned to Hell must be brought across the River Acheron by Charon the ferryman. Dante and Virgil are soon within a large crowd at the side of the river and Charon speaks to them: "you wicked souls here," the ferryman exclaims, "do not ever hope you will ever again see the sky (*cielo* – that also means 'Heaven'), for you are to be led to the other shores, the place of fire, ice, and shadow." (*Inferno* 3:84-87) After Charon separates Dante and Virgil from the crowd, we see the crowd respond to Charon's proclamation: they curse God, their parents, the time and place and 'seed' of their conception and the day of their birth. (*Inferno* 3.100-106) We will return to this scene below when we discuss fortune and divine justice. The condemned are led weeping and wailing to the boats that lead them to Hell.

> ### Hell's Plumbing
>
> It is unclear how Hell is lit, because the Sun's sweet light, the *dolce lume*, does not enter there. Nor is there a night sky; we get neither the pale light of a Moon nor the night sky's encompassing beauty. Without Sun, Moon, planets, or stars, we cannot find ourselves in time or direction of space. Both divine and celestial guidance have been lost, no direction from appearance, intellect or faith is forthcoming. The *Inferno* in its privation of light gives us an important contrast to the other two realms.
>
> Hell has nine circles plus Lucifer at the bottom. Hell's bottom three circles have their own subdivisions. Purgatory also has nine areas (seven on the mountain) plus the Earthly Paradise; Heaven has nine apparent circles (including the seven planetary spheres) plus the Empyrean.
>
> Hell's form has many features of the worlds above but they are inverted. Hell is shaped like a funnel or an upside-down cone that extends from the surface of the earth to its center. This giant hole in the ground was created when the rebellious Lucifer was hurled out of Paradise. The earth displaced by his fall erupted on the other side in our southern hemisphere as the mountain of purgatory.

After crossing Acheron, Dante and Virgil first meet the virtuous pagans whose eternal fate is simply not to see God. They have neither punishment nor hope. Their destiny reminds me of being in a so-so motel with great company but nobody has much to say. *Inferno* Canto 4 lists many historical figures from the 'pagan past' – philosophers, poets, epic heroes.

They then cross into regions of punishment. Those in Hell have lost the "good of the intellect" (*Inferno* 3.16-18) and the first several circles consist of people whose vices had run wild and had distorted their souls. Those who inhabit these regions are those whose lives were marked by incontinence. Circles Two and Three are inhabited by those who lost control through excessive lust or romantic indulgence and gluttony. Dante uses the symbolism of their punishments to show us the true nature of their sins. We see the lustful blown around chaotically by a fierce wind, the gluttonous wallowing in filthy rain.

Lust and gluttony are the ills of the first two regions of punishment in Hell; they are the mildest vices worked in the two upper regions of Purgatory. Lust and gluttony are the least evil offenses in Hell and the last vices to lose in Purgatory. It is not a coincidence that the astrological symbols for them are **Venus** and **Jupiter** respectively. They are the two 'benefics' – doers of good – in astrology. Yet in Hell they do no good.

> ### Venus and Jupiter, Lust and Gluttony
>
> The windy storm of the Second Circle clearly imitates the unstable behavior of those prone to lust or excessive romantic longing. In the violent wind the gentle noble qualities of romantic love have gone amuck. In the Third Circle for the gluttons, life-giving rains that are signs of abundance and the Earth's fertility – and the astrological Jupiter – have become filthy and foul.
>
> One could also say that the ill destiny of those governed by the astrological Venus may well take them to the Second Circle; those governed by Jupiter may go to the Third.
>
> In the medieval era the most learned weather prediction used astrology, not satellites and chaos theory. Astrometeorology has historical roots in Mesopotamia but was made systematic by Ptolemy of the second century, who was one of Dante's sources for his poem. In *Tetrabiblos* Book II Chapter 8, Ptolemy lists the effects of various planets when they have rulership of a previous eclipse. He considered eclipses strongly determinative of mundane effects that would include changes in weather.
>
> Here's what he says about Jupiter in this context.
>
> "He makes the air temperate and healthful, windy, moist, and favorable to the growth of what the earth bears: he brings about the fortunate sailing of fleets, the moderate rises of rivers, abundance of crops, and everything similar."[1]

> What is the weather of *Venus* like? Here we read about gentle winds and pleasant temperatures and instead in Hell get swirling winds in a disordered pattern so that this Circle's inmates blow about wildly.
>
>> "In general [Venus] brings about results similar to those of Jupiter, but with the addition of a certain agreeable quality… as to the winds of the air, of temperateness and settled conditions of moist and very nourishing winds, of good air, clear weather, and generous showers of fertilizing waters: she brings about the fortunate sailing of fleets, successes, profits, and the full rising of rivers…"[2]
>
> Using Venus and Jupiter as correlates with the lustful and gluttonous in Hell will correspond nicely to their use above in the upper ledges of Purgatory's Mountain.

Circle Four contains the hoarders and spenders, the parsimonious and profligate whose punishment is to shove large boulders to one another, enacting a depressing game without end. In their opposite ways they attempted to interfere with the turnings of Lady Fortune's wheel; we will return to this canto and its discussion of Lady Fortune at the end of our discussion of Hell.

Circle Five is the muddy swamp of the river Styx where the intemperately angry sulk and the sullen wallow. The angry hurl mud along the river and the sullen are submerged in the swamp, gurgling.

If I was going to find planetary correspondences I would see **Mercury** governing the hoarders and spenders and the **Moon** governing the sullen and wrathful. Mercury is the planet of the marketplace and is associated with avarice, as we will see. Moon symbolizes our bodily and emotional states as they constantly change. We all become sullen and angry but we do not make a lifestyle of these afflictions. Those on the banks of the Styx clearly have done that.

Phlegyas, another irritable ferryman, transports Dante and Virgil across the river Styx to the walled city of Dis. It takes an angel from above to gain Dante and Virgil entry into the foul city. Within the city walls, the sins and punishments are worse. Hell has become more intense: its inhabitants are characterized not by weakness, as above, but a hardened will.

A ledge forms the boundary of the heretics' realm that is Circle Six. Heresy is the activity of espousing your own creation as wisdom and constitutes a perversion of Truth. Just within the city walls Dante and Virgil encounter many tombs from which flames arise. If one were to look at the organization of Hell and the planets of astrology, the circle of the heretics is the most like the **Sun**.

We meet the Ghibelline Florentine leader Farinata, the proudest and noblest man in Dante's Hell, holding the underworld in distain from his throne that is a fiery grave. *Inferno* 10 with its heretics corresponds to *Purgatorio* 10 and its depiction of the proud and to *Paradiso* 10 and its entry into the Sphere of the Sun and the wise saints of the Church.

A steep rocky cliff downwards takes us to Hell's Seventh Circle for the violent. Canto 12.1-10 likens this decline to a notable rockslide in eastern Italy – except that this rock slide in Hell was caused by the earthquake at the Crucifixion. Below in Circle Seven are those who were violent against themselves, others, nature or God.

Everything about the Seventh Circle is the nature of the astrological **Mars**, the 'lesser malefic'. Ibn Ezra, a twelfth-century scholar and astrologer and a source for Dante,[3] depicts some of the attributes of the red planet.

> "Mars is hot, dry, burning, harmful, and destructive. He indicates ruin, drought, fires, rebellion, bloodshed, killing, war, fighting, blows, separations, and in general everything that is not right as it should be. Of the human nature he denotes anger.... Of people in his share are all men of war and those who command it, robbers, ironsmiths, blacksmiths, makers of lances and swords, bloodletters and attendants of animals, and the like... of crawling creatures [he rules] everything that is harmful such as the snake and scorpion, and everything that has a deadly venom.... of plants [he rules] the brier... and every tree that has thorns." [4]

In the Seventh Circle, the river Phlegethon begins as a *boiling river of blood* awaiting the violent ones; *centaurs* shoot the souls with *arrows* if they ascend above their allotted levels in the river. The River flows onward, cutting through a *lifeless landscape with gnarled trees*; these trees are the remnants of those who killed themselves and the encased souls are preyed upon by *harpies*. Further down is a *dry desert of flaming rain* for the "sodomites", prodigals, and usurers. The "sodomites" – or homosexuals – run within the dry desert avoiding the rain of fire. The usurers sitting in the *hot sand* are unrecognizable except for moneybags decorated with family insignia that hang around their necks.

Astrological Mars is affiliated with excess heat that brings sterility and diminishes life. Mars is not just its psychological attribute of anger; Mars has an entire range of qualities that Dante has used to depict Hell's Seventh Circle.

Phlegethon eventually leads to a long waterfall into the realms below, toward the *Malebolge* or 'evil ditches' that constitute the Eighth Circle. To get there Dante and Virgil cannot climb down by themselves but descend on the back of Geryon. This is a strange beast whose composite form resembles the nature of fraud that characterizes those in these ditches: it has the head of a righteous man, a serpentine middle decorated with multicolored and multi-designed fabric, and a scorpion's tail. Geryon's coat also reminds one of the leopard that obstructed Dante in the dark wood.

Canto 18.1-18 describes these ditches, each one containing a separate type of fraud. They descend from an iron-colored cliff as concentric circles. Arched bridges (and another rock slide) connect the different ditches in this Eighth Circle. This pattern of ten concentric regions below the earth imitates Heaven above: here in Hell, it consists not of planets and stars but of the densest earth and is like a fortress.

James Nohrnberg (1998) uses this image to show how the structure of the Eighth Circle inverts the Heavens.[5]

"The files of seducers and panderers, like the sun and fixed stars, move in two opposed directions. Moreover, the two rings encircle the nine remaining ditches of Malebolge, as the ecliptic and celestial equator circumscribe the nine remaining heavens – which in turn enclose the four layers of air, or the four sublunary elements, as Malebolge hems in a fourfold ring of ice. At the motionless dead center of either of these configurations, Satan finds his natural place." (p.241)

In these ten concentric ditches of Circle Eight dwell those who in one way or another used their God-given intelligence coldly for evil gain or bad purposes: seducers and panderers, flatterers, people who trafficked in public positions ("barrators") or church offices ("simonists"), hypocrites, thieves, evil counselors, schismatics or sowers of discord, and counterfeiters of various kinds.

Here we encounter varieties of the astrological **Saturn**, the 'greater malefic'. Like Mars, Saturn has a quality of dry, but Saturn's dryness is cold, not hot. Although modern astrologers affiliate Saturn with melancholy and emotional repression, the planet does much more. Its coldness and dryness associates it with the element earth with its leaden heaviness and resistance to penetration and movement. Saturn gives these evil ditches increasing density and sense of claustrophobia. Ibn Ezra tells us Saturn rules "[of places] caves, and wells, and pits, and prisons, and every dark and uninhabited place, and the cemeteries."[6] As we descend the *Malebolge* the situations of the sinners become more and more confining until we arrive at the very bottom of Hell that Dante names Cocytus, an icy lake that encases the traitors forever: Hell freezes over.

Saturn is also the planet of corruption and defilement, quite suitable for exposing the inner essence of fraud. Continuing with Ibn Ezra's description of Saturn, its occupations are "robbers, those who clean lavatories, slaves, the inferior, ditch and grave diggers, and undertakers… His occupation is every work that is exhausting and of little reward." The great malefic is associated with chronic illness as well as filth. With Saturn in mind let's explore the *Malebolge*.

These souls here endure a variety of outcomes. Panders and seducers, placed within two lines opposing each other, are whipped along by hellish creatures. Flatterers drown in a pool of excrement (spouting shit in life, they drown in it in death); those guilty of simony are placed upside down in flaming baptismal fonts; "barrators" who bought and sold public office are cast into ponds of hot sticky pitch by a squad of sadistic devils; (churchly) hypocrites walk around weighed down in leaden ecclesiastical garb; thieves exchange their bodies with serpents and snakes; evil counselors are trapped in flames, those who incited discord walk around mutilated and dismembered; and finally the counterfeiters suffer hideously from disfiguring ailments.

Magicians, astrologers, and other diviners are also found in the *Malebolgia*, below the simonists and above the barraters. In Canto 20 they spend eternity walking around with their heads twisted backwards so that their faces are above their shoulders and backsides. They say nothing as Virgil identifies them to Dante the pilgrim. The *Inferno's* depiction of astrology is in a one-sided moralizing manner, as is fitting the nature of Hell. The *Divine Comedy* will develop its astrology much further as the pilgrim's ability to understand increases. This canto gives the context for our extended discussion of astrology in Part Three.

In this section of the *Inferno*, the poet has trapped one of the *Divine Comedy's* most memorable characters, the great Ulysses. He is the only figure from the ancient Greek world in Hell, and he is cast as an "evil counselor" in Canto 26. Speaking from a tongue of flame, he relates his final voyage, a foolish quest for the limits of human experience and possibility. Sailing to the sight of the Mountain of Purgatory in the South a wave upended his ship and he died. We will return to Dante's Ulysses later.

At the edge of *Malebolge* are giants, creatures from ancient mythology or the Bible who once had rebelled against the pagan god Jupiter or the Christian God respectively. Dante and Virgil hitch a ride from the giant Antaeus and they descend to the fourth and final of Hell's waters, Cocytus. This river does not flow but is a large lake of ice, the cold center and bottom of Hell.

Souls here violated special bonds with a murderous result. They are encased in a lake of ice: some have their heads above the ice but can speak; others have faces that are half-frozen, their eyes frozen with tears; some are completely within the ice and cannot speak or move. We modern people would call all of them 'cold blooded killers' because we recognize the depth of their evil. Here human relationships have degenerated into cannibalism as the shades 'feed' on each other. The scenes depicted are nightmarish to the point of being traumatic to behold. Here the Poet has placed those whose betrayals of country, kin, guest, or benefactor have resulted in a nearly complete loss of their humanity. Indeed, at the beginning of Canto 32, Dante states that he does not possess the language that can reflect the utter coarseness of this deepest Hell.

At the bottom of Hell is Lucifer himself, the great angel who betrayed God. He is mammoth but immobile and insentient, with three heads chewing the bodies of Cassius, Brutus, and Judas, the traitors of Rome and Christ respectively. The wind from his futilely flapping wings is the source of the cold in the Ninth Circle. It is a common teaching in the medieval world that evil is not an entity in itself but the privation of good. In the bottom of Hell there is privation of warmth as well as light. In this spirit Dante has cast Lucifer as pure negativity – simply and savagely nothing.

> ### Rivers in the Divine Comedy
>
> The downward flow of rivers is a frequent motif in the *Divine Comedy*. Their flow parallels human decline and the accumulating force of human misery, reflecting the tendency of Earthly life to decay. If we recall the medieval period's vertical sense of the four elements, we note earth at the bottom, water above earth, air higher than water, and fire uppermost. (The stars and planets are 'ethereal'.) When presenting the lower realm of reality – our world – it is appropriate to refer to the lowest elemental levels of water and earth – rivers and landscapes.
>
> Rivers do not flow in neat circles but more randomly, conditioned by their respective mountain origins, the landscape along their sides, and their eventual destinations into sea or marsh. Contrast this with the orderly and circular flow of the planets and stars that make up the realms of Heaven. Dante is using landscapes, and especially rivers, to help depict our world as least orderly and most lowly: furthest down from God. As the *Divine Comedy* flows upward we see rivers eventually give over to the orderly planets and stars.
>
> Hell's rivers serve as downward crossings: Acheron and Styx mark the entry into Hell and into the inner confines of Hell, the city of Dis. The lower rivers give us crossings between evil and even more evil until at the bottom, the lowest place for the greatest evil, the river's water has turned to ice.
>
> In *Inferno* 14.94-120 Virgil describes to Dante the source of the rivers of Hell: they are from tears that fall from the Old Man of Crete, a colossus within Mount Ida. His head made of gold, his chest and arms are silver, below to his "fork" is brass. Below is

iron except for a right foot of clay. The tears fall through a fissure that begins below the Old Man's golden head and flow into Hell forming its rivers. Although the sequence of metals derives from ancient depictions of the four ages of mankind's decline, Dante's creation symbolizes the suffering of humanity since the fall of Adam and Eve. In *Inferno* 20.67-99, in their visit to the evil ditch containing sorcerers and diviners, Virgil clarifies the origin of Virgil's home town Mantua. After describing an idyllic area of mountains and streams and an island lake, he explains that it was below in a marsh that the sorceress Manto practiced her magic until she died there. The city of Mantua was built above this marsh.

We also see more downward flow in *Purgatorio* 14. Among those purifying the ill will of envy, Guido del Duca condemns the entire region of Tuscany by depicting the flow of the Arno and its local citizens steadily *downstream*. The population becomes more debased, animal-like and finally fraudulent and treacherous as the Arno moves westward from its source – downhill through Florence, to Pisa, finally to the sea. The course of the Arno imitates the structure of Hell.

What happens to the rivers in the higher realms of Dante's regions of the afterlife?

In *Paradiso* 10 and 11, rivers and landscapes are presented idyllically to describe the birth places of Frances of Assisi and Dominic, the founders of the Franciscan and Dominican Orders. In both cases, however, the Sun's image seems to overcome the landscape and rivers; the Sun rising in the east is connected to Francis in Italy and Sun setting in the west to Dominic in Spain. Like the Sun touching down upon the horizons of earth, Heaven is depicted as descending to benefit humanity's course.

When we get to Canto 14 of *Paradiso*, the opening likens Heaven's redeemed souls to ripples from concentric rings of water; soon Dante tells of three concentric rings bearing the saved souls in the Sphere of the Sun. The arbitrary shapes of rivers are transformed into perfect circles. This culminates in *Paradiso* 30 when the circular river of light transforms into the Empyrean or Highest Heaven.

Hell's Drama

If these descriptions of Hell's structure and inhabitants were the totality of the *Inferno*, it would be a fascinating document, perhaps a guilty pleasure for medievalists, but not the esteemed literary classic we take it to be. It is the personalities of Hell and the pilgrim's interactions with them that give us much of the poem's brilliance and relevance. It is in the psychological and moral ambiguity of character and drama where much of our modern interest in the *Inferno* lies.

The inhabitants of Hell are not ciphers for their sins but are cast as real people with discernible personalities. Many characters seem to have fine qualities: Francesca's sensitive nature, Farinata's love of his family and the city of Florence, Pier della Vigne's elegance and loyalty to his emperor, Brunetto Latini's devotion to his former student Dante, and even a heroic and questing spirit from Ulysses. Everything they say and do is also marked by their presence in Hell. Figuring out these people is not easy for Dante or us.

What are the responses of Dante's character through Hell? How does the pilgrim change during this first third of the journey through the afterlife? What does he learn? How, by touring Hell, does Dante provide the foundation for the spiritual progress to follow?

Although the pilgrim interacts with many of Hell's inhabitants, sometimes he is there simply as a witness. In the circle with the sorcerers and diviners neither he nor Virgil talk to anyone as they survey people condemned there (Canto 20). Often the pilgrim has a more active role and this itself provides many dramatic moments in the *Inferno*. He sometimes quizzes Hell's inhabitants, exchanges information with others, and argues with a few. As the *Inferno's* poetic voice changes between cantos, so do his responses to what he sees and his behavior toward those he meets.

Dante does change during his journey through Hell but I would not call it growth. Later we see that Dante's true development is from contrition and faith based on reflection and buttressed by the support of others – and the support of divine grace. These are the matters for Purgatory. In Hell Dante does become less gullible, less fooled by its inhabitants and indeed he does harden toward them. But Hell has also become harder.

In Hell, the pilgrim does not learn from reflection but largely through *imitation*. The changing situations and the souls he encounters bring out different facets of himself, especially different propensities toward evil. In showing different responses from the pilgrim, the poet gives us a diversity of dramatic moments. The poet thereby demonstrates that otherwise good people can do bad things not from conviction but from passivity to what is around them.

In Canto 4, for example, we return to the "virtuous pagans". Dante's character finds himself in good company with fellow poets Homer, Horace, Ovid, and Lucan, and, of course, his guide Virgil. He is happy to be included and they converse together. Interestingly, there is nothing written about the content of their conversation, although later in *Purgatorio* Dante gives us much conversation between the pilgrim and other poets. Here, like the ancient poets in limbo, the pilgrim is dignified but there is nothing to say.

In Canto 5, Dante meets Francesca di Rimini and her lover Paolo, who are bound together flying randomly in the wind. Francesca does the talking and she is attractive and compelling yet self-absorbed and shallow; she is very much the nature of astrology's Venus, illustrating the problems that Venus can bring. Her presentation is high on melodrama; their eternal destinies simply extend the melodrama.

Here are some well-known lines by Francesca from lines 100-105 and translation by Mark Musa (1984). Musa's translations are typically straightforward and clear.

> "Amor, ch'al cor gentil ratto s'apprende,
> prese costui de la bella persona
> che mi fu tolta; e 'l modo ancor m'offende."

> "Love, quick to kindle in the gentle heart,
> seized this one for the beauty of my body,
> torn from me. (How it happened still offends me!)"

By implication, Love, *amor*, not any individual, is responsible for this sad turn of the lovers' lives. Love seized Paolo's gentle heart (*cor gentil*) from her fine form – *la bella persona* – to a bad result. Francesca blames love and takes no responsibility. The words *cor gentil*, implying that love particularly afflicts the gentle soul, is from an earlier poetic tradition that Dante had adopted as a young man. Francesca continues and Musa translates.

"*Amor, ch'a nullo amato amar perdona,
mi prese del costui piacer sì forte,
che, come vedi, ancor non m'abbandona.*"

"Love, that excuses no one from loving,
Seized me so strongly with delight in him
That, as you see, he never leaves my side."

Their love led to their death together. Paolo's brother was Francesca's husband and he killed them both: he will eventually reside in the icy part of Hell named after the Biblical Cain.

The pilgrim falls for Francesca's melodrama completely. When Dante's character hears Francesca's production he expresses shock that such sweet thoughts and desires could have led to this. Soon, after Francesca reminisces about the lovers' first kiss, he swoons.

Most commentators and readers see Dante's swoon at the end of this canto as evidence of gullibility and naivety; I ask whether this also fits into a pattern of imitation throughout Hell. You decide.

Canto 8 gives us an example that is unambiguously imitative. Dante and Virgil have dropped further to the marshes of Styx amidst the angry and sullen. As they are being ferried across by an ornery Phlegyas, a muddied sinner approaches the boat; he identifies himself simply as one who weeps. The pilgrim recognizes this man from life and curses him; Virgil shoves the grimy sinner away from the boat and then greatly praises Dante for his antipathy toward him. Dante, who wants to see this soul suffer even more, soon gets his wish: the condemned man is torn into by those around him and he is last seen madly biting himself. We now see Dante in *his own* realm of anger.*

The muddied and now mangled person was the once-proud temperamental Florentine gentleman Fillipo Argenti, whose last name

---

* Giuseppe Borgese, in his article "The Wrath of Dante" (Clements, ed., 1967), cites this incident as an illustration of a developmental release of anger by the pilgrim and thus it is praised by Virgil and remembered fondly by the poet writing about it afterwards. Yet there are moments to come when the pilgrim is not aroused to anger. Dante's wrath is more in keeping with the imitative qualities of his responses in Hell.

was taken from his riding a horse shod with silver shoes. (Argenti's brother may have helped himself to the poet's property after his exile; Argenti's family also opposed Dante's return. Our poet had a personal grudge.[7]) Once a haughty and difficult person, Argenti is now covered with mud and is miserable – in Hell his true condition reveals itself.

Dante enters the realm of competitiveness in Canto 10. Just inside the city walls of Dis among the open flaming tombs are the heretics. Dante is curious about its souls. Holding all Hell in distain is the Ghibelline leader Farinata degli Uberti who we referred to previously. Farinata's forces were victorious at the battle of Monteperti five years before Dante's birth. Dante had told Virgil he would speak little to the inhabitants here, but when Farinata asks him who his ancestors were, Dante unreservedly tells all.

Having established that they were on opposite sides of Florentine politics, Dante boasts that the Ghibellines had not learned the art of returning from exile. There is a noteworthy interruption by Farinata's tomb-mate who was the poet Guido Calvacanti's father. Farinata continues by giving Dante a prophecy: within fifty rekindlings of the Moon – fifty New Moons – Dante himself will have to learn the art of returning from exile. We will consider this later when we discuss the role of prophecy in the *Divine Comedy*.

The conversation between Farinata and the pilgrim then moves to Farinata's family. Dante attempts to justify the Guelfs' harsh treatment of Farinata's family, and Farinata counters by recalling that he had once saved Florence from being destroyed after the battle of Monteperti. Both Dante and the condemned Farinata compete with each other and cast themselves in the more favorable light – both actively practice 'spin'. Again see that the pilgrim's behavior has changed by reflecting the patterns of the different realm.

We go from competitiveness and spin to empty rhetoric in a canto that is often misinterpreted. In Canto 15, Dante and Virgil have dropped to the realm of the sodomites. Bands of sinners run about in the burning sand and try to ward off the descending flames. One looks at Dante and says, "*Qual maraviglia!*", "What a wonder!" To which Dante replies "*Siete voi qui, ser Brunetto?*", "Is this you, Ser Brunetto?" Dante recognizes his former mentor as an inmate of Hell. Attempting to converse with Latini and not fall into the burning sand, Dante arches his neck as if bowing in reverence.

The pilgrim tells of his current spiritual impasse that has necessitated his journey and introduces Virgil who will help him back 'home'. Latini meanwhile assures Dante that if he navigates by his star he will reach a glorious port.* There is a fascinating disjunction early in their conversation. Brunetto stresses his former students' possibilities of future worldly fame and success; Dante, however, is talking about his errant ways to be corrected by means of visiting the Christian afterlife. Between Brunetto Latini and the pilgrim, this feels not like conversation but parallel rhetoric.

Their subsequent conversation does have grandness to it – or is their conversation instead overblown and grandiose? One could read their conversation either way. Yet one must look at the physical background of their conversation; the contrast is heavy between the affected high-mindedness of their speech and the degraded arid environment that surrounds it. Canto 15 resounds with themes of sterility and futility.

In contrast to the conversation with Brunetto Latini, on at least one occasion Dante's conversation parodies the sinner with whom he is speaking. Canto 19 explores the fate of the simonists, those who bought and sold church positions. Dante is biting in his criticism of ecclesiastical graft. Inhabitants here are upside down in baptismal fonts, their feet, kicking back and forth as flames erupt from their soles. Here Dante is positioned like a priest hearing confession as he converses with Pope Nicholas III who is awaiting his successors, especially Pope Boniface who was pontiff in 1300. Although the Pope was the highest priest of the medieval Catholic Church, the pilgrim talks as if the Pope is beneath him; this reverses on the upper levels of Purgatory.

Moving on toward the very bottom of Hell we see Dante's behavior becoming more coarse and treacherous like the environment he has entered. We take up the action in Canto 32.

Walking upon the frozen lake amidst many people trapped in the ice, the pilgrim's foot strikes the head of somebody who cries out, "Who tramples me?" The iced sinner refers to the battle of Montaperti and

---

* This is perhaps not a navigational metaphor alone but probably tells us that Latini had known the young Dante's astrological chart. I will take up this matter in Part Three.

Dante has an idea about who this person is, but the sinner will not divulge his name – he wishes to be forgotten. Dante then grabs the sinner's hair and promises to tear off his entire scalp if he doesn't tell who he is. One of the sinner's icy neighbors notices the commotion and, calling him by his name, Bocca, asks "*Qual diavol ti tocca?*" "What devil is at you?" (Canto 32:108). The man who Dante kicked is Bocca degli Abati, traitor to the Guelfs (Dante's party) at the Battle of Montaperti not long before the poet was born. Dante lets go of his hair: his revenge will be to tell others about the ill fate that had befallen this evil doer. He has betrayed the betrayer.

The next canto begins with a speech by Count Ugolino who is up to his neck in ice chewing on his former ally and adversary Archbishop Ruggieri. Ugolino wipes his mouth on Ruggieri's hair and tells Dante how Ruggieri had locked up Ugolino and his children and starved them to death. At the end of his horrible tale Dante walks away, says nothing to Ugolino but instead condemns the city of Pisa from where both traitors came. Dante expresses a malevolent desire – or casts a curse – that the nearby islands block the mouth of the Arno so that the entire city floods and its inhabitants drown (*Inferno* 33.79-84).

The pilgrim and his guide now enter another part of the frozen lake of Cocytus. We find souls so deep within the ice that they are completely immobile and their faces are turned upward above the ice. Their previous tears had frozen and no further tears can escape. This makes their suffering even greater, for now their grief is turned completely inward.

One such person asks Dante to remove some ice so he can shed tears. Dante says he will if the sinner will tell his name. If the pilgrim does not follow through, he says, may he too also travel to this ice. The sinner tells that he is Fra Alberigo, who had murdered his guests. The pilgrim exclaims in surprise that this sinner still appears among the living even though his soul is deep in Hell: a devil now inhabits his body on Earth. The two men converse further and as Dante is about to depart Albergo reminds Dante of his promise to take some ice off his eyes. Dante now double-crosses the frozen sinner: instead of removing ice from Alberigo's face, he walks away from him and tells us "*e cortesia fu lui esser villano*", to be rude to this kind of person would be courtesy (Canto 33.150).

Past those thoroughly encased in ice, Virgil asks Dante to look upon Lucifer himself. Facing the ultimate expression of evil, the pilgrim had become *gelato e fioco* (34.22) chilled and weak,* and *Io non mori' e non rimasi vivo* (34.25), not dead or alive. He has become like the immobile and insentient Lucifer himself.

At the bottom and the center of Earth, Dante and Virgil turn around and now begin a long ascent to the earth's surface. They are heading for the southern hemisphere where they will find the realm of Purgatory. Dante follows Virgil on a path upward to the world. Toward the top of the path, Dante finally sees through a round opening the beautiful things that the heavens carry (*de le cose belle che porta 'l ciel*) – to once again see the stars (*a reverder le stele*), for it is the stars tell us that a better world is ahead.** Having finished the ascent of the Mountain and before entering the Earthly Paradise, Dante will once again view stars through a narrow view of the sky.

Fate and Fortune in Hell

We now return to the upper levels of Hell to focus on Fortune and her Wheel. But first we need to introduce an important source for Dante and his entire era: the sixth century writer Boethius.

Boethius was an important intellectual, a Christian who endeavored to educate his fellow Romans about Plato and Aristotle. He was also active in political life as an advisor to Theodoric, the Ostrogoth ruler of Rome. However, Boethius lost the confidence of the king, due to political intrigue and possibly finding himself on the wrong side of contemporary political and religious controversies. Boethius was cast into prison and later executed. While in prison he wrote *The Consolation of Philosophy* which combines philosophical argument with verse and is written in a compelling literary style. This short work became one of the seminal philosophical works of the entire medieval era and was a major contributor to Dante's poem.***

---

*   There goes my taste for Italian ice cream.
** Hollander (2000) notes that the word for this small opening, a *pertugio*, was last used by Ugolino (*Inferno* 33) to depict an opening in the dungeon through which he and his starving children could see the sky. Hollander (2000), p.641.
*** The motif of the successful politician losing favor and being cast out is duplicated in the *Divine Comedy*'s depictions of Pier del Vigne in *Inferno* 13 (who killed himself) and Romeo who we will meet in *Paradiso* 6 (who did not). The poet clearly finds his own life's calamities reflected in Boethius and these two characters depicted in the *Divine Comedy*.

The work begins with the imprisoned Boethius in despair, having watched his fortunes change from very good to extremely bad: this was sudden, decisive, and brought about by evil men who seem to be doing very well while this famous writer and thinker languishes in jail.

> "In my salad days, I was rich, and whimsical Fortune smiled for a little while, but then she turned away
> That faithless face of hers, and my bitter life drags out
> Its long unwanted days. My fair-weather friends
> Admired me, paid compliments, and envied my luck,
> But now they see how my foothold was always uncertain."[8]

A woman appears, elegantly dressed with symbolic letters on her garment and bearing an otherworldly, perhaps angelic, presence. She is Lady Philosophy. She first casts out the Muses who are busy helping Boethius with his self-pitying song. Lady Philosophy and Boethius now converse, and their conversation encompasses the rest of *The Consolation of Philosophy*.

Boethius wants to know how his reversals in fortune and the apparent better fortune of bad people can be reconciled with a universe of divine order and goodness. Lady Philosophy admonishes Boethius for his narrowness of vision and for not understanding the purpose and larger context of fortune. Her arguments are cast as medicine for Boethius' sick soul; she presents them from the mildest to the most difficult, from the personal to the more conceptual and universal. Lady Philosophy's presentation eventually closes with an important discussion of free human will in the context of God's foreknowledge.

Early in her presentation, Lady Philosophy speaks for Lady Fortune who also admonishes the despairing Boethius. In this manner, Lady Fortune remarks on the ever-present cycles in nature shown in alternating day and night, seasons, and weather patterns. She then remarks:

> "That my nature is changeable you know perfectly well. I have a wheel, and I turn it so that what is low is raised high and what is up is brought down. You ascend? Fine! But you must acknowledge that it can't be wrong for you to have to descend again. You were not unaware of how a wheel works."[9]

Lady Fortune (or the Latin *Dame Fortuna*) was the fickle and capricious lady who was the only pagan deity who survived the fall of

Rome.[10] During the medieval era she was not an object of worship but continued to be a powerful symbol. We are already familiar with the image of Fortune's Wheel spinning good and bad fortune for people. Indeed from a narrow personal point of view our changes of fortune appear disorderly and arbitrary, far more a process of dumb luck or cosmic whimsy than design. Lady Fortune, as a whimsical and ever-changing entity, is a fitting symbol for a common experience in our lives.

All of us, like Boethius at the outset of *The Consolation of Philosophy*, enjoy and feel ourselves deserving of Fortune's Wheel's upward movements and feel shocked and outraged when things begin their slide downwards. We also try to make sense of it all, as did Boethius. In ancient times the stoics were particularly eloquent in explaining that the matters of fortune are temporary and partial by nature. Epictetus, the great second century stoic teacher, continuously reminded his students that it is counterproductive to fret over what is not within one's control for they have their origins in divine necessity. Much better, he taught, would be to bear life's troubles with equanimity and piety toward what has been ordained. Boethius, through Lady Philosophy, will pick up many of these themes. The goods of fortune (wealth, reputation, pleasure, or power), even if we attain them, do not even provide real happiness.

There is an important modern counterargument to all this: aren't these attitudes toward life unduly pessimistic and disempowering – 'fatalistic'? We do have choices in many matters of fortune: we can improve our health and longevity through diet and exercise, we can save and invest wisely, improve our career or relationship chances in many ways. That is simply the activity of prudence, one of the four cardinal virtues.

Clearly a path must be built between an attitude that implies personal powerlessness, and one of 'you create your own reality' that dismisses circumstances over which we have no power. At their best, contemporary psychotherapists and astrologers build paths between necessity and choice day by day, client by client.

The inmates of Dante's Hell who wail and curse God and their parents and their time and place of conception and day of birth do not acknowledge their own contributions to their final destinies. Hell's inhabitants have abdicated responsibility for themselves and in many different ways this is what landed them in Hell. They have "lost the good of the intellect", the faculty humans have to make free choices.

We now return to Dante and *Inferno*, Canto 7. In the background is the pathetic game between the "hoarders and wasters" whose teams are eternally pushing large rocks against each other. Their features are unrecognizable, for their obsessions with money have taken away their personal identities. (We find this feature also with the usurers farther below.) Virgil, in lecture mode, discusses the futility of our single-minded focus on matters of personal fortune, the cause of such great conflict among people. Dante then asks what is meant by Lady Fortune whom he had heard so much about.

Virgil replies that Lady Fortune is a cosmic minister, under God's direction, who distributes the "empty goods" of worldly fortune from time to time, from people to people, from family to family. Nobody can prevent this movement from happening or slow it down. Although Lady Fortune is frequently criticized she should instead be praised for she is indeed blessed. (Canto 7.73-96)

Later it appears that the pilgrim listened well to Virgil. We return briefly to *Inferno* 15, after Brunetto Latini had told Dante of the pilgrim's future disaster. Dante says he had heard such prophecies before and feels prepared for them. Fortune can spin her wheel however pleases her, he says. The remark, in line with that canto's preoccupation with fortune, has more than a little *braggadocio* and naivety to it. We will see that it is only in Paradise, where we might think the pilgrim would be above it all, that he learns the particulars of the catastrophe that will befall him. This will occur within the context of larger purposes of providence and divine foreknowledge, but his personal situation is also acknowledged for what it is, not dismissed or minimized.

Much of astrology's enterprise concerns the spinning of Fortune's Wheel, issues of money, reputation, romantic possibilities, and general success in life. Astrologers trace Lady Fortune's arrivals and departures, her inclines and declines, and give predictions as to the timing and extent of her activity.

By making Lady Fortune a minister of God, *Inferno* 7 renders fortune god-given even while acknowledging the shallowness of many of its concerns. At their best, modern astrologers respect their clients' needs to understand the turnings of Fortune's Wheel, but also convey that there is a larger more universal context upon which these turnings occur.

Astrologers may also recognize one of their own symbols. The glyph for the 'Lot of Fortune' in a birth chart looks like a wheel and depicts the quality and sources of fortune during a person's lifetime. This Lot is computed from the natal Sun, Moon, and Ascendant degrees and is fundamental to the natal astrological chart. Thirteenth-century astrologer Guido Bonatti describes the Lot of Fortune this way:

> "This part signifies the life, the body, and also its soul, its strength, fortune, substance, and profit, i.e. wealth and poverty, gold and silver, heaviness or lightness of things bought in the marketplace, praise and good reputation, and honors and recognition, good and evil, present and future, hidden and manifest; and it has signification over everything."[11]

We now need to explore the concept of 'fate', especially since some accuse astrologers – and some astrologers accuse other astrologers – of being 'fatalistic', implying a kind of personal powerlessness. Fate has a long and complex history but some main points are relevant here.

The word 'fate' comes from a Latin verb for 'what had been said', and implies an unalterable destiny that one cannot prevent. Originally a fate was a decree from the gods and in the literature of antiquity it often had a capricious nature. Achilles was to live a short life and attain great fame or a long life and be unknown afterwards; Oedipus was to kill his father and marry his mother. The justice of the ancient gods' decrees was unfathomable to human understanding, yet to doubt their goodness would be impious.

This provided fertile ground for the later development of astrology: the periodic and predictable movements of the stars and planets could help us understand and even anticipate what the gods have decreed for us. Astrology replaced the seeming-capriciousness of the gods with a system that assumed a divine order. It is no accident that stoic attitudes strongly influenced astrology in late antiquity.

The advent of Christianity moved the caprices of Lady Fortune into the direction of an all-powerful God who by nature cannot get it wrong. We see this in the *Consolation of Philosophy*, when Boethius gives 'fate' a specific role within the scope of both fortune and providence. Fate, according to Boethius, is simply how God has ordered the particulars of the world, how all things are bound with each other through providence.

Boethius has transformed the idea of fate into the necessary details of God's workings on earth. As we will discover later, for Dante this becomes the circling of the stars and planets.

In the *Divine Comedy* Dante's orientation is not toward fate but *divine justice*. According to the inscription on the gates of Hell, it was justice that moved God to create the dark realm of God's punishment. Dante posits a relationship of reciprocity between man's activities in life and God's judgments of those activities. Yet divine justice is ultimately unfathomable to the human intellect.

The greatly-lamenting new arrivals in Hell curse their eternal calamity as if they had no part in it; divine justice is far away from their conceptions, for justice actually validates the implications of the choices people had made in life. For the newly-damned, 'fate' has become a product of their 'bad faith', responsibility always being that of somebody (or Somebody) else.

It is important to emphasize that the doctrines given in the *Inferno* are all provisional, subject to further development in the later two canticles. Further along in *Purgatorio* 15.49-75, upon leaving the terrace of envy for that of anger, Virgil gives fortune's goods a wider focus. Although ordinary worldly goods move from person to person and family to family, the more important goods are not one's own but *can be shared with others*. In the center of the *Purgatorio* and the entire poem, narrow preoccupations with our ordinary sense of the goods of fortune – those that happen to one person at a time – widen into a discussion of shared goods of love that prepares the reader for the *Paradiso*.

Time-Keeping in Hell

On Earth the days and seasons are reckoned by the changing light of the Sun. According to ancient and medieval doctrine, time and the planets began simultaneously and through the planets' motions time keeps pace. The Sun in particular is the time's maestro. Time-keeping in Hell, where the Sun does not shine, must be different. Virgil refers to stars and the Moon when depicting the sky he cannot see from Hell.

The first time reference in *Inferno* is in Canto 7 after its discussion of Lady Fortune. After the end of Virgil's speech on Lady Fortune and just before they arrive at the swamp at the edge of the Styx, Virgil says, "every star is sinking that was rising when I set out", i.e. since Virgil first left to meet Dante in the dark wood in *Inferno* 1. It is unclear what stars would have been rising then and it is unclear what time it would have been at the end of Canto 7. A look through stars' times of rising and setting in spring 1300 may yield some information.[12]

In the early morning at about the time when Dante would find himself lost, the stars rising are Aldeberan and the shoulders of Orion, and in mid-morning the twin stars in Gemini would rise.

Dante and his medieval readers would have had good sense of when constellations and stars rise and set at springtime in Italy. By midnight Orion and the stars of Taurus that rose in the mid-morning would have been setting in the west. Close to the western horizon and setting after midnight are the stars of Gemini. (In Paradise we will see Dante astride these same stars praising them for giving rise to his talent.)

At the end of Canto 11, after their discussion of the structure of Hell, Virgil gives another time reference. This one also uses the fixed stars: the Fishes are rising and the Wain (the Big Dipper) is in the direction of the northeast wind named Caurus. Indeed when the stars of Pisces are rising the Big Dipper is visible in the northwest. The time would be in the hours before dawn since Aries would rise soon with the Sun – at least in Jerusalem.

Dante and Virgil visit the realms with different categories of violence and finally descend upon Geryon into the Malebolge. At the end of Canto 20, having visited the ditch of the sorcerers and diviners, Virgil tells Dante they must leave, for the Moon, referred to as "Cain with thorns," is *setting* in the west. If the day before was the Full Moon, the Moon would have set at sunrise. This next day's Moon, now waning and moving closer to the Sun, would set after sunrise, roughly 7:30 AM in the springtime. But, as we will see in Part Three, all information that comes from *Inferno* 20 is suspect.

Dante and Virgil tour the pits of the Malebolge containing the shades of the fraudulent. The last of the ditches brings them among the counterfeiters and again Virgil uses the Moon's position. He tells Dante that the Moon *is now beneath them*, what we might call anti-culminating (Canto 29.10). This would be about six hours later than the setting Moon (if it was) from Canto 20, so that it is early or mid-afternoon. In

Hell Virgil cannot directly see the stars of Pisces nor the Wain nor the Moon; he has but a mental sense, not a physical sense, of the movements of the sky that are obscured under the earth in Hell.

Things change at *Inferno's* end. In Canto 34.68, after Virgil has identified the traitors who are being chewed on by Lucifer, he states that they now must leave for night is rising. The pilgrim and his guide head *down* Lucifer's flanks then suddenly they are going up and Lucifer is now beneath them. Virgil once again hurries up Dante, surprisingly telling him that the Sun is already at mid-terce. What is "*terce*"?

'Terce' marks the first three-hour interval in the medieval day that begins at sunrise; this time was punctuated by prayer at the local churches and monasteries. As they turn around to move up toward Purgatory,

> ### Knowing and Time among Hell's Inmates
>
> We return to *Inferno* Canto 10, one of the most interesting cantos in the entire poem. In lines 94-108, Dante the pilgrim is talking with Farinata and wonders how those in Hell seem to know the future and the past but not present circumstances on Earth. Farinata replies that they see things better when they are at a distance but less clearly when events are closer in time. At the Last Judgment, when the future comes to an end, their knowledge will be completely gone. Dante puts this to good dramatic use in the *Inferno* but there is something more interesting happening here.
>
> Much about the *Inferno* is an inversion of Heaven and God, including the vision of Lucifer at the bottom being an inverted Christ. Here the *Inferno* inverts eternity. In Paradise we will see its citizens infallibly read the future from the eternal mind of God and so our dimensions of past, present and future are simultaneous. Our main access to eternity is as a continual 'now' that are the fleeting moments that continually come and go: in their knowledge of the world, this is what Hell's inmates are deprived of. Instead they have access only to those dimensions of time – past, future – that are secondary to and contained within our present experience.

Virgil's reference is no longer the Northern Hemisphere or the darkness of Hell but the Southern Hemisphere and movement toward light and the Sun. Now Virgil refers both to the Sun and the liturgical day. This is the first time reference using the Sun since Virgil and Dante entered Hell at sunset two days before.

Now we arrive at Purgatory, where all will take place on a human scale within the framework of human time. In Purgatory we trace the movement of time by the motions of the heavens, particularly the Sun and Moon.

Purgatorio: Light and Shadow

Grand Opening

We now begin the upward journey toward God. To mark this occasion, *Purgatorio* begins stunningly. After a brief statement of purpose and invocation to Calliope, the Muse of epic, the early morning sky appears.

Virgil and Dante are near a shoreline across from the Mountain of Purgatory. Above the horizon is Venus, the star that strengthens love and whose beauty tells of better things to come. The nightmare of Hell is over. Appendix 1 examines these lines closely to illustrate Dante's poetic form and the many ways the poet's words can be rendered into English.

Robert Durling (2003) has given us a very good prose translation that I use here, for the English follows the Italian closely.[13]

> *"Dolce color d'orïental zaffiro,*
> *che s'accoglieva nel sereno aspetto*
> *del mezzo, puro infino al primo giro,"*

> "The sweet color of eastern sapphire, gathering in the cloudless aspect of the air, pure to the first circle,"

> *"a li occhi miei ricominciò diletto,*
> *tosto ch'io usci' fuor de l'aura morta*
> *che m'avea contristati li occhi e 'l petto."*

> "…began to delight my eyes again, as soon as I came forth from the dead air that had weighed my eyes and breast with sorrow."

> *"Lo bel pianeto che d'amar conforta*
> *faceva tutto rider l'orïente,*
> *velando i Pesci ch'erano in sua scorta."* (Purgatorio 1: 13-21)

> "The lovely planet that strengthens us to love was causing all the east to laugh, veiling the Fish, which were her escort."

Dante looks to his right and sees four stars that are would be invisible to all of us in the northern hemisphere. They are not the stars of the

Southern Cross; most likely Dante didn't know anything about them. Later we learn that these stars represent the cardinal virtues of courage, temperance, wisdom, and justice. They are guidelines from the ancient world that apply to the work upon the mountain; later they are seen in perfected form in Heaven.

On Dante's left toward the north suddenly appears a stereotypical Capricorn, i.e. a man who appears venerable but severe. This is Cato the Younger who is the guardian of Purgatory's entrance. Much ink has been spilt explaining Cato's surprising appearance here: he was an opponent of the Roman Empire and a pagan who committed suicide, an odd figure to guard a Christian realm. Here is one explanation that seems right: "He is a man who died for the benefit of human society and in a time of discord and ruin, affirming before the world, by his own sacrifice, the supreme law of liberty – not only civil but metaphysical."[14]

Cato confronts Dante and Virgil and asks "has someone changed the rules so that somebody can enter Purgatory from Hell: are they fugitives from Hell?" Virgil uses much rhetoric to get past this skeptical Roman, most of which Cato ignores. But if their presence has been commanded by a lady from Paradise, as Virgil states, her desire is good enough for the stern gatekeeper.

Cato instructs Virgil to guide Dante eastward to a shoreline, where Virgil is to wash away Dante's tears and the grime from Hell. Dante must gird himself with a reed plucked from a marsh. This scene, portrayed as a ritual of humility, closes the first canto and sends Dante and Virgil on their way. In this canto the pilgrim does not speak a word.

Mount Purgatory's Form

Purgatory is where one becomes purged of the stain of sin and becomes worthy to ascend to heaven (*Purgatorio* 1.4-6). In so doing, the penitent restores his or her freedom and reclaims their naturally virtuous nature, the symbol for which is the Earthly Paradise at the top of the mountain. Between the grotesqueries of Hell and the otherworldly splendors of Heaven, Dante's Purgatory has a more ordinary feel to it.

In Dante's time, Purgatory was a fairly recent concept and there was little tradition upon which the poet could build. He placed Purgatory's location in the unmarked southern hemisphere and its structure is wholly of his making. This massive re-education camp is a high steep mountain, rounder toward the top with a large but steep base below. Astrology's symbolic Saturn makes a strong presence in the *Purgatorio*: the activity entails a long climb up a hard mountain. The central failing of the Mountain's pilgrims is spiritual laziness in its many (about seven) different forms. (Laziness is affiliated with Saturn, the planet slowest in motion and of the element of earth.)

Souls at the mountain's base, in "Ante-Purgatory", await the torments above: their waiting is a form of reorientation. They include those whom the church excommunicated, and also the indolent who must wait for as much time as they wasted in their lives in meaningless pursuits. There are many people here below Purgatory's gates, in "Ante-Purgatory".

The seven terraces on the Mountain proper are divided by the seven tendencies we call the Seven 'Cardinal' (more accurate than 'Deadly') Sins – pride, envy, anger, laziness, greed, gluttony, and lust. Traditional designations of planets with cardinal sins, in the order of the ledges of the Mountain of Purgatory are Sun, Moon, Mars, Saturn, Mercury, Jupiter, and finally Venus.

We're Not in Hell Anymore

In Purgatory, there is a purpose for the suffering that occurs. In Hell there is no learning, no improvement or decline, nothing other than eternally repetitive punishment. Hell's inhabitants, from the noncommittal pope to the wisest of the "virtuous pagans" down to Lucifer himself, live in futility. Only spectators like Dante and us can benefit from who they are and what they endure.

In contrast, all of Purgatory's citizens will go to Heaven – someday. Because of their previous lives and wills, this day may be a long way away, yet all of Purgatory's citizens are nonetheless infused with a sense of purpose, great or small. This renders the emotional atmosphere as different from Hell as Purgatory's moving sunlight is from Hell's continual shadow.

Purgatory is a human community: its people are all citizens of the 'one true city'. Hell has no citizens, only inhabitants who are oblivious, hostile or even destructive to one another. All of Hell's inhabitants have what is the opposite of community: an unflagging self-absorption. Their narcissism psychologically accounts for their suffering's futility – they are closed off from anything inside or outside themselves that could impel change, just as they were in life.

In *Purgatorio* the interpersonal environment is completely different. We see this from the very beginning. People in Purgatory often recognize Dante as a person still alive, marvel at him, and greet him with wonderment as a comrade. There is a clear sense that everybody is on the same team. Dante uses well the Catholic doctrine that the prayers of others can help the deceased get to Heaven more quickly. Many ask Dante to put in a good word for them to friends and relatives they have left behind. Thus the poet stresses the dependency of those in Purgatory upon others. Acknowledging dependency – on each other and on God – is a key to purification and eventual salvation.

The *Purgatorio* is a drama of many meetings and reunions, which gives this canticle a sweetness that brings to mind our own lives' moments of happy reunion. Yet our reunions can touch on sadness and longing; we find this especially below Purgatory's gates.

In Canto 2 Dante meets his old friend Casella who once had put some of Dante's poems to music and Casella sings one of them to the group. All have a fine time until suddenly Cato appears and hurries them along. In Canto 4 Dante exchanges barbs with Belacqua, an old acquaintance and purportedly the laziest man in Florence. In Canto 8 the pilgrim goes into the Valley of the Rulers with Nino Visconti, an old friend from Pisa (nephew of Count Ugolino who we met deep in Hell). Later, in the terrace of the gluttons Dante recognizes his old friend Forese Donati; clearly they had gotten into some trouble together in life.

Purgatorio also contains poignant encounters between poets of different eras. In ante-Purgatory Virgil meets the poet Sordello: both are from Mantua. In the upper terraces, Virgil meets the later Roman epic poet Statius whose poetry and conversion to Christianity were both inspired by Virgil. After this, Dante meets his poetic ancestors Guido Guinizzelli and the earlier poet Arnaut Daniel. These are not only meetings but also reckonings of influence.

There are also political reunions. Soon we will note encounters with leaders he has known, not in an atmosphere of adversity but of common purpose. In Canto 3 the pilgrim meets Manfred, son of Emperor Frederick II, excommunicated by the church, who lost to the pope and French king in the battle of Benevento the year after Dante was born. Manfred is cast as a handsome and heroic figure and they talk as if they otherwise would have been friends.

In Canto 5 we hear from the Ghibelline leader Buonconte of Montefeltro, who, like Manfred, had only asked for forgiveness of his sins as he was dying. Buonconte was the losing commander in the battle of Campaldino in which Dante had fought for the Guelfs. In the Valley of the Rulers Dante meets political leaders, many of whom were once enemies but now are with each other waiting their turn to ascend the mountain: here they sing hymns together.

All these meetings and reunions help prepare for the big reunion on the top of the mountain between Dante and Beatrice. This forms the dramatic peak of the poem.

Time and the Mountain

Hell's spaces are confining and Heaven's spaces open up to great vastness; in Purgatory space is continuous and predictable and gives a sense of place, direction, and location. In Hell time is distorted, as its inmates can see into the past and future but not the present. Upwards in Heaven time is eternal and so past, present, and future occur simultaneously. In Purgatory, however, time is orderly and sequential and sensual – it is *our* time. Its physical structures, light, time, and location all provide the progressive and redemptive environment for the souls who are in Purgatory.

Throughout the *Purgatorio* the Sun's daily motion ripples through the entire world as a place of human redemption and return to God. This implies that *our world* is also potentially a place of purification and redemption; we don't have to die first.* Dante uses geography and the movements of the surrounding sky to illustrate this.

Purgatory is located on the Earth exactly opposite Jerusalem. When Lucifer was cast from Heaven, the impact of this fall onto the Earth created the huge hole that became Hell; the earth that was displaced became Purgatory. Jerusalem and Purgatory share the same horizon

---

* It is not by accident that Thomas Merton named his famous autobiography *The Seven Storey Mountain*.

(*Purgatorio* 4.70) so that when it is sunrise in Purgatory it is sunset in Jerusalem.*

The second canticle begins before dawn and the first day (of three) brings Dante and Virgil to the edge of Purgatory's mountain. After seeing Venus in the predawn sky, Cato's instructions bring Dante east toward the shore as the Sun is closer to the horizon. At the beginning of Canto 2, the Sun is on the horizon. By Canto 2.55-57 the Sun – the active principle in Purgatory's sky – has driven Capricorn from the Midheaven. This means that Aquarius is now at the Midheaven, Taurus is now rising and it's closer to 8 AM.

By the beginning of Canto 3 the Sun has risen sufficiently to cast shadows and Dante notices that only he casts a shadow, for he is still in his living body. Seeing only one shadow he had forgotten that Virgil, who can cast no shadow, is next to him. (Canto 3.16-28)

Canto 4 opens as the pilgrim recognizes that his previous conversation with Manfred had been so absorbing that he hadn't noticed the time, for now the Sun has risen fifty degrees. (4.13-15). In early spring it takes about six hours for the Sun to move from rising to culminating – from the Ascendant to the Midheaven. If the Sun's angle is forty-five degrees it would be about 9 AM, and an extra ten degrees would be about forty minutes of time, making it about 9:40 AM. This is a real but idealized sky.

At the end of Canto 4 (lines 136-139) Virgil ends Dante's conversation with the lazy Belacqua by telling him that they must go, for it is already noon (Sun is at its highest point that day) and night already covers Morocco. We shall speak more of this western location below.

During the daytime hours the Sun strikes the mountain and Dante at specific angles and he projects shadows in specific directions and lengths: Dante himself has become a sun dial. In this Purgatory nobody can make forward progress at the night, for the Sun who guides us on the right way is absent.

---

*   Where on earth is this mountain? To find Purgatory, one takes the coordinates for Jerusalem, go 180° of longitude and an equal number of degrees latitude south of the terrestrial equator. If so the mountain of Purgatory has a specific location on earth: equally from the equator and 180° from Jerusalem. By modern reckoning, if Jerusalem's coordinates are 31N46 and 35E14, then those of Purgatory are 31S46 and 145W46; this places the mountain in the middle of our Pacific Ocean.

Purgatory and the Axis of Redemption

We must discuss one further complexity that the Poet presents the reader in this canticle. Let us briefly return to sunrise of the first morning in Purgatory and the first line of Canto 2.

"Già era 'l sole a l'orizzonte giunto"

"The Sun had come to the horizon"

This line poses no problems. *If we skip the five lines that follow*, the narrative continues straightforwardly: the cheeks of Aurora (goddess of dawn) were changing from white and vermillion to orange and were becoming older. This is a simple visual description. There is nothing problematic or even interesting about this.

Yet the poet has far more in mind than just depicting sunrise. What follows is an example of a *periphrasis* whereby thematic material is added to otherwise ordinary description.

Having placed the Sun at the horizon, the first tercet continues:

"...lo cui meridïan cerchio coverchia
Ierusalèm col suo più alto punto;"

"Whose meridian circle covers Jerusalem at its high point"

Because Purgatory and Jerusalem are 180° from each other, they also share the same meridian circle. When it is noon in Purgatory it is midnight in Jerusalem. In the second tercet the poet gives us other dimensions of space and of time.

"e la notte, che oppposita a lui cercha,
uscia di Gange fuor con le Bilance,
che le caggion di man quando soverchia…" (Purgatorio 2:4-6)

"..and on the other side night is circling emerging from the Ganges with the Scales (Libra) which drop when she is dominant (after the autumnal equinox)"

If it is sunrise in Purgatory and sunset in Jerusalem, it is midnight in 'India'; if you were in India, Libra had passed the Midheaven and is descending toward the west. The geography that Dante is presenting is structured so that the half-way point between Purgatory and Jerusalem is

'India' or the River Ganges. Later we will see that Spain/Morocco is the other half-way point on the other side to the west.*

These locations are not the 'India' or the 'Spain' that we know but opposing points 90° from the Purgatory–Jerusalem axis that designates four specific locations on earth. Jerusalem, India, Purgatory, and Spain are all 90° apart from each other.*

With the Sun in early Aries, there would be six hours between sunrise, noon, sunset, and midnight – the Sun's cardinal points in its daily cycle. Thus as we have four points equidistant on the earth we also have four times equally distant in time. In these few opening lines of the second canto of the *Purgatorio*, the poet has given us three of the four locations. According to his sense of the Earth's geography and of redemptive time, he connects them with the cardinal directions and the cardinal points of the Sun. This returns later in the *Purgatorio* and in the *Paradiso*. Here are two conspicuous examples.

At the beginning of *Purgatorio* 27, Dante will use the four points Jerusalem and Purgatory, Spain and India to signal the final purification and departure from Purgatory. This passage has a strongly ceremonial feel to it, like casting the directions for a new cathedral. This will mark the moment for the pilgrim, his guide, and the accompanying Roman poet Statius to pass through the wall of fire to leave Purgatory. The depiction of all four places and times gives this moment a sense of cosmic auspiciousness.

Elsewhere in the *Divine Comedy*, India and Spain are thought of as the horizontal points that form the world's limits. Ulysses, in his mad voyage depicted in *Inferno* 26, sailed his ship beyond the western limits, signifying inappropriate adventurous excess. (We will discuss Ulysses and his voyage in Part Three.) More benignly these places are referenced later in Heaven's realm of the Sun. Thomas of Aquinas and Bonaventure respectively introduce the lives of thirteenth century Francis of Assisi and Dominic, founders of the Franciscan and Dominican orders (*Paradiso*

---

* Up to the European voyages of the fifteenth century, world maps showed Jersualem at the center India with China at the furthest East and the Straits of Gibralter to the West. Our modern locations of India and Spain are indeed equidistant from Jerusalem; both places, however, are 35° of longitude from Jerusalem, not 90° as Dante and his contemporaries would have it.

Cantos 11 and 12). When discussing their places of birth, Francis is likened to the Sun rising over the Ganges and Dominic's natal Spain is where the Sun descends in the west.

> ### The Astrological Chart as Personal Mandala
> Throughout this book, I provide figures that we generally know of as 'astrological charts'. They consist of a horizon line and a meridian line perpendicular to the horizon that divides the chart into four quadrants (that are generally trisected to make for twelve 'houses'). The position of the Sun within these charts tells us what time of day is depicted: moving clockwise from the Ascendant (the left-hand side of the horizon), the Sun rises through the morning, conjuncts the meridian at the Midheaven at (astronomical) noon, sets on the right-hand side of the horizon, and anti-culminates at the bottom side of the meridian.
>
> An astrological chart depicts planets and stars, in the counterclockwise sequence of the zodiac, and their location relative to a specific place on Earth that is designated by the horizon and meridian lines. Such a chart may be used to interpret the life of an individual, a natural or chosen human event, and even asking a question of significance.
>
> In *The Astrology of Transformation* (1980), Dane Rudhyar speculated about features of astrology having different relevance to an individual along different stages of spiritual development. He posits that the complete astrological chart, particularly the intersection of the horizon and meridian lines, parallels an 'individual' phase. This phase marks the emergence of the individual out of biological and socio-cultural matrices into a central reference point of one's individual uniqueness. For this person, his or her astrological birth-chart becomes a mandala of an individual's actualization.
>
> The *Purgatorio*'s use of time and place references evokes the same quality of uniqueness about which Rudhyar writes. This conforms well to the canticle's focus on individual life stories and interpersonal connections. The poet's use of multiple locations for the same time signifies that spiritual journeys are specific to

> us as discrete individuals but are also part of a far larger universal process.
> Rudhyar understood that the final stages of spiritual development (that he calls "transpersonal") bring the uniqueness of the individual onto a larger frame of reference. The *Purgatorio* shows the same sequence: beginning with the early cantos' emphasis on personal history and the dissolution of the material body after death, the penitent lets go of spiritual blockages on his or her way up the Mountain, and finally at the Garden of Eden has become fully oneself – and ready to ascend to and participate in the vaster universe of divine Being.

Halting Motions to the Mountain's Ledge

We now return to the travelers and their journey. Their first day is devoted to immediate human concerns and there is little room for stars and planets, cosmic symbolism and metaphysics of nature and God. The spiritual journey begins simply but methodically, encountering the naïve hope and inspiration, the backwards pull of hesitation and inertia, and the slow realization that no other challenge is greater. We begin to see a transition from personal narrative toward ritual that characterizes the second half of this canticle.

At first the pilgrim is bewildered and dependent, his guide has never been there before, and the way to the Mountain is not clear. The crowd is also disoriented and people are looking around for what to do next and will not be able to help the visitors find the right way.

Returning to Canto 3, the two arrive at a steep cliff but do not know what to do, for there are no signs of a trail. Eventually our travelers see a group of souls coming very slowly toward them and who eventually tell Virgil and Dante to turn around as they are going in the wrong direction. Within this group is Manfred who we discussed earlier.

In the following Canto 4 the pilgrim and his guide climb through some steep passes to proceed upward and Dante finds this part exhausting. Virgil suggests that they wait until a wise person can give the proper directions. The pilgrim, not understanding where they are, becomes confused when the Sun appears on his left toward the North. (He is facing east.) Virgil explains that they are in the *southern* hemisphere, that if the Sun was in northerly Gemini (instead of Aries) the Twins would appear even closer than it does now to the Bears – the farthest northern stars. This is where the pilgrim finds out that Purgatory and Jerusalem share the same horizon.

Encouraging Dante, Virgil assures him that at the upper places in Purgatory the climb is not so steep and they can rest when they get to the top. Then they hear someone nearby say, "*Forse/che di sedere in pria avrai distretta!*" "Perhaps you'll be obliged to sit before then!" (Canto 4:98-99: Durling translation).

This is Dante's friend Belacqua, a lute maker and famously lazy man who had died not long before, close to the action of the *Divine Comedy*. Belacqua and others are crouched under a rock and he can hardly lift his head to talk to Dante. With Belacqua embodying a humorous image of the astrological Saturn engaged in a parody of contemplation, the old friends have a warm exchange that is one of the most engaging passages of the *Purgatorio*. Belacqua also tells Dante that for people who put off their spiritual life they must hang out for a time equal to their procrastination before they can go through the gates into Purgatory.

The Cliffs and Corpses of Ante-Purgatory

Continuing on the topic of the elemental features of the afterlife we now look at cliffs and ledges. Here in Ante-Purgatory the terrain is rocky and sloping, once again showing that we are still fairly low in the elemental hierarchy.

At the beginning of Canto 3 Dante sees Purgatory's mountain rising from the sea into the sky. They arrive at a cliff impossible to climb, so difficult that the roughest landslides that the travelers encounter seem easy compared to this. Is there another way to go where one does not require wings? (3:46-54.)

At the beginning of Canto 4 they encounter further obstacles. Dante and Virgil climb through a gap impossibly small, the path they ascend by is steeper than any mountain roads Dante knows of, and finally they have to use their hands as well as their feet to go upwards (4.19-36). In what gives great relief to any mountain hiker, they finally reach an open hillside – but once again do not know where they are. Pilgrim and guide pause and converse about the structure of the mountain and it is here that they meet Belacqua and many others and finally Sordello who will show them where to spend the night.

Like the meanderings of rivers discussed earlier, this landscape before Purgatory's gates is chaotic in its structure. Unlike a metaphorical river's easy descending flow into further evil or corruption, the rocky landscape at the base of the mountain has an upward ascent, but it is difficult and confusing.

We also see Ante-Purgatory's dense and disorganized level of materiality reflected in its concern for the corpses of the deceased. One might think this would be of no interest to those in the afterlife, but even Virgil gets in on this. This illustrates an abiding concern with the vicissitudes of personal fortune but also prefigures *Paradiso*'s concern with reunion of soul and body after the Final Judgment.

At the beginning of Canto 3, Dante is struck that he has a shadow but those who are deceased do not. Virgil refers to his long-dead body in present tense, noting that his bones lie buried in Naples (3.25-27). Very soon Manfred discusses the final fate of his dead body. After being killed in the battle of Benevento, Manfred was buried under a heap of stones by a bridge. But then, probably under orders from the pope, the nearby archbishop ordered his body exhumed and his bones cast outside the Kingdom of Naples to the shores of the river Verde. (3.124-135; and Hollander, 2003, p.71-72)

We move to Canto 5 and the story of Buonconte da Montefeltro. After losing the final battle and fleeing to a marsh, Buonconte fell into the mud and in his last moment he prayed for divine forgiveness. After an angel and a devil debated the final disposition of his soul (the angel won), his body floated down the river toward the sea and finally it moved past the Arno's banks to its bottom. This process had undone his arms that were previously folded in prayer. This decaying path lines up nicely with the descending river motif we discussed earlier: the eventual fate of his soul is to ascend toward Heaven after his physical body had gone downstream to its final disposal.

> Both Manfred and Buonconte happened to be losers in battle, just as Dante happened to be on the winning side in battle when a young man. Their losses of battle, the suffering of dying and the degradation of their bodies after death are idle gossip compared to the last-minute choices both men made and their resulting path toward salvation. With Manfred and Buonconte we begin to see reliance on fortune alone modified by the ultimate issue of concern – their ability to take part in God's universe.
>
> All this reminds us that below the gates of Purgatory we are working with a low level of materiality. This will only help us to imaginatively ascend the Mountain toward Heaven.

Pilgrim and guide find themselves surrounded by people asking Dante to put in a good word for them so their prayers can shorten the time to get to heaven. They approach one standing apart from the crowd and that is Sordello, a poet from Mantua (like Virgil) from the previous century. After Sordello tells Dante that nobody makes any progress after the Sun goes down, he takes them to what is usually called the 'Valley of the Princes' where the three could spend the evening. From a nearby ridge they observe former rulers gathered in each others' company and in song.

Those gathered in this fragrant colorful valley are united in being pilgrims but also in grief – at previous opportunities that were lost. They were all too preoccupied to pay adequate attention to their own spiritual lives or to God's will on earth. The poet describes the princes in order of worldly stature. It was the turnings of fortune that, in life, made some of greater stature than others and some victorious or defeated by others. Here below the gates of Purgatory they are equals and on the same side.

This brings us to the first day's sunset. The opening of Canto 8 is well-known and brings together a time reference, a particular poetic mood, and a double sense of Purgatory's voyage. This opening illustrates the transitional nature of Dante's journey in Purgatory and an early period in an individual's spiritual journey.

Let's hear these lines from two American poets of different literary eras. This first is from the great nineteenth century poet Henry Wadsworth Longfellow.

" 'Twas now the hour that turneth back desire
In those who sail the sea, and melts the heart,
The day they've said to their sweet friends farewell,"

"And the new pilgrim penetrates with love,
If he doth hear from far away a bell
That seemeth to deplore the dying day."

Here's a free verse version from the contemporary poet M.S. Merwin from his translation of the *Purgatorio* (2000).

"Then it was the hour that brings longing again
to melt the hearts of those out on the sea
the day they have said goodbye to their dear friends,
and when love stabs the new pilgrim who hears
far off in the distance a bell ringing
as though mourning the day that is dying."

The ship has left during the day and sailors have left their loved ones home. At the end of the day the sailors hear the evening bell, a normal event in the rhythm of the village's day. One already misses home and longs to be back but the open sea lies ahead.

This dying day ends the journey through Ante-Purgatory. Those here seem to live more through their previous earthly lives than the heavenly second life to come. At the beginning of this final canto before entering the gates of Purgatory, one would like to return to the happy familiarities but the open sea, perhaps a dangerous sea, lies ahead. Longing for home intensifies the fear of what lies ahead and the fear intensifies nostalgia for being back home.

Previously, as Sordello had been pointing out the various people in the Valley of the Princes, Dante became distracted by the poignant sunset to the west. After these lines, Canto 8 continues by noting an unnamed person raising his hands in prayer *toward the east*, toward sunrise and the new day ahead. This is a uniquely transitional moment, for they are facing 'east' and 'west' simultaneously. They look backward toward the old familiar day that had died and ahead toward the open seas and unknown trials and a new dawn.[15]

Like the church bells that signal the rhythms of the village the sailor has left, it is the Sun and the other stars that signal the rhythms of a sacred universe. These verses embody a moment in Dante's journey and our own from the open sea of confusion back to one's true home, where the downward pull toward his previous life gives way to upward pull toward eternity. Will and inspiration alone cannot accomplish this journey, for our backward tendencies are deep.

In his introductory essay to the *Purgatorio*, Jeffrey Schnapp writes, "To reach and ascend Mount Purgatory requires human effort and superhuman support. Both are necessary if the gravitational pull of sin is to be transmuted into the levitational 'God-ward' pull of sacred love." These motions make up much of the psychological and spiritual drama of this canticle.[16]

As night begins to fall two angels appear in the color green (the color of hope) with broken-off swords. They will stand guard over the pilgrims overnight, and indeed there appears a snake in the grass they chase away. (See Appendix 1 for different English renderings of the snake's appearance.)

Dante looks hungrily to the sky, to where the stars are most slow, *pur l`a dove le stele son pi`u tarde*, like a wheel's spokes close to an axle, *s`i come rota pi`u presso a lo stelo*, You may remember the four circumpolar stars from Purgatorio 1. They represent the Four Cardinal Virtues of wisdom, courage, justice, and temperance; in their place are now three other circumpolar stars that represent the Three Theological Virtues of faith, hope, and love or charity. How is it possible for one set of circumpolar stars to replace another? We're not quite sure: perhaps the previous four stars are now hidden by the large mountain.[17] Perhaps at sunset in the spring the four stars would sink under the horizon for a time, making way for the three stars to dominate the beginning of the night. In Canto 29 we will meet all seven stars again, appearing as nymphs alongside the chariot that brings Beatrice to the Earthly Paradise and to Dante.

Even if the astronomy doesn't line up, the symbolism of these two constellations is clear: the four stars of the cardinal virtues introduce the morning and guide one's daytime activities, but it is faith, hope and love that can help one through the night.

Approaching the Threshold

As Canto 9 begins, finally it's dark and Dante prepares to sleep. During the daytime, the time and motions of Purgatory have been reckoned by the path of the Sun. Now appearing is the Moon, the paler planet who represents the night and had figured more prominently in Hell. The constellation Scorpio is the dominant figure in the eastern sky in spring's evening hours. A hint of violence by the Scorpion adds an uncertain quality of danger to this haunting image. Yet we also find beauty in a large white Moon garlanded by the stars of this night constellation.

Before Dante sleeps we are given a dream-like image:

"*La concubina di Titone antico
già s' imbiancava al balco d'oriënte,
fuor de le braccia del suo dolce amico*"

"The concubine of old Tithonus
Was turning white on the eastern balcony
From the arms of her sweet lover"

The first line refers to the concubine of old Tithonus. Aurora, the goddess of dawn, is depicted leaving the bed of her lover Tithonis each morning to greet the new day. But here who is Tithonis' "concubine"? Perhaps this is not the goddess of dawn but is a different Aurora who is white. This would be not Tithonis' wife, the Aurora of the Sun, but his lover or concubine, the 'Aurora' of the Moon. If so this depiction is not of sunrise but *moonrise*. There is dispute about this passage: many commentators wonder whether Dante would have invented a second Aurora myth to account for a lunar 'Aurora'.*

"*Di gemme la sua fronte era lucente,
poste in figura del freddo animale
che con la coda percuote la gente;*"

"Her forehead shining with gems,
Set in the shape of the cold animal
That strikes men with her tail."

---

* See Cornish (2000) p.62-78 for an eloquent argument for this position. That Dante is here describing a 'lunar Aurora' has been asserted convincingly by Moore (1903) p.76-79 and has widespread support. To me Dante's use of the myth of Aurora to depict moonrise is quite appropriate.

The constellation Scorpio as a crown of gems on the Moon's face.
Illustration by Penny Burke.

The first line refers to glowing gems on her forehead. They are in the shape (*figura*) of the cold animal (*del freddo animale*) that strikes with its tail. Dante is most likely referring to Moon rising bedecked with the stars of Scorpio.

This dramatic eastern Moon fits well into the context of the *Divine Comedy*'s progress. You may remember that it was the morning of the full moon when Dante was lost in the dark wood; if the Sun was in Aries, the Moon was in Libra. We are now three days and nights later and the waning Moon would be seen arising in the East a couple of hours after sunset. Our old indolent spiritual selves re-emerge at night.

Dante falls asleep and, toward dawn, he dreams that an abducting eagle has captured him, taking him upward through fire. The reality is different: instead of being captured by an eagle he was gently carried upwards by Lucia, a lady of Heaven, to the gates of Purgatory. The process of purification is ultimately benign, not a dangerous abduction, yet the downward tendencies symbolized by night (and the Moon in the east) sense this ascension as personal threat. In a sense the pilgrim has been abducted by the grace of God who now forces the matter upward.[18] While the dreamer has been dreaming, the Sun had been above the horizon for some time and finally Virgil succeeds in waking up the sleeping pilgrim.

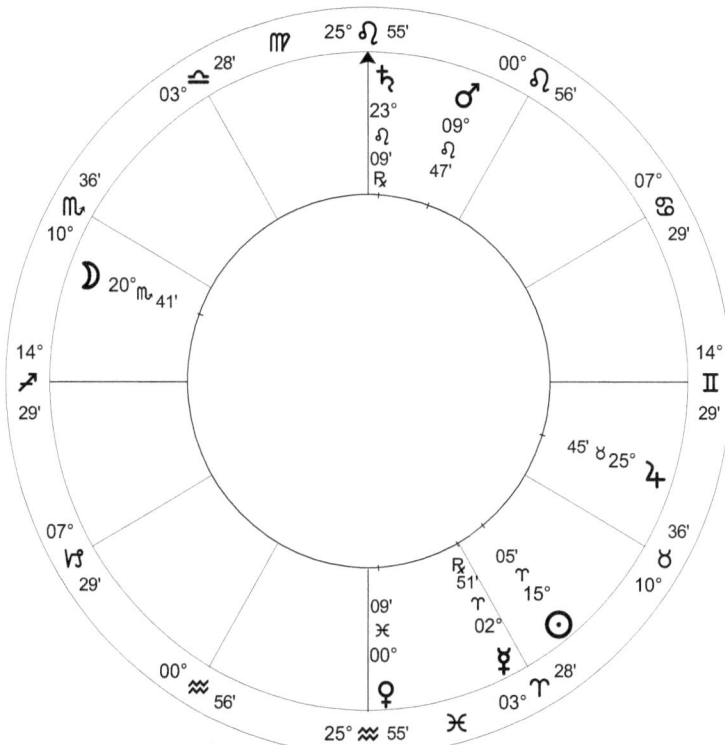

An Astrological Chart for Sun and Moon, *Purgatorio* 9.
Here is an astrological chart showing the approximate position of the Sun and Moon as described in the first lines of Canto 9. The planets' positions for *March 1301* illustrate this better than those for 1300.

Finding Purgatory's gate is not easy and the path is more like a gap in a sheer wall. Guarding the gate is an angel sitting atop three rock steps whose face is too bright to look at. One step is so white and radiant that Dante can see his own reflection; the second is a darkest purple that is cracked; and the third is redder than flowing blood red. Over these three steps and seated on a throne of adamantine rock, the angel confronts the pilgrims. Virgil briefly explains that they are here on the command from a Lady from Heaven. The angel invites them toward the three stairs.

Dante lowers himself to his knees, beats his breast three times, and asks admission. The angel then traces seven "P's" on Dante's forehead with his sword. The angel then takes out two keys, one that is gold, the other silver. The first key is more precious, the second takes great skill to use, yet both are necessary to enter Purgatory. He touches the door with one and then the other and the door opens with a heavy cracking sound.

This scene is obviously rich in symbolism. There are some specific images and rituals from church doctrine but Dante does not spell them out to us – he would expect his medieval reader to know them already. With the angel as confessor and Dante as penitent, they are components of the Christian ritual of confession. The steps would symbolize the acts of confession, contrition, and satisfaction (or the penance itself). The gold and silver keys symbolize the Church's power to grant absolution and that, on a personal level between priest and penitent, it takes great skill to untie the knot of sinfulness.

There are other possibilities. One may also see from the first step the mirror-like clarity of understanding, the second step the darkness of acknowledgement, and the third step the blood red of sacrifice. Helen Luke (1989), in a Jungian interpretation of the *Divine Comedy*, likens the colors of the steps to the alchemical processes of *albedo, nigredo, and rubedo.** She also notes the colors of the two keys. Gold is the color of the Sun and represents conscious will; silver is the color of the Moon and signifies our unconscious or hidden tendencies that take great skill to master.

Either way, the cleansing process in Purgatory is no self-initiated self-improvement project but is instead an act of surrender to divinity. Purgatory's entrance is well guarded but accessible to one who desires to enter. The carving of the seven "P's" (probably for *peccata* or 'sin') is a general acknowledgment of faults that are the first step toward purification. They represent the Seven Cardinal Sins.

Careful not to look back, pilgrim and guide enter through Purgatory's gates and the gates shut behind them. Their first steps are not easy, for they are surrounded by rock on all sides twisting back and forth like

---

* In an interview quoted by Edinger (1985), Carl Jung discusses the alchemical process. Its aim is (1) the rescue of the human soul, and (2) the salvation of the cosmos. At the beginning one meets the Dragon and the stage is *nigredo*, or blackness, where there is great suffering. The process first dissolves the *nigredo* and what's left is the *albedo* state – the 'whiteness' of an abstract and idealized state. The soul comes to life to become fully human by enrichment by 'blood' and this is the *rubedo* stage. (p.147)

waves: the landscape is difficult once again. As they were making their way through this thin passage, they could see that the Moon was setting in front of them.

If the waning Moon had risen around 9:00 PM the night before, this Moon (*lo scemo de la luna*) now could be seen taking to its bed (*rigiunse al letto*) to lie down (*ricorcarsi*) in the West in the mid-morning. Most commentators treat this simply as a time reference.[19S] To my mind it is more than that. The Moon, symbol of the regressive tendencies of the night and the timekeeper for Hell and dark prophecy, is now taking her bed in the west. At this moment the Sun in the east has overcome the Moon in the west. The Sun is now ascending and the Moon descending; it's a new day and new beginning for the pilgrim.

On Sin and Penitence

As Virgil explains to Dante at the end of Canto 17, all seven sins are privations or poor relatives of love: pride, envy, and anger are contaminations of love; sloth is characterized by not enough ardor in one's love; the final three are based on excessive love: for wealth (avarice), food and drink (gluttony), and sex (lust).

There are planetary correspondences to these seven sins that the poet would have had in mind writing *The Divine Comedy*. We begin with the two luminaries – pride, the desire to be at the center, is represented by the Sun itself; the Moon, shining with borrowed light, represents envy or the delight in the ill fortune of others. Anger is obviously Mars, and sloth has Saturn's slowness and reluctance to change. Avarice is correlated with Mercury, the planet of the marketplace and the deal. Gluttony is of the nature of the planet Jupiter who loves abundance and superabundance. Lust, the least offensive of the seven, is Venus.

Now we purify the Seven Cardinal Sins. Each sin is addressed on a specific terrace of Purgatory's mountain and cleansed via specific 'remedies' – they are not 'punishments' but opportunities to confront and repent one's erring ways. The cleansing takes place by dual use of allegorical imagery and physical suffering.

Upon entering one of the ledges or terraces, there appear illustrations of the virtue that counteracts the sin that is purified there; upon leaving there are illustrations of the tragic consequences of the sin itself. These examples of virtues are taken from the Bible (particularly the life of Mary) and from antiquity. They follow the process of penance, whereby one is inspired by examples of virtue. At the end, encountering illustrations of the ill effects of the sin, one feels complete revulsion toward the sin and cannot go back.

The Burden of Pride and Blindness of Envy

In the first three ledges the sinners' negativity toward neighbors had compromised their natural love: the prideful hope to exalt themselves by comparing themselves to others, the envious fear of the positive qualities of others and therefore they rejoice in their suffering and difficulties, and the angry hunger after vengeance. Their ordeals all carry a quality of blindness. On these lower ledges Dante's activity is more reflective; later he will be more active.[20]

The first moments upon the first ledge – for the proud – are stunning. Dante and Virgil suddenly see wall paintings along the mountain which have been executed with amazing artistry. It seems that they can hear the figures speaking and even smell the smoke of incense; the scenes themselves seem to move. Three examples of humility are given: from the life of Mary and the Annunciation, from King David in the Old Testament, and the Roman emperor Trajan from antiquity.

Those purifying pride cannot see far because their bodies are lowered by the large boulders they are carrying. Dante also bends down to talk with them; at least by ritual gesture he participates with others in the process of purification. As the pilgrim states in Canto 13, he will have to spend quite a bit of time here among the proud. Dante hears from those whose pride in family, talent or power has become the burden that they now must carry, just as their pride burdened them in life.

In Canto 11, Dante recognizes a formerly famous manuscript illustrator named Oderisi whose work, he says, has only a fraction of the repute given to another. Oderisi carries on eloquently about the flimsiness of worldly fame, citing examples of how various famous artists are eclipsed by others who are then themselves eclipsed. Fame is just a gust of wind that blows in one direction and then another. Fame is simply a category of fortune and subject to its seemingly-random turnings.

After viewing many painted examples of pride's downfalls Dante and Virgil begin to leave this area. On their way out, an angel plucks off one of the "P's" from the pilgrim's forehead, and his footsteps have become far lighter as they move along: purification, at least in ritual, is taking place.

As they emerge onto the next ledge they see no shades or carvings; they see only the livid color of rock.* While waiting for a sense of what to do next, Virgil turns counterclockwise and gives a short prayer of praise to the Sun addressing its sweet light that warms the world and also guides it. They do not see art but now hear voices flying by that give examples of merciful love and later, on their way out, they see examples of envy's tragic consequences.

This ledge contains sufferers appearing like blind beggars who lean upon each other. Their eyes are sewn shut with wires like Dante's contemporaries would use to train a falcon.

Their sin, envy, is called *invidia*, a word that means 'not-seeing' or even 'seeing against'.[21] This is different from how 'envy' usually appears in our ordinary parlance – wanting what somebody else has. Today we even cite envy to complement another's possession or situation. *Invidia* is more malevolent, taking delight in the misfortune of others and we have imported the German *Schadenfreude* to depict this. Although we usually consider this kind of response a guilty pleasure, Dante would consider it poisonous. The virtue that undoes this kind of envy is love or mercy.

We meet Sapia, a Sienese noblewoman of the generation previous to Dante. Addressing Dante's rather overblown introduction to her, Sapia's words are to the point but gentle. When Dante asks to speak to somebody from Italy, she replies that all are citizens of the one true city (*d'una vera città*). She recounts her joy when in life she saw some of her fellow Sienese fall in battle. Her short time thus far in Purgatory was brought about by the sincere prayers of a humble comb-setter who knew her. When Sapia finds out that Dante is still alive touring Purgatory, she rejoices in God's love for him. Dante and Virgil are ready to depart.

Having heard examples of envy turned ruinous, Virgil notes how the heavens call out their splendors and yet we fix our eyes downward. (Canto 14: 145-151) Virgil refers to the sport of falconry whereby the falconer lures the bird down. Instead of being lured down, God attempts

---

* Compare the opening of *Purgatorio* 13 with *Inferno* 13 and their similar depictions of a lifeless and arid landscape.

to lure the person upwards but he or she has been baited down here instead. The stars above are God's lure for the return journey.

Let's pause here and ponder the Sun and Moon and their relationships with pride and envy. Our two most basic failings that can be the root of the others are purified on the two lowest and most crowded ledges of Purgatory.

The traditional astrological Sun differs somewhat from the modern designation of the Sun being one's 'basic identity'. In an astrological birth chart the Sun traditionally represents one's father. In ancient times it was through one's father that the continuity of family and family property was assured over generations, hence the tendency of families even today to take on the father's surname. According to ancient biological doctrine, the male provided the active principle in the formation of an embryo. We can extend these concepts further: on an outer level the Sun represents one's public manifestation; on a physical and psychological level the Sun is the conscious and intentional activity of life. Sun is an astrological principle of engagement.

The Sun's association with pride is clear. When we swell with pride we inflate our outer qualities and take too seriously the fine things the public or even our intimates may say about us. We shine inappropriately and later meet Lady Fortune's down-turnings with outrage. These cantos, however, emphasize pride in one's ability and accomplishment. We use our abilities for personal aggrandizement and not in service to others or to higher divine authority. Instead of looking at the vast sky, those once-proud, now carrying heavy boulders upon their backs have a much narrower view that mimics their former lives.

Bringing together the Moon and envy or *invidia* appears a bit more complicated, since the Moon is more the feminine principle and is the astrological symbol of physical and emotional existence. The modern reader may be unimpressed by the rationale that the Moon's light is borrowed from the Sun and more pale in comparison to the Sun and therefore the Moon is about envy. Instead, think that the Moon is the most changeable and the most adaptive body of astrology's planets: this is its strength as well as its weakness.

To illustrate the difference between solar and lunar responses, I consider a modern Italian, Angelo Siciliano, who was born in 1892, immigrated to America, and died in 1972. He is better known as 'Charles

Atlas', body-builder and successful marketer of body-building programs and education. Mirroring events from his own life, his publicity contained the famous scenario of a '97-pound weakling' who suffered sand being kicked in his face by a bully. Humiliated and angry about the incident – especially because he is usually depicted accompanied by a young woman – this mythical weakling purchases the Charles Atlas training program and begins to work on his conditioning, and we know the rest. The Charles Atlas myth and program perfectly illustrates a *solar* response to humiliation – the skinny guy develops his strength and eventually outshines those who harass him. This vignette is an example of *positive pride*, an inherent self-confidence it takes to reach one's potential.

What would be a *lunar* response to this situation? Our 97-pound weakling would not fight the bullies but *adapt* to them: he pouts, becomes resentful, maybe works on his non-muscular areas of talent, and probably never goes to the beach or sees the woman again. Although he may achieve other successes in life, malevolence lingers subtlety, so that later he rejoices when bad things happen to his former bullies and even to his former female companion. Our lunar friend has chosen the safest but most passive and cowardly path, incurring less risk in the short term but a far greater handicap in life. Such is the envious dynamic of the Moon that many of us also share.* I will touch on this again in the forthcoming presentation of the Sphere of the Moon in Heaven.

In the Middle of the Great Poem

Purgatorio 15-18 recaps much of what has preceded and sets the direction for the remainder of the *Divine Comedy*. The following cantos contain much dialogue, some astronomical configurations, and very little drama.

The sequence of the middle cantos begins with Canto 15 and a look at the sky. Not surprisingly, this is a complex but rich passage. On Purgatory's Mountain it is three o'clock in the afternoon. At this time the Sun's afternoon position is 45° declining from the Midheaven

---

* Shantideva, a ninth century Buddhist sage who wrote *The Way of the Bodhisattva*, notes that we tend to be proud with those inferior to us in some way, resentful of those with qualities superior to ours, and otherwise competitive with equals. Shantideva seems to have reduced four cantos of the *Purgatorio* into one phrase.

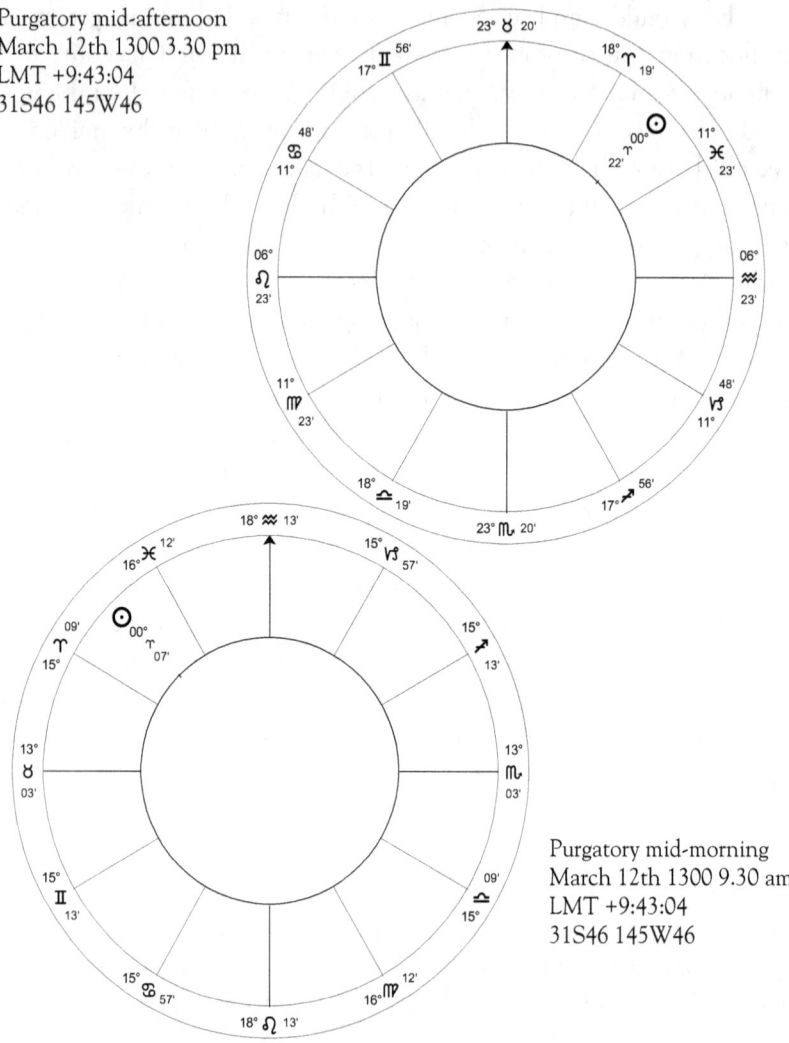

Purgatory mid-afternoon
March 12th 1300 3.30 pm
LMT +9:43:04
31S46 145W46

Purgatory mid-morning
March 12th 1300 9.30 am
LMT +9:43:04
31S46 145W46

Here is the symmetry between the Sun's mid-morning and mid-afternoon positions in the sky. In order to allow this to resemble the more idealized sky of the *Divine Comedy*, I have used *the sky of the spring equinox prior to the narrative of the poem*. In that way the position of the Sun in the sky corresponds most precisely to the time of day.*

---

* If the latitude was at the equator and the Sun was closer to 0° Aries exactly and, the altitude and azimuth of the morning and afternoon Sun would exactly mirror one another.

toward the Descendant. Dante depicts this by referring to the Sun's position *on the other side of the Midheaven*: the Sun has as much left of its daily journey as it had between sunrise and mid-morning. He has set up a relationship so that the previous morning Sun mirrors the current afternoon's position of the Sun.

Then Dante refers to the Sun's path as *la spera/che sempre a guisa di fanciullo scherzo* – the sphere (or circle) that always plays like a little child. (Canto 15.2-3) What is this sphere or circle, this *spera*? This is most likely the ecliptic, the apparent path upon which the Sun and other planets move that goes counterclockwise from west to east. Each day the other motion – the clockwise diurnal motion – traces a different line in the sky. Over the course of a year the path of the Sun and other planets form a spiral as they move along both paths.

In Dante's era, with life spent outdoors or indoors with little light, it would be easy to discern the movements of the Sun in the sky throughout a year. We could see it like a child playing – bouncing a yellowish red ball comes strongly to mind. Not only is his image of the child at play light-hearted (in accord with much of the mood of this canto) but brings to mind how the celestial sphere is organized. This is the beginning of many references to these clockwise and counterclockwise motions that continues to the very top of Paradise.

The symmetry he sets up is in line with other multiple time and place references in the *Purgatorio* that we have discussed already. Suddenly Dante sees a blinding light that he mistakenly thinks is the reflection of the Sun shining off an approaching angel. In a literal way he is mistaken because the angel has its own light. Yet he is intuiting the truth: the angel is indeed a reflection of God. The angel strikes off the mark of envy from Dante and they are on their way to Purgatory's next terrace.

Halfway Between Fortune and Providence

On their way to their next destination pilgrim and guide have a discussion about fortune, articulating the distinction between what can be shared and what cannot (the goods of fortune). This discussion becomes an extension of the discussion from *Inferno 7* of Lady Fortune and her distributions of the world's goods. Virgil makes the distinction between that which money can buy and that which money cannot buy. Here you may also be reminded of the element earth in which no two particles can inhabit the same space; recall that the 'higher elements' of air and fire can blend into the same spaces more easily.

Worldly goods, Virgil tells us, reduce one's share when divided. They are money and property, fame and reputation, a good family or marriage. It is the pursuit of these goods that also make us vulnerable to the downfalls purified on the two ledges below. So it is that the goods of worldly fortune are kept to themselves and our preoccupation with worldly fortune serves to cut ourselves off from others.

Virgil contrasts worldly goods with those that are closer to God that can be shared. In Heaven and ideally on Earth, love is not divided when shared but increased and made greater. Consistent with the theme of brightness of this canto, God moves toward love like sunlight to a shining body (*Purgatorio* 15.67-69). Human love circulates and reflects divine love like mirrors and jewels reflect and augment the light of one another and the light of the Sun (God).

The Angry and Slothful

Cantos 15 and Canto 16 are respectively like the white and black boxes of a checkerboard. Although the time is mid-afternoon, Canto 16 begins by using the night sky to establish a strong contrast with what had come before.

> "*Buio d'inferno e di notte privata*
> *d'ogne pianeto, sotto pover cielo*
> *quant' esser può di nuvol tenebrata*"
>
> "The darkness or gloom of Hell or a night deprived
> of all planets, under a barren sky,
> where everywhere the clouds cast shadows upon it."
> (*Purgatorio* 16.1-3)

Things have changed from the dazzle of the angel's light and Dante's inner visions to a new kind of darkness, a smoke darkness. Here, upon the terrace of anger, they cannot see anything at all because this terrace is engulfed in black smoke. While reading this, we must imagine the protagonists conversing in total darkness.

From the dark smoke someone approaches Dante and Virgil. It is a rather irritable fellow named Marco from Lombardy. He describes himself as somebody who knew the world, who loved virtue even though people have now slackened in its pursuit. Now comes an important moment in the development of astrological themes in the *Divine Comedy* (Canto 16: 58-141).

The pilgrim asks Marco why there is so much evil in their world. Is it the movements of the stars that have caused the world to be such a mess? Marco gives a long and complex answer. This irritation is not at the ideas about stellar causation – that he agrees with – but that people use it as a convenient excuse for their failures in life. You also have free will (*lebero voler*) that can distinguish good and evil and through which you bear responsibility for the choices you make.

For the roots of his day's evil ways, Marco cites political and cultural factors. Because of institutional decay by religious and secular authority, moral guidance is lacking in the contemporary world. We will take up this conversation in detail in Part Three.

Ironically Marco speaks much truth through the thick smoke. As with many people prone to anger, it is easy to attend to the anger and not attend to the content of what is being said. Astrological Mars, although considered a malefic, has a striking range of effectiveness. The fiery red planet pertains to all kinds of human arousal and engagement – and is most often effective when it chooses its battles and when restraint and confrontation are calibrated. After Marco retreats back into the smoke, a light begins to appear – it is the Sun that is about to set. Another angel appears who shows the way to their next destination and wipes another "P" from Dante's brow. We are now in Canto 17.

Because night has begun to fall, they can go no further and must stop and rest. Dante asks Virgil who is in the next area. Virgil responds that its inhabitants' love of the good had fallen short of what was required: they are the slothful. The ensuing conversation between pilgrim and guide takes up much of the next several cantos. This conversation follows Marco's emphasis on cultural factors but with an emphasis on personal desire and responsibility. Virgil's remarks take up the topics of human and divine nature and human and divine love and we will also comment upon them in Part Three when we discuss nature and super-nature.

While Dante and Virgil are talking it is getting later into the night and the Moon is present in the sky. What follows is one of the strangest time references in the *Divine Comedy* (*Purgatorio* 18.76-81).

The Moon dwells in the eastern sky like a *secchion*, a brazier holding coals or a copper bucket on fire (a gibbous Moon) and blots out all the nearby stars. So far this is purely visual and straightforward. But here is the second tercet that further locates the Moon in the sky.

> "*e correa contra 'l ciel per quelle strade*
> *che 'l sole infiamma allor che quel da Roma*
> *tra' Sardi e' Corsi il vede quando cade.*"

> "[The Moon] is running against the heavens on that path
> That the Sun inflames when the Roman
> Between Sardinia and Corsica sees it set."

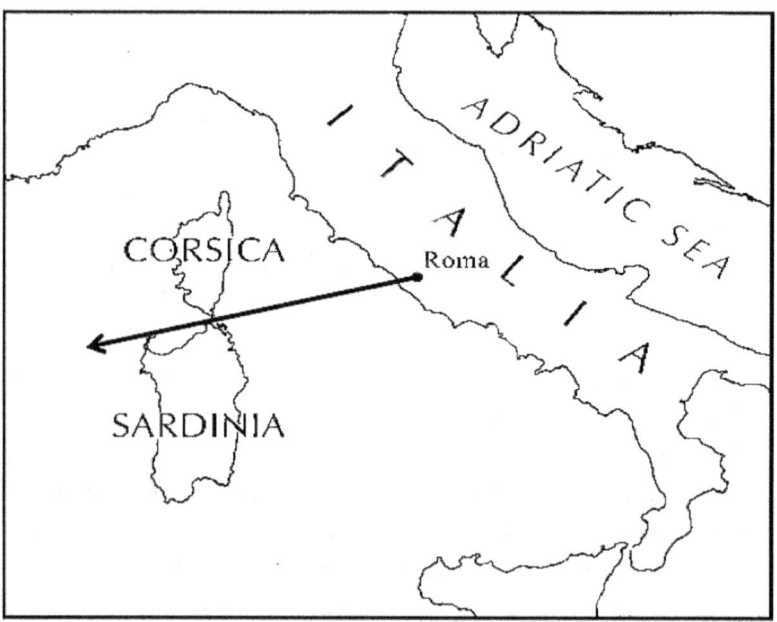

Map of Italy with Sardinia and Corsica to the West /Southwest of Rome

You may note that from Rome one can draw a line between Sardinia and Corsica that goes west and somewhat south. The Sun sets to the south of West when it is in one of the southern signs of the zodiac: Sagittarius and Capricorn. You may recall that the night before the stars of Scorpio formed a head band of pearls for the Moon; tonight the Moon is likely in Sagittarius.

The first line of this tercet refers to the Sun's path being *against* the course of the sky or heaven (*correa contra 'l ceil*). What does he mean by this? In line with Platonic teachings from the *Timaeus* and elsewhere, the path of the clockwise daily circle is thought of as closer to God and eternity. (This was the common medieval understanding and informs Dante's depiction of the upper realms of Paradise where the Sphere of the Fixed Stars contains the Earth's diurnal motion.) The counterclockwise circle is that of the zodiac, along which the Sun and planets move at their own speeds.

The Moon's appearance like a fiery bucket on the eastern horizon is ominous and foretells difficulties in the night ahead. The poet refers not to a springtime Sun emerging with light and warmth but one that is setting and becoming visually remote as the Sun does when it approaches the Tropic of Capricorn: its light and heat are declining.

Suddenly a new set of penitents appears: these are the formerly slothful who are now engaged in their nightly long-distance sprint and hardly have time to speak to the visitors. One former abbot from Verona makes the briefest hurried appearance. Instead of seeing or hearing or having visions of traditional examples of zeal and the evil results of laziness, they shout them out like military recruits at boot camp.

The sin of laziness appears precisely in the middle of the poem. Laziness – moral, spiritual, and political – is indeed one of the central concerns of the entire poem: laziness burdens us all. We have seen laziness demonstrated earlier in the *Purgatorio* by Belacqua and others, and now we see what awaits the slothful when they have made it to the Mountain. The planetary correspondence of laziness is, of course, Saturn, that slow planet moving heavily through the sky. Having procrastinated once, these penitents have not another moment to waste.

After the formerly lazy have run off, Dante's mind begins to drift and the opening of Canto 19 moves toward a second dream.

A Transitional Dream

As with the previous night's dream from Canto 9, this dream is transitional and begins with a description of the heavens. The sequence starts chillingly; I use Durling's prose translation of the first tercets (2003):

> "Ne l'ora che non può 'l calor dïurno
> intepidar più 'l freddo de la luna,
> vinto da terra, e talor da Saturno"

"At the hour when the heat of the day can no longer warm the cold of the moon, vanquished by earth and sometimes by Saturn"

The poet brings us back to how it feels very late at night when the last vestiges of the previous day's warmth are gone. Citing both Moon and Saturn brings out the fact that this coldness is not just from an earth deprived of the Sun but it seems to come down from above.

In the eastern sky appears a configuration of stars:

> "Quando i geomanti lor Maggior Fortuna
> veggiono in orïente, innanzi a l'alba
> surger per via che poco le sta bruna –"

"when the geomancers see their Greater Fortune in the east, before the dawn, rising along a path that stays dark for it but a short while…"

Geomancy came to the medieval Christian world from the Arabs. According to this divinatory art, patterns appearing in sand or elsewhere, or formally cast, may yield one or more specific images that one may use to answer a question or 'read' about an area of life.

The asterism Fortuna Major is formed from a pattern or grouping of stars from the constellations Aquarius and Pisces (or Pegasus[22]) and certainly these stars would rise very early in the morning before the springtime Sun rises in Aries. This asterism is considered quite fortunate, indicating success, fulfillment of desires, luck, and money. Although this asterism appears to Dante in the dark of the night it is also associated with Leo and the Sun.[23] Usually we think of stars in Aquarius and Pisces producing cold, not 'good fortune'.

There is a contradiction between the cold part of the day and noting an asterism that diviners associate with worldly good fortune. Most commentators remind us of the poet's previous treatment of soothsayers and diviners from *Inferno* 20. Because geomancy is divination its interpretations are deceptive and herald the deceptive dream that follows.

I differ from this conclusion. We are no longer in Hell but rather approaching the higher reaches of Purgatory's mountain and we can take in more complex realities. *Purgatorio* 19's opening is auspicious but intentionally disorienting, as is the dream that follows. I divide this dream into four parts.

There appears a woman who is deformed and ugly: she stammers, is cross-eyed, has crooked feet, crippled hands and a pale complexion.

The dreamer gazes at her. As the Sun strengthens cold limbs that the night has made numb (*e come 'l sol /le fredde membra che la notte aggrava*), his gaze has corrected all her deformities – as love desires (*com' amor vuol*).

Now she appears as a beautiful woman and begins to sing to him. She identifies herself as the sweet siren that had steered Ulysses off course, who beguiles sailors, whose voice is so enchanting to hear that rarely can one leave her.

Suddenly appears "a lady" who indignantly asks, "Virgil, who is this?"

Virgil moves to this lady but seizes the 'siren', rips open her garments and exposes her belly and its foul smell awakens Dante.

No, this is not a misogynous dream nor is it even particularly about lust.

Virgil, upon seeing Dante troubled by this dream, states that the woman is the "ancient witch" who is the source of all the ill that is purified above. (Canto 19.58-60) She represents *all* the objects of inordinate desire that are purged in the ledges to come. These objects include wealth for the greedy, food and drink for the gluttonous and beguiling women for this pilgrim's lust.

This dream is about desire in its complexity and our complicity with it. From a disfigured woman the pilgrim fashions an object of beauty, *as love would have it*, but then this woman tells the truth about who she is. Dante's gaze has made her an object of desire; she has become the deceptions that follow. Although the dreamer makes this woman beautiful and she even identifies herself as a cause of misery, he cannot stop this process he has brought about. An "honest" lady (Beatrice to come?) must identify the situation and Virgil must tear away the siren's surface comeliness for the pilgrim to wake up to her nature.

This dream constitutes a wonderful picture of ambivalence, like a compulsive gambler dreaming of being in a casino who then dreams that he or she is in bankruptcy court. This dream shows progress – Dante sees his own mind projecting the woman's beauty, she tells him who she really is, and she is uncovered at the dream's end. In spite of the pilgrim's subsequent discouragement this dream is a *Maggiore Fortuna*.

In the middle of Canto 19 Virgil once again uses metaphors from falconry but also the stars and planets to cheer up and guide the disheartened Dante. In this status sport of medieval Europe, the trainer summons a falcon from the sky by waving a brightly-colored lure toward the bird.[24] Here, however, it is the "great wheels" *above* that are the lure and God who is the falconer summoning us *not down but up*. The wheels of Heaven orient the otherwise worldly person away from temporary conditional goods toward goods that are complete and eternal. To achieve one's destination – Paradise – one needs to survey it with one's eyes. This appears to be the role of the stars and planets in the *Purgatorio*.

Throughout the preceding cantos Virgil's eloquent explanations have not turned Dante's mind away from creating and being seduced by habitual longings for pleasure. A valid philosophical approach can only go so far – further surgery is needed. Thus we begin the final three terraces of Purgatory.

The Easier Part of the Climb (Not Counting that Wall of Fire)

The top three areas of Mount Purgatory are devoted to purifying avarice, gluttony, and lust. Those who are expiating avarice lie face down on the ground. The formerly gluttonous walk around emaciated and are hardly recognizable through their fleshless faces. Those purifying lust walk in fire. They correspond in astrology to Mercury and the benefics Jupiter and Venus, respectively.

In contrast to Virgil's admonition to aim one's gaze upwards toward God's lure, Canto 19 finds Dante and Virgil with those who are face down upon the earth and are unable to look up. These are the avaricious – because their gaze was once set so firmly upon the things of the world now they cannot see above the ground. Dante converses with a pope and a king, once-successful people who now spend their time looking at dirt.

The pope identifies himself, "*scias puod ego fui successor Petri*": "know that I was a successor to Peter" (19.99). He is Adrian V, who was pope only for a short time when he died in 1276 when Dante was 11. Dante attempts to bow to him reverently (something that didn't happen with Pope Nicholas in *Inferno* 19), but Adrian corrects him, saying that they were both fellow servants of one Power. Adrian then wishes to resume his penance, and Dante reluctantly leaves him. Adrian shows the papal lineage in decline: from its promising beginning with Peter, the papacy has degenerated due to its over-involvement in worldly matters.

At the opening of *Purgatorio* 20 there is a denunciation of the she-wolf of avarice – we met her much earlier in the dark wood. Dante hears positive examples of generosity from one of the prone penitents. The speaker here is Hugh Capet, founder of the dynasty that had ruled France up to Dante's time. Capet died over two hundred years before the narrative of the *Divine Comedy*.

Capet introduces himself as the root of the bad tree that casts a shadow over Christendom: *Io fui radice de la mala pianta/che la terra cristiana tutta aduggia* (Canto 20:43-44). Capet then proceeds to denounce his heirs Charles I of Anjou for killing Conradin, the last Hohenstaufen and even poisoning Thomas of Aquinas. (These events would all be considered mistreating Italy.) Hugh Capet takes on Dante's contempories in the form of prophecy of 'future' events (that happened since the *Divine Comedy*'s narrative): Charles of Valois will capture Florence and turn it over to Dante's hated Black Guelfs and his brother, Phillip IV 'Phillip the Fair', who, Dante alleges, was responsible for Pope Boniface's death. Capet then rehearses biblical, mythical, and historical examples of the bad results of avarice and their conversation ends.

Back on the mountain with our pilgrim, the poet gives us a surprise: an earthquake followed by joyful shouts of "*Gloria in excelsis Deo!*" This is not how people usually respond to an earthquake.

During Canto 21 this strange event is explained by another surprise. Walking up to Dante and Virgil from behind is somebody new. This person explains there can be no earthquake here from an earthly cause because Purgatory is Heaven's domain and therefore all causes are from above. Instead, the earthquake signifies the moment when one of Purgatory's penitents rises from his suffering and is now ready for Heaven. *He* is this former sinner, the one standing in front of them.

> **Mercury: the Avaricious and the Honor-Seeking**
> At first glance it seems a little odd to associate astrological Mercury with avarice or with the popes, kings, and the other luminaries upon this terrace. In Paradise's Sphere of Mercury, we will find redeemed souls who in life were distracted by seeking honor.
>
> Consider the conditions required for Mercury to be visible in the sky. Sometimes Mercury is in the east about to become hidden by the beams of the rising Sun in the morning sky; otherwise it may be in the west, hardly visible in the light remaining from the Sun that had just set. Unless one has an unobstructed view of an eastern or western horizon over water, a desert, or down from a mountain, Mercury is difficult to see. The small planet's elusiveness is part of its astrological signification as a fast thinker and talker and as a trickster. Here we also find the planet of the deceptive 'art of the deal'.
>
> On the fifth terrace of Dante's Purgatory, the earthly status of pope and king – solar beings – had settled for the dimmer possibilities of personal gain when there was a far larger range of possibilities available to both. The contrast between the luminous Sun and the dimmer radiance of Mercury symbolizes this. For a king or pope, attending to personal or family gain is like holding out a flashlight when the Sun is already shining.

He identifies himself as Statius, the Roman epic poet. He states that his poetry was inspired by and measured itself by that of Virgil and he would gladly spend another year in Purgatory for the privilege of meeting this great man. The union – or reunion – of Statius with his poetic mentor is a touching moment.

Statius and Dante are metaphorical half-brothers – they have a father in common, Virgil. When Statius credited Virgil for helping him become a Christian as well as a poet, he likens him to one who goes forward in the dark holding a lamp behind him, illuminating the path for others that he cannot see himself (22.67-69). Throughout the *Divine Comedy* Virgil has been Dante's guide and teacher yet he will never get his own taste of Heaven's bliss that is available to his Christian student. Statius' arrival signals that Virgil's ability to teach Dante is coming to an end.

The inclusion of Statius reaffirms the *Purgatorio*'s emphasis on friendship. We had seen this previously in the earlier cantos but not since then. Upon the upper ledges of Purgatory the three share a common calling or vocation – they are all participants in poetry's long-lasting grand enterprise. In order for Dante to accomplish the *Divine Comedy* and especially the upcoming *Paradiso*, he needs to fully harvest the fruit of all traditions of poetry and the blessings of its greatest poets.

Toward the end of Canto 22 we arrive at the area for the gluttons where a tree covers the middle of the road. This is no ordinary tree; its branches face downward so it is impossible to climb; it is nourished by a clear liquid from a high cliff above; and it permeates the air with the delicious odor of sweet fruit. This tree is nourished not from roots below but a water spray from above. Botanically speaking we are closer to the higher realms of the supernatural.

A voice intoning "You shall not eat this food" tells us that this tree represents – and is descended from, actually – the Tree of the Knowledge of Good and Evil from the Garden of Eden. A voice within the tree continues to talk: it exclaims examples of the virtues of abstinence in matters of food and drink. It is the tree itself that is the penance of the former-gluttons: its fragrance and the water's spray brings about feelings of hunger and thirst and emaciates their bodies. Unlike the previous area for avarice, which emphasizes the base nature of the wealth that is longed for, here the object of intemperance is given its best qualities: the fruit has a sweet fragrance and the water is like nectar.

Yet these objects of craving stimulate not satisfaction but hunger: is not more craving the result of craving? The penitents are confronted with the painful qualities of attachment but without the temporary and illusory satisfactions its objects may offer. In Indian mythology the penitents are similar to some inhabitants of the *Preta-loka*, the 'hungry ghost realm', who have huge bellies but tiny throats so they are always hungry and thirsty. With the tree they witness the abundance of creation and the concomitant desire, yet there is no satisfaction but instead the frustration of desire. As with the final terrace immediately above them that purifies lust, the sin of gluttony overextends itself in pursuit of some of the best things in life.

Among those with skeletal faces somebody approaches Dante and exclaims, "*Qual grazia m'è questa!*", "what grace is this for me?" (Canto 23:42)* Dante hears a familiar voice and he finally recognizes his old friend Forese Donati. Here is a different kind of friendship from that between Virgil and Statius, for Donati is from Dante's personal life. Their ensuing conversation is animated and shows an easy familiarity with none of the epic poets' loftiness. Once upon a time Dante and Forese were up to some trouble together. These two are like two former drinking buddies who, both now sober, find each other at an Alcoholics Anonymous meeting.**

During their conversation Donati points out some of the other penitents. One was a former pope who had a famous weakness for eels marinated in wine. Another person approaches Dante, Bonagiunta of Lucca. He was a poet from a generation before Dante, and a critic of the style of poetry that Dante had inherited from Bonagiunta's contemporary Guido Guinizzelli.

The poet Dante has given himself a chance to (1) show off, and (2) begin establishing his poetic credentials and lineage. Bonagiunta asks him if he was the author of a famous canzone from *La Vita Nova* and tells Dante that he and some others had missed out on the "sweet new style" of which Dante is a part. He tells Bonagiunta that he is one who, when love breathes within (or inspires), he takes note and writes down according to its dictation (24:52-62).

This statement leads us to ask, "*What love?*"; "*Whose love?*" Is it the particular love made lofty by Dante's early verses? Is it the love of God and the universe that pervades the next canticle? I find this tercet delightfully ambiguous and can include both possibilities. I also take this to mean that as long as he is taking dictation faithfully and simply, he is on solid ground. Otherwise, he would surely get things wrong.

---

* Contrast this to Brunetto Latini's greeting from *Inferno* 15: Latini and Forese are both significant people in Dante's past and their greetings tell us much about the differences between Hell and Purgatory.

** Dante and Donati may have written poems together called the *tenzone*, which was basically a good-natured off-color exchange of insults. As revealing and humorous as these poems are, Dante does not mention them or allude to them here. It seems that they had gotten into enough trouble without the *tenzone*.

Now they find themselves at a second tree, another shoot from Eden's Tree of Knowledge of Good and Evil. On their way out an angel appears who takes away the second to last "P" on Dante's forehead and they begin moving toward the final ledge of Purgatory.

As we approach the ledge where lust is purified, Dante uses an elaborate astronomical depiction to signal a transition to an important matter for discussion. Canto 25 opens with this time reference.

"At this time of climbing,"

"*ché 'l sole avëa il cerchio de merigge
lasciato al Tauro e la notte a lo Scorpio*" (Canto 25:2-3)

"The Sun had left the meridian
to Taurus and the night to Scorpio."

At noon in the early spring, the Sun and Midheaven would be in Aries; by this time, though, the Sun has descended and Taurus is upon the Midheaven. Therefore it is early afternoon. By evoking the night and the zodiacal sign opposite Taurus, the poet reminds us of Purgatory's opposite location, Jerusalem. This prefigures the cosmic configuration depicted soon, as they become ready to leave Purgatory for the Earthly Paradise.

This astronomical depiction serves to stop the reader's mind and subtly orient him or her to a change of focus. Before going further, however, the poet first gives us some conceptual heavy lifting: the pilgrim asks about the status of minds and bodies in the afterlife. This becomes a lecture by Statius on the divine origins of the soul and the origin of bodies' forms from the stars and planets.

Toward the end of Canto 25, the three poets suddenly see a bank throwing off flames and a wind blowing upwards so the flames fly along a well-defined path. Through the flames they hear a sacred hymn and hear examples of chastity, including penitents calling out by name their chaste marriage partners. ('Chastity' here simply means sexual activity in accord with social convention.)

The poet's depiction of the purgation of lust is primal and unforgettable – the sinners walk through fire. Being 'on fire' with lust is a basic human experience that we all share. But fire, as in the activity of metallurgy and alchemy, also can be part of a purifying process: the fire expunges impurities by burning them away so the pure essence remains. Purified love itself can be like a fire that burns brightly and ardently.

> ### Interlude for Myth
>
> Some of the *Purgatorio*'s previous time references have not been from astronomy but from mythology. Dante draws from Ovid's *Metamorphosis* that depict the Hours, Days, Months, Years, and Centuries attending upon Phoebus, the charioteer of the Sun (Book 2.29-32). Dante also draws from Statius.*
>
> The day before, pilgrim and guide were leaving the cornice of the proud. Virgil hurried Dante by noting that the "sixth handmaiden" (*l'ancella sesta*) had returned from serving the day (12.80-81). This meant that it was after noontime. A few hours earlier in this second day, as the three poets were about to arrive in the area of the gluttons, Dante's image drew from the Hours taking turns steering the Sun's chariot: the fourth *ancella* has left, and the fifth was at the chariot's pole – the helm of a large chariot – whose "horn" was pointing up toward the meridian (22.118-120). It was around 11:00 AM.
>
> This seemingly decorative way of depicting hours of a day hides some consummate literary artistry. Like an accomplished composer who takes a small motif or single chord earlier in a piece to create its grand conclusion, Dante will soon give us another chariot, and the Sun's chariot in particular, in grand fashion.

---

* Statius, Thebaid 3. 406 ff (trans. Mozley) (Roman epic 1st C.E.): "Far on the sloping margin of the western sea sinking Sol [Helios the Sun] had unyoked his flaming steeds, and laved their bright manes in the springs of Oceanus …and the swift-striding Horae (Hours), who strip him of his reins and the woven glory of his golden coronet, and relive his horse's dripping breasts of the hot harness; some turn the well-deserving steeds into the soft pasture, and lean the chariot backward, pole in air." http://www.theoi.com/Titan/Horai.html

On the seventh ledge we find an elemental sameness between the original offence, its purgation, and its purified form. According to ancient and medieval understanding the natural inclination of fire is to go up: upon the ledge for the lustful we are close to being out of Purgatory, up to the Garden of Eden and our lost innocence.

At the beginning of Canto 26 are two groups of people who are walking through the fire. They are in two files going in opposite directions and

> ### Love and Cosmic Circles
> The choreography of Canto 26 is part of a larger pattern with its two intersecting circles of penitents from opposite directions, like the equator and ecliptic circles moving opposite each other but also connecting at the Aries/Libra axis. When the poet wishes to depict love and the universe he presents us, directly or indirectly, with the wheels of the sky. With the lustful in the highest reaches of Purgatory, we find the same interlocking circular structure like the Heavens.
>
> In *Inferno* 5 we saw lustful also in circling motion but in their circle the wind was billowing them about chaotically. Canto 18 is concerned with those who had been involved in what today we would call 'sex trafficking': the seducers and panderers (or pimps). These people are also divided into files going opposite one another, like the equatorial and ecliptical circles. They used sexuality fraudulently, and their punishment mimics the motions of the Heavens. Here in Hell people in file are whipped by devils so they move more quickly.
>
> This pattern presents itself in perfected form in the *Paradiso* in the form of perfect circles. The Circle of the Sun invokes the majestic harmony of both circles. But there the form consists of two (later three) perfect circles containing twelve souls each that revolve around one another. At the very last canto of the *Divine Comedy*, in its final vision, these two cosmic circles symbolize the harmony of the soul's will and intellect. It is love, exalted or degraded, from down in Hell to the highest Heaven, which is the nature and ultimate purpose of the cosmos.

as they encounter each other they exchange brief welcomes and kisses as they pass each other. The first surprise is that one group contains homosexuals and the other contains heterosexuals. Although within a medieval tradition that forcefully condemned homosexuality, Dante's treatment is surprisingly fair.

One of the penitents in the fire speaks with Dante and suddenly discloses himself as Guido Guinizelli. He was the lyric poet of the previous generation whose verse was criticized by Bonagiunta on an earlier terrace, who exerted a strong influence on Dante and others. Dante first gazes admiringly at this man whom he considers his poetic father and finally, as close to the fire as he can get, speaks with him in praise. Addressing Dante as "*Frate*", brother, Guinizelli deflects Dante's praise toward the direction of another penitent, the true father of their vernacular poetry of love – the Provencal Arnault Daniel. Dante ends Canto 26 by having Arnault introduce himself in his native Provencal tongue, asks Dante to remember his pain, and vanishes into the fire that purifies.

Now we have had the *Divine Comedy*'s last conversation about poetry. Like ethical philosophy, poetry can point the way but cannot account for the complete expression of the nature of the world and of the best life possible for humans. For that we need to climb from the natural to supernatural and from reason to revelation and from the vicissitudes of fortune to the decrees of providence. In the *Paradiso* theology supersedes philosophy and astronomy/astrology replaces poetry.

At the beginning of Canto 27 it is time for the pilgrim and the others to leave Purgatory. It is sunset in Purgatory, it is sunrise in Jerusalem, and noon in India and midnight in Spain. The moment is filled with cosmic auspiciousness: the earth is perfectly aligned with Heaven to link the redemption of one man with all of humanity.

> "*Sì come quando i primi raggi vibra*
> *là dove il suo fattor lo sangue sparse,*
> *cadeno Ibero l'alta Libra,*"

> "At sunrise ('where the first rays strike')
> where its Maker bled [Jerusalem],
> the Ebro falls under high Libra (midnight in Spain)."

> "*e l'onde in Gange da nona rïarse,*
> *sì stava il sole; onde 'l giorno sen giva*"

> "And the noontime Sun is scorching the Ganges
> and the day was departing."

An angel appears and invites Dante and the others to cross the wall of fire. The pilgrim freezes: he remembers having once seen people being burned. Virgil tries to reassure him that no harm can possibly occur here, that not one hair on him will burn when he walks through the fire. However, Dante's fear is more persuasive than Virgil's appeals. Virgil finally reminds him that Beatrice is on the other side of the fire and Dante is then able to enter it – and come out on the other side. After a short walk that was so hot he would dive into molten glass for relief, he and the others are on the other side and another angel, brilliant with light, congratulates them.*

What is the signification of walking through fire to depart from Purgatory? Aside from walking some rough terrain, bending down a few times, and getting stuck in some smoke, Dante hasn't really been uncomfortable during his journey up the mountain. The wall of fire does take the measure of him. Before entering the Garden of Eden one's purification must be complete: those parts of us that hang onto our harmful tendencies must be burned away completely. Purifying our defects deprives us of a part of who we think we are – and that too must be burned away.

It was sunset when Virgil, Statius, and Dante crossed the fire and now they must stop as night descends. Instead of the astronomical complexity preceding the dreams of the two nights before, we get a simple picture: the stars above appear bigger and brighter than before. (This takes us back to the moments at the last tercets of the *Inferno*, when Virgil and Dante were moving out of Hell and from a small opening saw the stars above them. Here the opening is larger and the stars are brighter.)

---

* There is no mention of either angel taking the final "P" from Dante's brow, nor is it mentioned that the fire has burned it away. We may consider this an omission but instead it's probably a purposeful ambiguity – for our hero, purging lust and getting beyond Purgatory would be the same thing. Or perhaps the living poet writing the *Divine Comedy* didn't want to pretend that lust had been removed from him.

He and others fall asleep on the steps leading to the Earthly Paradise. It is at the rising of Venus, the planet that inclines us to love, that Dante falls asleep and begins to dream. His third dream on Purgatory contains no hints of evil or creepiness: the dream is a soothing vignette from the Bible.

The dreamer sees a young lady walking in a meadow singing that she is Leah (Jacob's wife in the Hebrew Bible) and she is making a garland for herself. She is different from her sister Rachel (Jacob's second wife) who sits in front of her looking-glass all day. Leah says that Rachel is as desirous of seeing as she is desirous of making something beautiful for herself. Leah finds satisfaction in doing and her sister finds satisfaction in seeing. (Canto 27.97-106)

To the medieval imagination Leah and Rachel were the active and contemplative lives respectively. Leah and Rachel are cast as two different people whose styles neither oppose nor blend but complement each other. In Paradise we will find right engagement and then right contemplation preached and modeled. This is the best life possible on earth. Gone are the complexities of the previous dreams; this is a dream like that of a child.

When they awake Virgil has his last words with Dante. So far this journey through Hell and Purgatory has been one of moral education and improvement. Virgil, spokesperson for ancient wisdom through the prism of medieval revisionism, tells his charge that his will and desire are now in alignment and from now on he can trust his own desire and his own pleasure. Virgil, referring to the symbols of state and church (crown and mitre) confers upon Dante the status of a new man who is sovereign over himself, with a will that is now "free, upright, and sound." (*Purgatorio* 27:139-142)

Paradise Descending

The last cantos of *Purgatorio* parallel the last cantos of *Inferno* and *Paradiso* – all bring us into different worlds than what we previously encountered. *Inferno* concludes in the icy pit of Cocytus, an ugly surreal landscape with Lucifer at its center; *Paradiso* above ends beyond the stars, beyond space and time in an empire of light with God at its center. *Purgatorio* ends in the Earthly Paradise, the original Garden of Eden. This is a realm of nature that has always been perfect because all its causes are directly from the Heavenly Paradise, the realm of super-nature. These final cantos anticipate much of what comes in the *Paradiso*, and provides the environment for the emotional core of the poem, the long-awaited meeting of Dante and Beatrice.

We begin with the opening of *Purgatorio* 28. Now in front of Virgil and Statius as if leading them, Dante finds himself in a forest – not an *ocura selva*, a 'dark wood' but "*la divina foresta*", and, a few lines later, "*la selva antica*", the 'old wood'. Instead of being hurried along as before, Dante walks very slowly. This grove of trees pleases all the senses: Dante feels a cool breeze that inclines the trees' branches toward the East; he hears the sweet sounds of birds in the trees balanced by the lower-pitched sounds of the breeze flowing through leaves. His path is stopped by a stream, clear and pure, darkened only by being in the shadow of the grove of trees so lush that neither the Sun nor Moon can penetrate it.

This sensual pastoral scene is missing only one thing – a *pastorella*! – a 'shepherdess'. Across the stream Dante sees a solitary woman. She moves as if she was dancing, laughing and singing as she gathers flowers. Her eyes look as if she's in love. After all the weirdness upon Mount Purgatory it's nice to get a sweet and relaxed setting brought alive by a beautiful woman. Dante thinks this woman to be like Proserpina before Pluto abducted her; he resents the stream for keeping her at a distance from him.

The woman – whose name we will hear later – begins by saying "you people are new", "*voi siete nuovi*", remarks that her love is rejoicing and singing gratitude to God, and offers to answer any questions he may have. Immediately Dante regains perspective (maybe the last "P" is gone after all) and asks her how this place, so close to God, could have earthlike weather.

She becomes teacher and Dante becomes student. She tells him that they are in the Earthly Paradise, the original Garden of Eden, showing what humans had before the fall of Adam. She explains that here their elevation is so high that this realm is closer to God: there could be no disturbances here to harm any human. The breeze here does not come from nature's turbulence but from the first turning of Heaven (the path of the fixed stars and the zodiac) and the resulting breeze turns in its own circle and accounts for the forest's sounds. The wind strikes plants here so that the air itself becomes impregnated and causes the various trees to come about and to grow.

The poet is rendering a purified and elemental physicality to us. The water here is not from ordinary evaporation and condensation but emits from a fountain that pours directly from the will of God. On one side of this fountain flows the river Lethe that erases the memory of sin; the other river is Eunoè that strengthens memory of previous good. Like the original Age of Gold in ancient poetry, this is an earthly realm that is primordial and beyond corruption. The pilgrim and the ancient poets have stepped onto a transformed world.

At the beginning of Canto 29, a bright light like lightning flashes through the forest. On one side of a river is Dante and on the other side, to his right, a solemn procession begins to appear.

We have now entered a realm of pure allegory: everything in this procession has a specific meaning that would be familiar to Dante's contemporaries.

The sudden light that begins the procession is from seven large candles whose blaze creates seven streams of light above; they symbolize the Seven Gifts of the Holy Spirit. These gifts, which are loosely correlated with the four cardinal and three theological virtues, are: wisdom, understanding, counsel or right judgment, courage, knowledge, piety, and fear or awe of God.[25] Behind are twenty-four elders in white who symbolize the twenty-four books of the Hebrew Bible. Behind them are four creatures with wings, each wing containing six eyes. These are the four men who wrote the four Christian gospels. Their images – the Bull, Lion, Eagle, and Angel or Man, are traditionally correlated with the fixed zodiacal signs of Taurus, Leo, Scorpio, and Aquarius. Behind them and drawing a grand chariot is a griffin, a mythical animal with wings and the head of an eagle and the body of a lion. The griffin, with its twofold nature as creature of earth and air, symbolizes Jesus Christ. The chariot itself represents the Church. It is of greater brilliance than any that drew a triumphant Roman emperor and out-dazzles the mythical Chariot of the Sun (29.115-120).

Along the chariot's left wheel are four women, all dressed in purple, who represent the cardinal virtues of wisdom, fortitude or courage, justice, and temperance. Along the chariot's right wheel are three women who symbolize the theological virtues of faith, hope, and charity; they are dressed in glowing red, green, and white respectively. Behind the chariot are four, then two, then one man of different colors and characters; they represent the later books of the Christian Bible or New Testament. The one at the very back looks like he is half-asleep or in a trance – he is John of Patinos, the writer of the Book of Revelations from which much of this pageant's symbolism is derived.[26]

Suddenly we hear a thunderclap, just as at the procession's beginning we saw something like lightning. The procession suddenly comes to a halt. Dante continues this lengthy rollout to open Canto 30 with an astronomical allusion.

"*Quando il settentrïon del primo cielo,*
che né occaso mai seppe né orto
né d'altra nebbia che di colpa velo" (Canto 30.1-3)

"When the Septentrion (7-star constellation) of the first heaven
That has never had occasion to rise or set
Or wear the veil of any other fog except for sin"

These lines tell of seven stars from the first Heaven (line 1) that have never risen or set (line 2) or been veiled by anything but sin (line 3). The first Heaven is the Empyrean, the realm of Paradise beyond time and space wherein the redeemed are truly present and at whose center (and circumference) is God. The seven gifts are of the Holy Spirit, which is also God.

In the following tercet (3-6) we hear of the *lower* Septentrion: this is either the constellation Ursa Major ('Great Bear', or 'Big Dipper') or Ursa Minor ('Little Bear', or 'Little Dipper'). These constellations are close to one another in the northern sky. It is likely that Dante meant Ursa Minor, for its brightest star is Polaris the North Star: this star guides navigators to port as these Seven Gifts guide humans to salvation. The poet likens the Empyrean to these circumpolar constellations, hinting at the ultimate Paradise while staying within the range of conventional mind.

Lines from the Bible and from Virgil's *Aeneid* are now sung. The area becomes more crowded by the sudden appearance of many angels upon the chariot who surround the lead character. Dante sees a woman within the chariot; she is dressed with a green crown above a white veil covering her face and a green mantle over a bright red garment (the colors, once again, of the theological virtues). Dante recognizes Beatrice and, turning to Virgil in amazement, discovers that this guide has disappeared. Beatrice then begins to address the pilgrim.

There have been many reunion scenes in the *Purgatorio* and most have joy, nostalgia, and humor. This one is different from all of them. Beatrice's bearing is not loving but regal. She says that yes indeed she is Beatrice but what are you, Dante, doing here in the Earthly Paradise? Do you not know that here men are happy? (*non sapei tu che qui è l'úom felice?*) Dante showing up in the Earthly Paradise, without having acknowledged and repented his life's wrongdoings, would be like attending an event at Buckingham Palace or a state dinner at the White House dressed in dirty jeans and a t-shirt. When the surrounding angels implore Beatrice to be merciful Dante begins to melt into tears.

Addressing the crowd of angels Beatrice states her case. This is a man, she says, who came into life well-favored by the great wheels of the Heavens and with an abundance of grace but he misused his many advantages and had gone far astray. During her lifetime Beatrice had attempted to sustain him through her beauty, but after she died he soon followed false images of the good, (*imagini di ben seguendo false* 30.131). He had fallen so low that Beatrice sent Virgil to rescue him.

Then, at the opening of Canto 31, Beatrice addresses Dante directly and asks him to account for himself. After first being unable to speak but soon in tears, he admits that once she died he had pursued those present things with their false pleasure (*Le presenti cose/col falso lor piacer volser miei passi* Canto 31:34-35).

Beatrice upbraids Dante mercilessly. She accuses him of abusing his God-given gifts, including her own presence in his life, and becoming a moral and spiritual slacker of the worst sort. Like a mother scolding a young child, she asks him to look at her. As his gaze moves upward to see her, she turns her eyes toward the griffin and, when he looks at her for the first time

> "*Sotto 'l suo velo e oltre la rivera
> vincer pariemi più sé stessa antica,
> vincer che l' altre qui, quand' ella c'era.*" (31.82-85)

> "Under the veil and on the other side of the river she seemed to surpass her former self more than she surpassed others when she was here."

The pilgrim now feels regret at the core of his being, hatred toward all that had once pleased him so much. He faints; when he comes to he is being taken across the river Lethe by the woman of the forest. He drinks of Lethe's water and forgets his former sinfulness – at least for now.

Think of Beatrice as Dante's personal incarnation of divinity. His falling in love with her was not just a worldly affectation but also provided him with a personal opening to God. Dante's personal experiences of youthful sexuality and romance, focused on this unattainable woman, had become an opening to divinity for him. She is divine love, an emanation of God's glory, undivided from the young Dante's attractive neighbor who was married off to a banking family and who died too soon. The poet has brought together the longings of the troubadour poet and the Christian doctrine of the Incarnation.

Dante's personal situation represents many things about us: our mismanagement of spiritual good fortune, our lost opportunities from youth, becoming distracted by temporary gratification (sensual or intellectual) and forgetting what truly brings happiness. These situations are spoken of in every spiritual tradition and, to some extent, they are all our stories.

The pilgrim's confession also makes good his previous ascent of those three steps on the way onto Purgatory's ledges (Canto 9). Renunciation and repentance need to be personal and immediate to have any value. This helps move Dante the pilgrim from a focus on feeling better into the realm of true personal transformation.

The narrative continues, and Dante is now on the same side of the stream as the procession. It is time to see Beatrice for who she is, and the four beautiful women who are the four cardinal virtues begin to take him to her.

The women identify themselves in this way: "*Noi siam qui ninfe a nel ciel siama stelle*" (31.106) – "here we are nymphs but in the sky we are stars."

You may remember from the beginning of *Purgatorio* that Dante, looking to his right, saw four stars in the southern sky; he finds out that these are the four virtues of courage, prudence, temperance, and justice. These virtues are not the result solely of hard work but are also gifts of divinity. This line also reminds us what we are witnessing: a pageant from

Heaven itself, Paradise descending to make itself available to Dante and to us, providing a worldly transition to an otherworldly Heaven. Soon it will not be the stars that come down to Dante, but Dante himself, guided by Beatrice, who will go up to the stars.

Having led Dante to Beatrice, the four women in purple ask Beatrice to reveal herself for who she is. Once again she looks at the griffin and

> ### River Crossings
> Previously we looked at rivers flowing – mostly downwards. Rivers are powerful symbols of crossings into a new life. It was the River Jordan where the Israelites crossed into the Promised Land and also where Jesus was baptized.[27] The ritual of baptism (from the Greek 'to dip') became the Christian rite of initiation and incorporates motifs of purification and also crossing.
>
> Upon the Earthly Paradise the river Lethe – forgetfulness (of past sins) – divides where Dante and the others enter and where we find Beatrice and the pageant. It is across the river that Dante and Beatrice first converse and it is across the river where Dante is led to look upon her directly. We could say that on this side of the river is the natural and the other side is the supernatural or the divine.
>
> The four nymphs, representing the four cardinal virtues, are on the other side of the river with Beatrice. Singleton (1967) deduces that they do not represent the virtues of wisdom, courage, justice, and temperance that are natural, but as 'infused' or bestowed by divine grace.* Otherwise, he posits, these nymphs across the river could not be the same as the four stars in the southern sky that we saw in *Purgatorio*'s opening lines.
>
> Dante crosses the river Lethe to forget past sins and the river Eunoè to remember better previous good. In the *Paradiso* Dante drinks from his eyes a river of light to enter the Empryean. This river of light marks not a physical but perceptual crossing as Dante can now gaze upon the eternal splendor of highest heaven.

---

* There is a parallel between the presentation of these virtues and within Mahayana Buddhism. The six *Paramitas* are the activities of generosity, discipline, patience, exertion, meditation, and wisdom. Usually these six are

Dante now sees the two natures of the griffin are reflected in her eyes. Beatrice is now seen as transformed – transfigured – into a creature of heaven. Three women who represent the theological virtues of faith, hope, and charity – who "see more deeply" than the others, ask her to reveal her mouth and therefore her smile. The poet has no words to describe this experience: the aesthetic, romantic, and the divine all converge as the face of one particular woman.

The procession now begins to move to the right – clockwise. Beginning with the seven candles they begin to turn east toward the rising Sun. When all had passed before them the griffin-drawn chariot begins to turn its pole that corresponds to the North Star and the circumpolar stars.

Here the procession's 'still point' or 'pole star' is the chariot. Christ and the church are now like the spot in the sky that allows sailors to find port. The still point and the pole star both signify the high heaven that is the First Motion and both also anticipate the highest Heaven, the Empyrean.

The procession stops by a tree that is decayed and stripped of its leaves – this is the original Tree of Knowledge. At this point there begins a ritual of re-enactment and redemption performed by the griffin who is the stand-in for Jesus Christ, who speaks of divine justice, and the tree is new again.

Then Dante does what many of us do when overwhelmed by profound truth – *he falls asleep*. When he awakes the procession has gone except for the chariot, Beatrice who is now sitting by the tree, and the seven nymphs who represent the seven cardinal and theological virtues. The medieval allegory play continues but with a less happy story: it enacts the various crises of the Christian Church up to that point.*

---

called 'transcendent actions' or 'perfections', yet the word itself also means to go beyond, or to the other side – to the other shore. The Paramitas serve purposes similar to the four cardinal virtues: they are specific disciplines for the advancement of the practitioner *and* they are natural attributes of a realized person or *bodhisattva*.

* The chariot continues to represent the church; twice there are incidents in which an eagle – representing empire – leaves feathers on the chariot. This is the church becoming too infused with secular authority and worldly goods – that leads to its becoming corrupt. At the end is an image of a harlot

In the *Inferno* and *Purgatorio*, the poet had taken on civil authority of different kinds – Florentine, 'Holy Roman Empire', and French. Although he has taken on a few individual popes he has not yet taken aim at his current Catholic Church. This little drama anticipates the more thorough (and searing) treatment of the Church by the citizens of Paradise.

By the end of *Purgatorio* Beatrice has established herself as Dante's guide and teacher, although for Dante this takes some getting used to. Beatrice gives an opaque prophecy of a "messenger from God" (*messo di Dio*) who will end the present madness of church and state – the stars are already near that will secure this event (Canto 33.40-45). Dante does not understand much of the previous allegory play or Beatrice's teaching and prophecy: he is to note things as he witnesses them.

Dante asks about the Earthly Paradise's second river and Beatrice tells him to ask *Matelda* – we finally have a name for the *pastorella*.

> ### Dancing Matelda
> Dante scholars have puzzled over the identity of the forest lady for a very long time; centuries later there is still no consensus. In recent critical editions of the *Purgatorio*, Hollander (2003) tells us that this name is less important than her role as Eve before the fall; Musa (1985) tells us that the subject of her identity is pointless, for she is more symbol than person. Because she had been nameless from her appearance in Canto 28 until almost the end of the *Purgatorio*, scholars and readers have correctly stressed her symbolic attributes; she is part Eve, part angel, and part forest goddess. She may also parallel Leah, who represents the active life, who speaks of Rachel, who represents the contemplative life and is likened to Beatrice. Charles Singleton (1967) talks of Matelda as Astraeia, a goddess of justice – a principle of the soul's harmony – and the last creature to leave the ancient paradise at the end of its Age of Gold.

---

and giant in the chariot; after abusing the harlot, the giant carries her off into the forest. The harlot is the corrupted church; the giant is the French monarchy; the forest that the harlot is being carried off to represents the relocation of the papacy from Rome to Avignon in France.

Dante does supply this woman with a name and we must take this seriously, for a name can supply us with richer layers of meaning. Perhaps, some write, Matelda was a friend or relative of the historical Beatrice who is lost to history.

Many scholars associate the name Matelda with Countess Matelda of Canossa from the eleventh and early twelfth century but do not know what to make of it. This Matelda was present for an important moment in medieval history. In Matelda's courtyard, Holy Roman Emperor Henry IV spent three days barefoot in the snow supplicating her guest, Pope Gregory who previously excommunicated him. Their conflict was about whether pope or secular authority had the right to appoint bishops and this incident settled the matter for awhile. By using this name, the poet was possibly alluding to the ongoing relationship between Church and Empire that are twin political concerns of the *Divine Comedy*.

I wish to add yet another dimension, an astronomical one. For Matelda is also Venus, the goddess and the morning star.*
Matelda is not the wanton and lustful goddess familiar to ancient mythology who was thought to drive people crazy (see the opening to *Paradiso* 8) but has been 'updated' to a Christian context. This *bella donna* sings and dances and has love in her eyes, is indeed presented as a warm, flowing, and loving person; the love in her heart, like the song she sings, is an affirmation of *divine sources* of love. The metaphors around her do not associate her with Diana, the chaste forest goddess with whom the poet would be on safer – and far less interesting – ground.

Matelda is also Venus the planet, evoking memories of the first beautiful object seen in Purgatory's early morning sky: the

---

* In their critical edition of *Purgatorio* (2003) Durling and Martinez provide a translation of a poem by Guido Cavalcanti, a friend and contemporary of Dante, p.589. Its beginning contains one clue about who this woman is:

   "*In un boschetto trova' pastorella
   Pi`u che la stella – bella, al me'parere.*"

   "In a little wood I found a shepherdess, more
   Beautiful than the morning star, it seemed to me"

> sight of this planet lightened the dark memory of the visitation to Hell and she was causing the entire sky to laugh as she veiled the stars of Pisces. Venus, the planet that strengthens love, heralded the soon arising Sun, just as Matelda's presence heralds the arrival of Beatrice in the chariot that surpassed the Chariot of the Sun. And just as Love heralds and makes way for the radiance of Wisdom, Venus heralds the Sun rising in the east.

At the very end of the *Purgatorio*, Matelda takes Dante to the river Eunoè to drink: drinking from this river magnifies the memory of all former good acts and allows him to understand his previous sin as occasion for God's grace.

The canticle concludes with the verse below. Just as Dante saw the Tree of Knowledge made new in a little drama of human redemption, the individual has also been renewed. Notice the repetition of *novelle*, new, and that it is made to rhyme with *stelle*, stars. The translation that follows is from M. S. Merwin (2000, p 331).

> "*Io ritornai da la santissima onda
> rifatto sì come piante novelle
> rinovellate di novelle fronda,*
>
> *puro e disposto a salire a le stelle.*" (*Purgatorio* 33:142-145.)

> "From the most sacred waters I returned
> remade in the way that trees are new,
> made new again, when their leaves are new,
> pure and ready to ascend to the stars."

Afterword: Cardinal Sins and Planets

I have a assumed a specific correlation between the seven Cardinal Sins and the seven visible planets and their astrological symbolism, although this is not stated directly in the *Purgatorio*. Yet this concept has a long history that goes back into antiquity and endured well past Dante's lifetime. Below are two suggestive references of planets and sins from that era.[28]

One is from the *Corpus Hermeticum*, an influential text in ancient times that was unknown in Dante's day. This body of teachings came from Egypt roughly during the time of the rise of Christianity. Part of the *Corpus* is the *Poimandres*, a short dialogue between the student Hermes and Poimandres, the principle of *Nous* or divine intellect. Poimandres tells Hermes that the universe had descended from primal being through (archetypal) Man into Nature and Earth to give rise to individuals with both physical bodies and immortal souls. Upon death, somebody with wisdom who has led a virtuous life is now free from the burdens of body, senses, and emotions. In a journey similar to that in Dante's *Paradiso*, this person goes back home through the planets. (For clarity I have placed the planetary spheres in brackets.)

> "Thus a man starts to rise up through the harmony of the cosmos. To the first plain [Moon] he surrenders the activity of growth and diminution; to the second [Mercury] the means of evil, trickery now being inactive; to the third [Venus] covetous deceit, now inactive, and to the fourth [Sun] the eminence pertaining to a ruler, being now without avarice; to the fifth [Mars] impious daring and reckless audacity and to the sixth [Jupiter] evil impulses for wealth, all of these now being inactive, and to the seventh plain [Saturn] the falsehood which waits in ambush."[29]

We see traditional meanings of the planets and some interesting twists. In its common astrological depiction, the Moon stands for the vicissitudes of a human body. To astrologers past and present, Mercury is a clever conniving planet; the Sun represents leadership; Mars gives qualities of daring and recklessness; Jupiter is associated with wealth. Venus is usually linked with love, lust, and luxury but here it's called "covetous deceit". ("Covetous deceit" in this context seems more emotional entanglement than physical desire.) Saturn, the cold and dry outermost planet is the planet of falsehood, perhaps symbolizing the deception of materiality itself.

The following paragraph from *Poimandres* seems to foreshadow Dante's *Paradiso*. The *Paradiso* is but one example of a spiritual journey rendered through the stars and planets, for there is a long history in the ancient and medieval eras for this literature.

> "Then, stripped of the activities of the cosmos, (the man of virtue) enters the substance of the eighth plain [fixed stars] with his own power, and he sings praises to the Father with those who are present; those who are near rejoice at his coming. Being made like to those who are there together, he also hears certain powers which are above the eighth sphere [empyrium], singing praises to God in a sweet voice. Then in due order, they ascend to the Father and they surrender themselves to the powers, and becoming the powers they are merged in God. This is the end, the Supreme Good, for those who have had the higher knowledge to become God."

More available to the medieval poet was a commentary on Virgil's *Aeneid* by Servius from the fourth century. Here we find another set of correspondences. Discoursing on line 714 of Book VI of the *Aeneid*, (depicting Aeneas' journey through the underworld) Servius comments:

> "Astrologers conceive that the body and soul are connected by powers of individual divine qualities in this fashion because when the souls descend, they attract to themselves the torpor of Saturn, the anger of Mars, the lust of Venus, the desire for gain of Mercury, and the longing for power of Jupiter."[30]

This list is closer to medieval and modern astrological depictions of the planets. Mercury's vice appears to be avarice and Jupiter's focus is not on wealth, as in the *Poimandres*, but on power. The Sun and Moon do not appear.

The Hermetic text and *Aeneid* commentary both refer to a spiritual journey through the planetary spheres. In the *Poimandres* the good and wise person ascends and releases his or her worldly vices; the *Aeneid* commentary goes the other way: one descends and takes them on. In both texts we see these seven sins all complicating our true nature. The planets symbolize these faults and also express the transition between worldly and divine being.

I now offer a third example that is more contemporary with Dante. It is from an English manuscript about a century after the *Divine Comedy*.[31] In this text we read about an allegorical battle for the soul between charity and the seven cardinal sins; the sins divide into pride and sloth (from the devil), envy, anger, and avarice (from the world), and gluttony and lust (from one's own flesh).

According to this text, each sin has assistance from a particular planet: *the Sun aids pride, Moon envy, Mars anger, Saturn sloth, Mercury avarice or covetousness, Jupiter gluttony, and Venus lust.* I have reordered the sequence of sins and planets to the order of the seven ledges of the *Purgatorio*. It is this correlation, I feel, that we can find in the *Purgatorio*. But it is indirect.

If we keep to the classification of sins and planets cited above, there is an order to the ledges of Purgatory. We can see the sequence of ledges if we classify the planets into the luminaries (Sun and Moon) and the starry planets, into benefics (Jupiter and Venus) and malefics (Mars and Saturn). Like the *Sun* and *Moon* the faults of pride and envy (or ill will) are pervasive and foundational for the others. Pride and envy are the means by which the other vices have greater ability to cause damage. Anger, represented by malefic *Mars*, fits right above the bottom two. The higher ledges of the mountain represent those vices characterized by excessive love and are therefore more redeemable. Avarice relates to the neutral planet *Mercury*. The two lightest (but not most infrequent) vices, gluttony and lust, are the matter of the benefics *Jupiter* and *Venus* respectively. The two benefics represent the goodness of sensual existence taken to excess.

But what of *Saturn*, in the middle position and here affiliated with sloth? In the structure of Paradise the central planet is the Sun, the maestro of the other planets and representing wisdom in its many forms. In Purgatory, however, the middle ledge is inhabited not by wise people but by spiritual underachievers whose efforts were too little or too late. Laziness may be the common quality to all of them and thus Saturn would justly be given a central place in the mountain's structure. This also befits the mountain's earthly structure and its difficult climb only made easier by direct help from above.

Is there a connection between Saturn's quality of contemplation in heaven and an affiliation with laziness in Purgatory? The reader may want to return to *Purgatorio* 4 and find that Belacqua is still crouched under a rocky ledge, thinking.

Did Dante know of this set of attributions of seven planets? This seems very likely. Why did he not use them directly? Perhaps he takes from the Neoplatonic tradition that criticized astrologers for thinking that some heavenly bodies could be malefics when all Heaven is divine by nature. Although the visible planets and their astrological significations are not directly mentioned in the first two canticles they seem indispensible to their structure. If by increasing aspiration to and descending love from God one moves upward in Purgatory, it is only in Heaven that the planets provide levels of perfection. In Paradise the motion between planetary spheres is effortlessly upwards. Here the planets have not elemental meanings as in the *Inferno* or psychological meanings as in the *Purgatorio* but instead are connected with spirituality and ultimate good.

Paradise is our next destination.

Notes
1. *Tetrabiblos*, Robbins translation p.18
2. *Tetrabiblos*, Robbins translation pp.186-187
3. Kay, R. (1994) p.14
4. Ibn Ezrz, *The Beginning of Wisdom*, trans. Epstein (1998) pp.96-97
5. Nohrnberg, J. "Canto 18: Introduction to Malebolge" in *Lectura Dantis: Inferno* (1998) Ed. Madelbaum. Berkeley and Los Angeles: University of California Press.
6. Ibn Ezrz, *The Beginning of Wisdom*, trans. Epstein (1998) p.91
7. Durling/Martinez (1996) p.124; Reynolds (2006), p.141
8. Slavitt, D. (2008) p.2
9. Slavitt, D. (2008) p.32
10. Patch, Howard (1927/1967) p.3
11. Translated R. Zoller (1980) p.85
12. See *Solar Fire* astrology software program
13. Durling/Martinez (2003) p.19
14. Raimondi, Ezio "Canto 1: Ritual and Story". Mandelbaum et al. p.5
15. See Quinones, R. "Canto VIII: In the Valley of the Rulers". Mandelbaum et al, pp.74-76
16. Schnapp, Jeffrey "Introduction to *Purgatorio*". *The Cambridge Companion to Dante*, ed. R. Jacoff. p.93
17. Durling and Martinez (2003) pp.137-138

18. See Luke, H. p.71
19. See Singleton (1973) pp.199-200; Durling/Martinez (2003) p.166
20. See Ferguson, *Dante's Drama of the Mind*
21. Hollander (2003) p.287
22. Martinez/Durling (2003) pp.316-317
23. "The Astrological Origin of Islamic Geomancy." Van Binsbergen, V. (2003) http://www.shikanda.net/ancient_models/BINGHAMTON%20 1996.pdf
24. Durling/Martinez (2003) p.320
25. Thomas of Aquinas, *Summa Theologica* II, 2
26. Martinez, Ronald, "Rolling Out the Apocalypse", from Durling/Martinez (2003) pp.623-626
27. See Freccero, John, *The River of Death*, 55-69, from Freccero, J. *Dante: The Poetics of Conversion*
28. See Bloomfield, 1967
29. Salaman, van Oyen, and Wharton, *The Way of Hermes* p.23
30. Bloomfield (1967) p.31
31. Bloomfield (1967) p.233

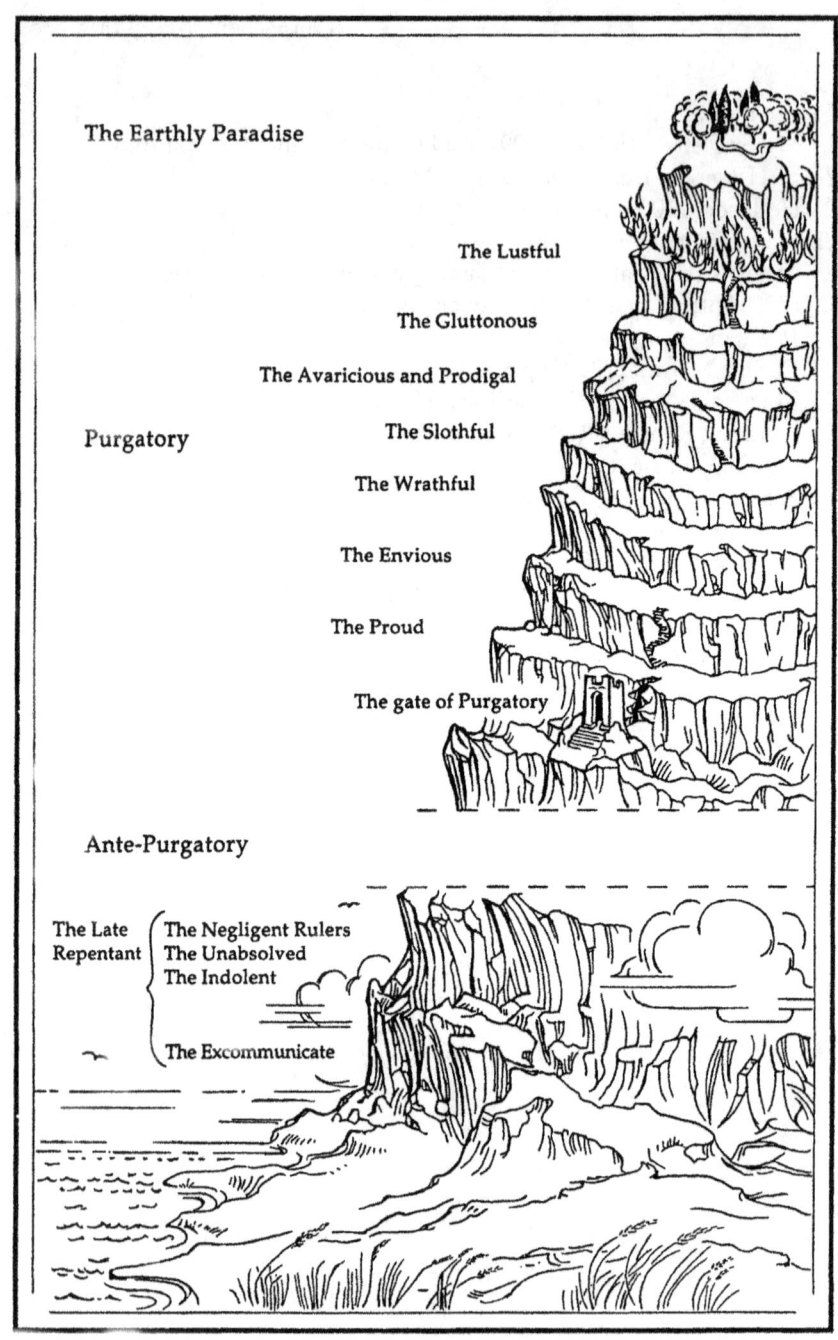

The Structure of Dante's Purgatory

The Divine Comedy of Dante Alighieri: Volume 2: Purgatorio: Purgatorio v. 2 by Dante Alighieri, Ronald L. Martinez, Robert M. Durling and Robert Turner (2004). Illustration p.xiv. Reproduced by permission of Oxford University Press, Inc.

Part Two

Paradiso: Empire of Light

Our Planetary Journey

Prelude to Bliss

As we begin our ascent into Heaven we ask a simple question: why is a *Paradiso* necessary?

Dante the pilgrim has gone through the awakening tour of Hell and the release of sin on the mountain of Purgatory. In the Earthly Paradise he has been crowned and mitred as lord over himself and has repented his previous moral wanderings and sidetracks. He no longer possesses a one-way ticket to damnation; his soul has been reclaimed and – if he doesn't backtrack – he is out of the woods and will eventually find Heaven.

Yet in the third canticle the pilgrim will ascend through Paradise. He will be educated by Beatrice and some of Paradise's prominent citizens. From his own ancestor Cacciaguida, he will learn about his personal fortune and his destiny. He will get a Heaven's eye view of our planet, be quizzed by the apostles, interview Adam, gaze upon Mary and pray directly to her, and will finally come to the sight and mind of God. Heaven will go through a lot of trouble to teach and transform Dante. Why?

Here is a partial answer. According to medieval thinking our highest good is the *direct* contemplation of God. This is something unavailable during our earthly lives but, as the result of salvation, is given to us in the afterlife forever. At the end of the *Paradiso* the pilgrim receives his share of the vision of God and it is some of the best poetry ever written. Yet this is not enough to explain the need for taking the pilgrim all the way up through Paradise.

A more complete explanation relates to the political and cultural themes that pervade the third canticle. The central concern of the *Paradiso* is not theological understanding or an experience of God for its own sake, but to make the most difference in a troubled and decaying world.

The prophecy and command given to the pilgrim by his ancestor Cacciaguida in the middle cantos of the *Paradiso* makes this clear. The pilgrim has been recruited and is being trained to engage in the political and spiritual battles of his time, to become a foot soldier in an ongoing war against the greed and corruption of church and state, against the degeneracy of its institutions.

To be an instrument of divine providence, the pilgrim's will and intellect must be reconciled with God. For this to occur, the pilgrim will receive a glimpse of the final reality that, in Dante's Christian view, is God's divinely-ordered universe. As the pilgrim scales Paradise his apprehension of God and his comprehension of reality increases and expands.

This changes the poem's focus from one man's story of alienation and salvation to world salvation and history's fulfillment, from a concern with personal fortune to the rule of our world by providence. Accordingly, in *Paradiso* Canto 28 Dante sees a universe no longer centered on earth but on God. The role of stars and planets evolves further. Previously we looked to them for personal inspiration and guidance – in Paradise, they become the carriers of time and the world within eternity. And then at last, we are above the stars.

Much that is different in the *Paradiso* begins immediately. The canticle begins not with narrative but proclamation of the nature of the universe. You may recall that first lines of the *Inferno* are about Dante the individual finding himself lost in the dark wood, and the first lines of the *Purgatorio* state the mountain's general purpose of re-education. Here we have entered a new realm of existence and poetic expression.

Paradiso's first lines provide the view of Paradise and indeed the rest of the universe. The main image for divinity is that of *light*.

> "*La gloria di colui che tutto move*
> *per l'universo penetra, e resplende*
> *in una parte più e meno altrove.*"

> "The glory of him who moves all things
> pervades – or penetrates – the universe, and shines
> in one part more and in another less." (*Paradiso* 1:1-3.)

The first line may remind the reader of Aristotle's depiction of the "Prime Mover" of all creation who cannot himself be moved. Aristotle would not have considered our world to be God's "glory", since his deity was more an igniting mechanism than an ongoing situation. Unlike

Aristotle's philosophical deity, the Christian God remains involved with the created world that reflects his light back to him.

Like others of his age, the poet Dante does not view the universe as dualistic, whereby matter is considered 'unspiritual', for God's glory penetrates everything and pervades everywhere. Nor is this a monism whereby everything is equally sacred. Instead, the universe is viewed as a hierarchy.

According to Dante and his medieval contemporaries, the highest heaven of the Empyrean receives most of God's glory. It includes the hosts of angels who run the planetary spheres but in descending order of receptivity. Then there's humanity and finally, on the more meager end, are the lower animals and the four elements of the Earth. However, since the natural world is pervaded by divine glory, anything can reflect God's glory back to Him, anything created can lead one back to God.

In the third tercet of *Paradiso* 1, Dante begins an account of the inexpressibility of the experience of Paradise: memory fails when intellect approaches its ultimate goal, when it fathoms the depths of its desire. This tercet is also packed with concepts that pervade the *Paradiso* as well as the *Divine Comedy* as a whole: intellect, will and desire, and memory. All these human faculties occur within sequential time. On the upper reaches of Paradise we will examine all these faculties from the viewpoint of Eternity.

Back in Hell Virgil referred to its inhabitants as those "who have lost the good of the intellect" (*Inferno* 3:18), and we proceeded downward further and further into the depravity of will that results from this loss of intellect. In Purgatory the will is gradually set right, and one's vision widens from the temporary and conditional toward the eternal and unconditional. At the peak of Purgatory the pilgrim is empowered as ruler over himself: the truly free will has been restored. In *Paradiso* there is now focus on purifying intellect to perceive truth (to receive divine light) according to one's fullest capacity. Because of its focus on intellect, the poet's rich philosophical and religious traditions are fully on display in this canticle.

Here and elsewhere in the *Paradiso* Dante writes from the viewpoint of somebody who has completed this journey and now must render it to others. Because Paradise's fulfillment is so remote from our and Dante's ordinary lives, he writes that he cannot reproduce his experience adequately for us, but relate only sensory and imagistic remnants. This trope of inconceivability could be banal but Dante uses it well. This conforms to the poem that is dreamlike but is also rendered with philosophical and theological precision.

Let's Get Astronomical
Paradiso's opening canto continues with a complex invocation of Apollo, god of poetry and prophecy, to guide Dante on his voyage. Then, when one would finally expect some narrative, Dante gives us a striking cosmic image.

> "The lantern of the world rises to mortals through diverse outlets, but from the one that joins four circles and three crosses...."
> (*Paradiso* 1.37-39 trans. Robert Durling (2010))

The Sun rising to join four circles and three crosses is when the Sun rises due East exactly at 0° Aries at the spring equinox. The poet invokes a fleeting cosmic moment that serves symbolic purposes; here in Paradise we have an idealized sky, not the naturalistic sky we saw previously in the *Purgatorio*.

During the journey through Hell and Purgatory, the Sun would have moved well beyond the first degree of Aries. Additionally, the time of day for Beatrice and Dante to ascend from Earth to Paradise is noon, not sunrise (*Purgatorio* 33.104, *Paradiso* 1.44-45). Departing at noon for Paradise corresponds to entering Hell at sunset and entering Purgatory at sunrise and is richly symbolic for all three canticles. Yet this tercet in *Paradiso* 1 invokes sunrise.

This image is not naturalistic but geometrical and we have to use our imagination to form it. We can't see these circles and crosses in the sky but must apprehend them with our mind's eye. The poet is signaling to us that we are entering a realm that is less sensory and more intellectual and imaginative.

What are these four circles and three crosses that join the Sun? For four circles to make three crosses, one circle must intersect all the others.[1]

When the Sun is at 0° Aries, at the spring equinox, it is at the intersection of the *ecliptic* and the *celestial equator*. The ecliptic is the apparent seasonal path of the Sun, divided longitudinally by the twelve familiar signs of the zodiac. The celestial equator extends due east-west and is perpendicular to the North and South Poles. Longitudinally the equator divides into 360 degrees of Right Ascension and is the daily cycle of the Sun.* This leaves us with two circles to determine.

At sunrise, the third circle would be the *horizon* of a specific place: unlike the circle of the ecliptic and equator, the horizon changes as our location on Earth changes. The poet specifically cites sunrise in Aries, locating the Sun on the horizon.

In my view, the fourth circle is the equinoctial *colure*. Commentators, following a citation in one of Dante's astronomical sources and a reference in Macrobius, have identified two *colures* as possibilities for the fourth circle. An *equinoctial* colure is a great circle around the Earth that goes from the North and South Poles through 0° Aries and 0° Libra on the ecliptic. The *solstical* colure is another great circle through the poles offset 90° from the equinoctial colure. The solstical colure crosses the ecliptic at 0° Cancer and 0° Capricorn. Both colures relate the ecliptic to the North and South Poles, and like the ecliptic and equator, they are fixed in the sky regardless of location on earth. The equinoctial colure intersects with 0° Aries, the intersection of ecliptic and equator.

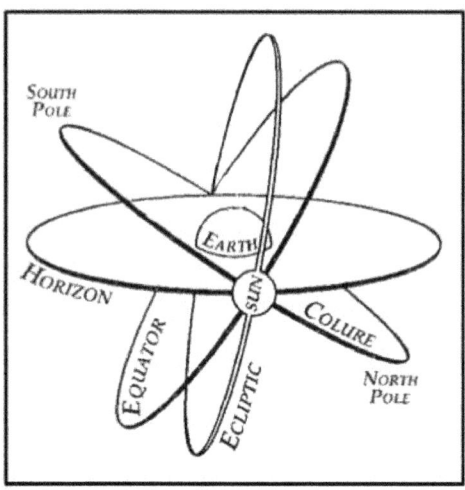

---

* This intersection of ecliptic and equator is striking in the context of some schools of modern astrology – this position is called the 'Aries point' and stands for the World as a whole.

Bring to mind that unique moment when the Sun rises at the spring equinox – which each year happens somewhere on the planet. At this time and place the circles of the *equator, ecliptic,* and *equinoctial colure* all connect to the circle of the *horizon* and this unites four circles and three crosses or points of intersection. Then the Ascendant would be exactly 0° Aries and the descendant 0° Libra of ecliptical longitude. By right ascension, the Ascendant would be 0° or 0 hours, the descendant 180° or 12 hours. (At the Earth's equator the horizon itself would be the equinoctial colure.)

Let's freeze this instant of time and place for a moment. 0° Aries on the Ascendant always gives 0° Capricorn at the Midheaven, because at this moment the meridian is exactly perpendicular to the Ascendant. The solstical colure, extending from the poles to the Capricorn-Cancer axis, is the meridian itself. *Heaven and Earth are perfectly aligned.**

We will encounter circles of the Heavens throughout the *Paradiso*. At the beginning of Canto 10, immediately before entering the Sphere of the Sun, Dante evokes the intersection of the ecliptic and equator – the Aries/Libra axis – to display the divine ordering of world and to exemplify God's beautiful work.

The configuration of *Paradiso*'s opening emerges again at the beginning of Canto 29. Before beginning to answer Dante's silent questions about the creation of the universe and the fall of the bad angels, Beatrice pauses – for the length of time it would take the Sun and Moon on Aries-Libra axis to straddle the horizon – a poignant instant (Canto 29.1-6). By then, however, our view of the universe has switched its center and its structure.

These stanzas also use the numbers "four" and "three", and these numbers occur throughout the *Divine Comedy*. "Four" may remind us of the cardinal virtues of courage, temperance, justice, and wisdom as well as the four angles of the sky. "Three" may remind the reader

---

* If you consider the third circle to be the meridian, conforming to a noon departure time, 0° Aries would be at the Midheaven with the Sun and the horizon would be 0° Cancer/0° Capricorn – *but only if one is at the equator*. This is a plausible but less elegant alternative reading. For a detailed discussion of these stanzas in the context of the entire poem, see Cornish, A, *Reading Dante's Stars* (2000).

of the theological virtues of faith, hope, and charity and also suggests Christianity's doctrine of the triune God.

Let's move now to the next lines that follow this grand image. At the place where Sun intersects with four circles and three crosses…

> "…it [Sun] comes forth with better course and joined with better stars, and it tempers and seals the waxy world more to its manner."   (*Paradiso* 1:40-42) Durling translation (2010).

You may recall the very beginning of the poem when Dante was lost in the dark wood. He noted that planets in Aries repeat their positions from the beginning of the world, and this was a good time for him to begin his journey upward – except the pilgrim was pushed back. Now, having descended through Hell and ascended the Mountain of Purgatory, this grandly auspicious time signifies the ascent to Paradise.

In Aries the Sun and accompanying planets are held by Dante and his contemporaries to produce greater effects. In Aries the Sun and other planets bear a closer semblance to divine order, like the imprint onto the wax being a close resemblance of the original.

Whenever we see a metaphor of wax and the imprint sealed upon it, we should immediately think of the wax being changeable *material* and *form* sealed upon it like the imprint from a stamp. As we move up through Paradise and the understanding of the pilgrim becomes greater, we will see that the stars (and their movers) have imprinted God's glory upon our lower world in the same way.

Concluding Canto 1, the pilgrim looks upon Beatrice who has directed her gaze toward the Sun and Dante joins her. Beatrice's gaze has dazzled the pilgrim; he senses that he has been rendered beyond the human (*transmunanar*). To the bewilderment of Dante, they are now being drawn upward through the Earth's atmosphere toward Heaven.

Beatrice, addressing her student's confusion, provides a glimpse of how the world works (*Paradiso* 1:103-135). The order that all things have among themselves bears resemblance to God and therefore all beings contain the footprint of Divinity. All things, however, are variously formed and have different destinations, moving to different ports along the great sea of being (*gran mar de l'essere*). For example, the element fire naturally moves upwards and the element earth moves naturally downwards.

As beings with intelligence and love, humans are carried toward God more directly through intention, like an arrow on a bowstring with divinity as its target. Yet we easily fall short when we become distracted by false pleasures. Heaven's intent may be perfect but outcomes in nature and in us are usually far from it.

Having been released from the downward tendencies that had been purified in Purgatory, the pilgrim now can move in the truly natural direction – upwards toward God. Unlike the opening lines of *Purgatorio* 8, there is no nostalgia for the home one has left behind but an effortless path upwards toward one's true home.

Heaven's Form: the Heavens Themselves
Before continuing our exploration let's briefly stop to consider how Dante built this Heaven and its use of astrological symbolism.

To construct Hell, there were already some basic structures for the poet to use, although he gave them greater complexity and psychological depth. To construct Purgatory Dante was mostly on his own, and the image of Purgatory being a Mountain opposite Jerusalem was probably his own invention. To construct Heaven, there was already much literature depicting the stars and planets between Earth and Eternity. What follows is one such source for Dante.

Cicero's *Dream of Scipio* (Latin: *Somium Scipionis*) with the commentary by Macrobius from the fifth century CE was popular throughout the medieval era. Cicero's *Dream* was part of a mostly-lost work called *De Republica*. The dreamer is Scipio who was the familiar general and hero of the Third Punic War of the 2nd century BCE and in this dream he is visited by his grandfather, the great Scipio Africanus, the hero of the Second Punic War of the century before.

In the dream Scipio's grandfather first takes the dreamer to a place from which he can look on Carthage, the city that the dreamer will someday destroy, and the young man is given a personal prophecy about his life. Grandfather takes him to a place from where he can see all the Heavens and its array of planets and stars. By fulfilling his duty to Rome, grandfather says, Scipio and others may return to the Heavens, particularly to those stars we call the Milky Way. Then Scipio is asked to look down on the puny Earth we make so much of. This leads to a presentation of the Earth's geography and the larger planetary ages. The dream ends on a note of admonition to lead a life of virtue and service to country so to return to the stars from whence he came. As we tour Dante's Paradise, it will be obvious that he took much from *The Dream of Scipio*.

Here is a passage from Macrobius' commentary that discusses the stars and planets. The dream comments on the downward journey of the soul from the Milky Way toward Earth, going through layers of planets. At each sphere the soul obtains a quality necessary for Earthly life, ordered from the planet closest to God to that furthest away. Note the positive qualities given to planetary spheres.

> "In the sphere of Saturn it obtains reason and understanding, called *logistikon* and *theoretikon*; in Jupiter's sphere, the power to act, called *praktikon*; in Mars' sphere, a bold spirit or *thymikon*; in the sun's sphere, sense perception and imagination, *aisthetikon* and *phantiastikon*; in Venus' sphere the impulse of passion, *epithymetikon*; in Mercury's sphere, the ability to speak and interpret, *hermeneutikon*, and in the lunar sphere, the function of molding and increasing bodies, *phytikon*."[2]

According to Macrobius and others in his Neoplatonic tradition, the soul can be drawn upwards toward immortality or downwards toward bodily existence. Upon Earthly death, the virtuous one leaves his body and "returns to the splendor of everlasting life."

The medieval Christian Dante could not go that far. In *Paradiso* 4 Beatrice disputes "Timeaus" (the interlocutor for which the famous Platonic dialogue was named),* that the soul returns to its star. If so it may result in the error of polytheism by naming planets after pagan gods. However, she says, if Timaeus meant that planets bestow qualities on us (e.g. temperament and talent), there may be some truth in what he says (*Paradiso* 4:58-60).[3]

In Dante's Paradise people are assigned to the different planetary spheres based on their similarities to the planets' astrological symbolism.

---

* The *Timeaus* is considered a late dialogue of Plato and concerns itself with cosmology and the foundations of science from a Pythagorean point of view. Up to the modern era the *Timeaus* was considered Plato's most important dialogue. Of all the writings of Plato, Dante and his contemporaries had access only to a commentary on this dialogue.

People who were of the nature of Mercury or Jupiter would likely be found within these respective planetary spheres. However, Beatrice states clearly, *none of them are really there on the planets*. All of Heaven's citizens are actually in the Empyrean, the highest brightest Heaven beyond space and time. From Christ's mother Mary to Piccarda, all live there forever in bliss, according to their capacity to receive God's love and light. *Paradiso's* characters literally condescend to Dante, appearing on planetary spheres as a concession to his limited capacity for understanding their true nature and home. *Paradiso's* depiction of people upon planets is thus an educational device for the pilgrim and a narrative device for the poet.

Here is a summary of the planetary spheres and the redeemed souls (or "lights") that appear there. Their correlations are straightforward and follow common astrological symbolism.

In the lower spheres – those that are closer to Earth – we find the citizens of Paradise presented not for their positive but for their limiting qualities. They are, however, all in the highest Heaven.

In the Sphere of the *Moon* we find women who were cloistered but in life went back on their religious vows to marry against their will. John Ciardi called them "The Inconstant."[4] Their presence on the Moon will lead to a subsequent presentation about free will and the sanctity of vows. As the lowest sphere its depictions and descriptions are the most physical.

Inhabiting the Sphere of *Mercury* are those who sought honor for themselves during earthly life. Here we meet people involved in the active life (especially Emperor Justinian of the Byzantine Empire) limited by their desire for personal glory.

In the Sphere of *Venus* we find those with affinity toward sensual love and luxury. It is on this sphere that we find the strongest presentation of astrological causation working the purposes of divine providence.

We then arrive at the middle of Heaven's sequence of planetary spheres. The four Cardinal Virtues are presented through the following four spheres as features of divine fulfillment. The lights that seemingly inhabit these spheres led exemplary lives; as we go further into Paradise, these lights are not presented as distinct personalities but as or within large assemblies.

In the Sphere of the *Sun* we find men who are wise church leaders, theologians and philosophers, or important scholars. The Sun is the conductor and organizer of the other planets as *wisdom* is to other positive spiritual qualities. The lights surround Dante and Beatrice in concentric circles of twelve lights each.

We find on *Mars* crusaders and martyrs, those who fought for God. They embody *courage* or *fortitude* and are in the shape of a large cross. Here the pilgrim will meet his crusader ancestor Cacciaguida and receive his life's assignment.

Jupiter is for those who embodied *justice*, particularly those who served God as rulers. Here the lights are arrayed as words from the Bible encouraging rulers to be just: its final letter transforms into an Eagle that speaks to the pilgrim.

On *Saturn* we find great monastics, those who served God through contemplation and discipline. They descend to the Sphere of Saturn and later ascend using a great ladder that extends upwards toward God. Here *temperance* is prerequisite for contemplation.

In Paradise the Cardinal Virtues are considered not worldly but "infused" – related to salvation, as they are on the other side of the rivers of the Earthly Paradise. *Sun's wisdom* is not ordinary discernment but the understanding that guides; *Mars' courage* is fearless commitment; *Jupiter's justice* aligns with Divine Wisdom; *Saturn's temperance* represents disciplined and complete focus on God, not just avoiding sweets and bad television.

The eighth Sphere is that of the *Fixed Stars* that are the constellations of the signs of the zodiac. Just as the band of stars is closer to Divinity than the planetary spheres, so are the Theological Virtues closer to Divinity than the Cardinal Virtues. The Theological Virtues are the subject of this starry realm. From the stars of Gemini, Dante and Beatrice will meet three apostles for the pilgrim's examination on *Faith, Hope, and Love or Charity*.

The ninth Sphere is the *First Motion* and it is featureless. At the origin of time there are no virtues to consider and Dante and Beatrice meet nobody there. From this vantage point, however, Beatrice will show Dante the stars and planets and the angelic orders that govern them. She will also talk about the world's creation and the fall of Lucifer.

> ### The Heavenly Spheres and the Sciences
> In his earlier *Convivio* that was in some respect a sketchbook for his *Divine Comedy*, Dante indulged in an interesting thought experiment bringing together the fields of knowledge and the heavenly bodies.[5] Dante gives different rationales for his correlations; some are clever, others seem rather labored. It is interesting because it illuminates Dante's interest in the hierarchies of Heaven and the planets astrologers know well. The first seven levels correspond with the medieval *trivium* and *quadrivium*: they are the seven planets themselves. Higher realms of knowledge are likened to higher realms of Heaven.
>
>> Moon: Grammar
>> Mercury: Dialectics
>> Venus: Rhetoric
>> Sun: Arithmetic
>> Mars: Music
>> Jupiter: Geometry
>> Saturn: Astronomy/Astrology
>> Fixed Stars: Metaphysics
>> Crystalline Heaven or First Motion: Moral Philosophy
>> Empyrean Heaven: Theology

With the image of the stars and planets fading into dawn and then the pilgrim drinking with his eyes from a river of light, we enter the tenth sphere, the Empyrean, shaped like a rose and with God Himself at the center. Beatrice departs and a new guide, Bernard of Clairvaux, will lead the pilgrim to the vision of God.

Nearer to us than the Sun

The First – or Last – Sphere of the Moon

Returning to the narrative of the *Paradiso*, Dante and Beatrice ascend to the Moon, the sphere closest to Earth. In Canto 2, they are *in* the Moon. Paradise's Moon is clear, very white, sensible and also otherworldly.

Paradiso's translators have a chance to translate some beautiful poetry. My selection for best translation of these lines goes to Jean Hollander (2007).

"It seemed to me that we were in a cloud,
shining, dense, solid, and unmarred,
like a diamond struck by sunlight.
The eternal pearl received us in itself,
as water does a ray of light
and yet remains unsundered and serene." (*Paradiso* 2.31-36)

As the lowest realm of Heaven, the closest to Earth, the Moon is cast as the most material body in Heaven. Here we get the most naturalistic environment and the most concrete visual depictions that we encounter in Paradise. The pilgrim wonders: how could the solid body of a living person penetrate the solid body of the Moon? Our usual sense of bodies obstructing each other, so basic to our lives on this physical plane, has dissolved. Welcome to Paradise.

As seen from Earth, the Moon is covered with marks or blemishes: to the unaided eye Moon appears even to have a landscape. Yet in Dante's Paradise, the Moon is bright and unblemished. Early on the poet is telling us that the imaginative realm of Paradise differs from our normal earthly perceptions.

Much of *Paradiso* 2 consists of the famous (or infamous) discussion about the spots that appear on the Moon from the Earth, a discussion we will take up in detail in Part Three. In this canto Beatrice refutes the pilgrim's assertion that the spots are caused by differences in consistency in the Moon's matter; instead she asserts that these appearances are differences in *light* as it diffuses from the Highest Being down through the ladder of creation. Beatrice discloses the structure of the universe from Heaven through the stars and planets and their angelic realms to Earth (*Paradiso* 2:112-148).

On the Sphere of the Moon we meet the first redeemed souls in Paradise. The pilgrim sees faces as if they were reflections in a mirror but there is nobody behind him; instead they are in front of him, white and translucent like pearls on a pale forehead. (*Paradiso* 3.10-18.) This is the opposite of the story of Narcissus, who thought he was looking ahead but instead he sees only himself. Unlike in the higher spheres the pilgrim can recognize their individual features. Now we meet them. One named Piccarda begins to speak; she was the sister of Forese Donati who we left among the gluttons in Purgatory. Piccarda had been removed from the convent by her bad brother Corso Donati and forced into a marriage of (Corso's) convenience. Piccarda introduces another figure named Constance. According to Dante's understanding, Constance, who later was the mother of Frederick II, was also forced from the cloister for a political marriage.

Why are they here on the Sphere of the Moon? From the Earth, the Moon is by far Heaven's fastest body, being six times swifter than Mercury at that planet's swiftest. The Moon's appearance is always changing, appearing predictably through its phases in different parts of the sky and in different sizes and shapes. Modern astrologers often look at the Moon psychologically: the closest heavenly body signifies one's feelings, emotions, and maternal relationships. They may also note the Moon's zodiacal sign position and corresponding element to say how one curbs anxiety and soothes him or herself. These features are instances of the Moon's changeability, adaptability, and varied responses. The Moon accounts for a changing situation as it contacts by aspect one planet and then another.

Let's consider one of Dante's sources, Guido Bonatti, whose *Liber Astronomiae* or *Book of Astronomy* provides an encyclopedic account of astrology in the medieval era. Bonatti was more than a generation older than Dante and often worked as an advisor to Ghibillene military and political leaders. Bonatti provides a possible inspiration for the first people who we meet in Paradise.

> "And of faith she signifies religion, wherefore Lunar men often become religious, especially in youth. But sometimes they do not well observe their promises to God, and they rarely persevere well in religions; and from thence arise the tales of the common people." (Tractate 3, Chapter 7, p.180)

According to Beatrice, those of the Moon had in life lacked those qualities of courage and fortitude that would have allowed them to hold to their previous vows – they could have remained steadfast. They had the free will sufficient for them to refuse to leave the monastic life and to allow themselves to die instead. From Beatrice's point of view, the Moon's inhabitants were too adaptable in life.

Reflecting our early discussion of the planets and the Seven Cardinal Sins, the topic of *envy* comes up in the realm of the Moon. The pilgrim,

> **Paradise Interpersonally**
>
> Often in the *Paradiso* one individual introduces and praises another who does not speak. This contrasts strongly with the previous two canticles. In *Inferno* one may be glued eternally to the introducer (Paolo with Francesca), roommates in the same flame (Diomedes with Ulysses), or, at the Hell's bottom, the person introduced is being gnawed at by the introducer (Ruggieri by Ugolini). This only serves to reinforce the isolation and resulting depravity of the inhabitants of Hell. In *Purgatorio* people often speak for themselves upon being introduced. In Purgatory there is a sense of common purpose but the activity of purification falls first upon the individual sinner.
>
> *Paradiso* focuses on the community of the saved. The few life stories we hear are for the purposes of instruction not drama. Unlike the partial understanding (and downright deception) of many of those in Hell and Purgatory, the saved souls of Paradise speak not with their own knowledge but with the correct understanding from God. Error is impossible in Paradise, therefore all of its citizens can teach Dante.

still more worldly than otherworldly, asks Piccarda if the citizens of Heaven's lower regions wish to attain a higher status.

It would be impossible for any of Heaven's inhabitants to wish a different state, she replies, for all are given the degree of beatitude and bliss according to who they are. She sums up this point in some of the *Divine Comedy*'s most unforgettable lines. Here's the Italian followed by Jean Hollander's version in English (2007).

> "E 'n la sua volontade è nostra pace:
> ell' è quel mare al qual tutto si move
> ciò ch'ella cria o che natura face."

> "And in his will is our peace.
> it is to that sea all things move,
> both what His will creates and that which Nature makes."*
> (*Paradiso* 3:85-87)

---

* *Soul* is what God creates directly, *body* is what God creates through the medium of stars and planets and their angelic movers.

Their eternal bliss may be objectively less than some others, although it is perfect for them.

The Realm of Mercury

Now we are ready to ascend to the realm of Mercury. This is our first starry planet and, together with Venus, one of the two planets on our side of the Sun. Those whom Dante meets in these 'inferior' (lower) planets are among the saved but, like those upon the Moon, their beatitude is limited, in this case by the limitations of ambition (Mercury) or excessive worldly love (Venus) in their earthly lives.

The canto before their ascent gives us a taste of the planet Mercury. Appropriate to this planet being that of ledgers and the marketplace, Beatrice casts theological issues (maintenance of vows and the sacrifice of Christ) into the language of debt and payment. At the end of Canto 4 Dante asks if somebody can compensate for having broken religious vows by providing a substitute. Beatrice, very pleased with this question, emphasizes the greatest seriousness with which all religious vows should be considered, for they are an offering to God of his greatest gift of free will. However, one may change previous vows on occasion if sanctioned by the church. Beatrice suggests what we might call a 50% interest penalty to change the terms of a religious vow to a different vow.

In Canto 5, at the end of their discussion, Dante has an "eager mind" with more questions – a Mercury moment – but now Beatrice's stillness silences him and they quickly rise to the Sphere of Mercury. Bright Mercury glows with even more radiance upon Beatrice's arrival. Its lights greet them in great numbers like fish coming to the surface of a pond expecting food. They heard from each one, "*Ecco chi crescerà li nostri amori*", "Here is one who will increase our loves!" (Canto 5.105)

Contrast this joyful greeting with the quiet pale figures that had appeared in the Sphere of the Moon – at Mercury we have quickness, playfulness, and a hint of jockeying for advantage. Dante is eager to know about them and they are eager to answer his questions: we see Mercury's focus on curiosity and gathering information.

Although Piccarda and Constance had visible features, those on Mercury are mostly hidden in their own joy's light that is consistent with the planet most hidden by the Sun's light. One half-featured light approaches Dante. He is none other than the sixth century (Eastern) Roman Emperor Justinian, whose words take up all of Canto 6.*

Justinian begins by placing himself in history. During his era, beginning with Constantine, the flight of the Eagle (symbolizing the Empire) had reversed its course: it had previously gone from East to West when Aeneas fled Troy to found Rome. By Justinian's time it had gone from West to East, from Rome to Constantinople, contrary to the superior 'primary' diurnal motion from East to West.

Justinian tells of his role in organizing the Roman law code and of his conversion from heretical views. Mercury, frequently hidden by the Sun, is a fitting place for the righteous rulers who also desired fame and glory. Mercury, the planet of cleverness and trickery, can depict those trying to get a little extra for themselves. Justinian is eclipsed in Paradise by the Sun, as individual fame is eclipsed by divine purposes in history. Even the great Emperor Justinian was merely a foot soldier in the larger cause.

At the end of Canto 6 Justinian introduces the person next to him who is named Romeo. This man had been court advisor to the Count of Provence in the early 1200's. Romeo had come into town and joined the service of Provence's ruler and had managed to marry off all four of his daughters – a very smart man! However, Romeo was upended by evil rumors from others, walked away from the count's service, and lived his last days a poor man. Justinian's exit is also noteworthy for its Mercurial qualities. At the beginning of Canto 7 he ends his discourse with a prayer that Dante devised from Latin and some (bad) Hebrew. Justinian gets ready to leave, wheeling to his own song and dance; he and others depart as if they were flying sparks fading away.

Dante's mind is now confused and scattered. Beatrice, reading his thoughts directly – as do the other citizens of Paradise – discusses central mysteries of Christianity: why did the Son of God need to die for the atonement of Adam's sin and its effects upon humankind? Why was it

---

* Justinian's prominence in history contrasts with the Moon's characters that were relatively unknown. Piccarda was largely unknown during her life; Constance, although quite politically adept in her own right, is better known as the mother of the Emperor Frederick II. Piccarda and Constance were also cast as victims of circumstances around them, conforming with the more passive symbolism of the Moon.

considered just revenge ("*vendetta*") upon the Jews who crucified Christ although this deed served as a just compensation for the sin of Adam? It is noteworthy that once again Beatrice continues to use the vocabulary of accounting and the marketplace – debt and payment – in service of Christian doctrine.

Upward to the Sphere of Venus
Paradiso 8 is an important stop for us, because of a conversation there about astrology, "circling nature," and our natural temperaments and gifts. This canto opens stridently by stating that the ancients erroneously empowered Venus as a deity and believed that from Venus arrived "*il folle amore raggiasse*", "beams of maddened love". (We are reminded of Francesca in *Inferno* 5, perhaps of Dido in Virgil's *Aeneid*). This lines up with his previous discussion of planets and free will from *Purgatorio* 16 and hints that Dante may use the planet Venus in different ways than previously. This also protects the poet from 'paganism' that might be inferred from the ensuing conversation about *la circular natura* and its role in shaping who we are.

We've already seen Venus twice in the *Purgatorio* as a rising planet. In the first canto Venus is above the eastern horizon and heralds the entrance into Purgatory from Hell; rising Venus also preceded Dante's final dream in Purgatory in Canto 27. Dante twice used Venus to presage what was to come, similar to Venus rising ahead of the Sun in the morning sky. In our previous discussion of the Earthly Paradise, we looked at the possibility that Matelda was like Venus and Beatrice was like the Sun.

Venus shines brightly in the sky either as a morning star, rising ahead of the Sun before dawn, or an evening star, setting after the Sun at dusk. Here the poet depicts Venus as being wooed by the Sun, ahead and behind (Canto 8:11-12). These contrasting conditions of Venus' appearances may have inspired Dante to emphasize *contrasts* in the cantos on Venus, contrasts that structures the poetic depiction of Venus.

Returning now to the poem, the pilgrim is on the Sphere of Venus where he sees lights circling about in harmonious motion as if they were acting out a musical polyphony. Contrast this harmony to the chaotic flying about and shrieking that Dante and Virgil encountered in Venus' area of hell for the lustful – those subdued by "maddened love" – in *Inferno* 5.

> **Venus as an Epicycle**
>
> Canto 8:3 depicts Venus as "*volta nel terzo epiciclo*", turning in the third epicycle. Why does Dante use the word "epicycle" here? Let's briefly shift gears onto astronomical theory and review ancient and medieval depictions of planetary motion.
>
> If, as the ancient and medieval eras insisted, the planets were superior forms that move in perfect circles, how would they account for planets' changing speeds of motion and changes of direction? Following previous speculations, the ancient astronomer Ptolemy presented a doctrine of "epicycles" whose complex and tedious calculations worked wonderfully to predict planetary movement and position. In addition to circles of the equator and ecliptic accounting for their motion diurnally and around the zodiac, each planet also moved upon another circle, its own circle, called an "epicycle".
>
> Consider John Carroll's commentary on these lines quoted by Hollander (2007). "Translating all this into its spiritual equivalent, the meaning appears to be: as Venus had one movement round the Earth and another round the Sun, so these souls had two movements of the heart, cyclic and epicyclic, one round some earthly centre, the other round God, of whom Sun is the natural symbol." (p.190). We will encounter this image again when we arrive at the final lines of the *Paradiso*.

Greeting Dante is the light of Charles Martel, whose father was Charles II of Anjou, King of Naples and whose mother was the daughter of the King of Hungary.* Dante asks Martel, an exemplary character from a noble family of questionable quality, about family differences: how can bad sons be born to a good father?

---

* Charles Martel had met Dante in 1294 as he was passing through Florence to see his father. He died the next year of a plague at the age of 24. Dante thought of him as a potentially great ruler cut down before his time; his early death destroyed what would have been an opportunity to restore order to Italy and Europe. Upon Charles' death his brother Robert became powerful to no good end – according to the poet. This Charles Martel should not be confused with another Charles Martel, king of the Franks who had defeated the Muslim army at the Battle of Tours in the eighth century.

Charles Martel replies that character and destination in life are produced not by one's family but by the movements of the Heavens. Because of needs for different temperaments and vocations for people to function in community, the Heavens decree different destinations for people. If people attended more to what nature fashions and less to family and class, people would do their rightful work and both individual and society would be better for it.

How do we attend to what the Heavens have fashioned? We can look at the natural inclinations of people; I think that perhaps we can also look at their astrological charts. Clearly the poet does not exclude such a possibility. From the miseries of *Inferno* 20 and the moralizing of Marco the Lombard and *Purgatorio* 16, the pilgrim and we are ready for a positive account of how astrology can tell us about human nature. The pilgrim is now better able to understand how the universe works without lapsing into error.

Why is Charles Martel in the place of Heaven reserved for those who were vulnerable to Venus' influence? The text gives no sense that there were complexities of love in his life: in fact Canto 9 begins with a short address to Charles' young wife Clemenza.

Perhaps we should look at other astrological meanings for Venus. We already know of Venus' association with all manners of love but there is more. Below is from Guido Bonatti's description of the astrological Venus. It focuses on many of life's enjoyments.

> "And he whose significatrix is Venus where Venus will be living in leisure, and he will know better how to conduct his own life, and how to live more delightfully and in a more courtly way than another much worse than he… And he will know how to put together crowns and garlands, and all ornaments, and particularly womanly ones; and he will freely wear ornaments on his own body, and he will go around covered with beautiful and clean clothing…
> And Venereal men are of games and laughter and dancing, and gladness and joy, and freely using food and drink in company…
> And Venereal men spend time in the houses of prayer, so that they may appear to be what they are not; and they restrain their faith, and long to hear the sounds of musical instruments, and they are strong in them more so than other men." (Tractate 3, Chapter 5, pp.170-171)

According to Bonatti's description, Venus does not connote a deep thinker but is instead the party-planet of astrology's planetary symbols. At her best Venus gives elegance and refinement; at her worst she renders one shallow and frivolous. Bonatti associates musical instruments with Venus, for it is the music and not the pious sermon that attracts Venus-like people to church.

Perhaps Charles Martel was an elegant and cultured young man who took well to the courtly life – perhaps a little too well. Alternatively, he was a kind man whose native temperament partook of the warmth and congeniality of the fair planet Venus.[6] Had Charles Martel lived longer, Venus could have made him a distinctive ruler when other rulers of his time tended to be calculating and cynical.

We move to Canto 9 where we meet three individuals whose lives recall Oscar Wilde's famous line that "every sinner has a future and every saint has a past". We first meet Cunizza, who Dante himself may have met when he was young and she was elderly. She had many a youthful affair and was subject of much scandal, having at one time run off with the Guido Calvacanti's father (who is in Hell with Farinata). Cunizza had since repented and became wise and esteemed later in life. Like Charles Martel, Cunizza also had an evil brother: she was sister of Ezzelino III da Romano, a brutal ruler whom Dante had put in a blood-drenched area of Hell. (*Inferno* 12.110)

We then meet Folquet de Marseille, a troubadour poet from Provence who renounced the life of court and pleasure, became a monk, and later in life, as bishop of Toulouse, carried on a brutal fight against the Albigensian so-called heretics. Dante does not mention this later stage of Folquet's life but his readers would have known of him in that context. We have an implied contrast: Folquet and the recently mentioned Ezzelino whose brutality was not for the holy cause of subduing heretics but for his own gain.

Rounding out those we meet in Venus is Rahab "the Harlot" of Jericho who had hidden two spies sent by Joshua and thereby helped produce a victory for the invading Israelites. She was not massacred with the others but saved when Joshua fought the battle of Jericho.

Like a composer who precedes a stirring finale with soft and unchallenging music, in *Purgatorio* 9 Dante seems to be holding himself back. The Sphere of Venus contains biography and personal depiction of salvation, but now we go from individual to grand ensembles. Beyond Venus we are henceforth outside the shadow cast by our Earth (*Paradiso* 9.118-119).

The Sphere of the Sun or, 'Heaven Lights Up: the Musical'
Wheels and Circles

Paradiso's Cantos 10 to 14 and the Sphere of the Sun are critical because the Sun has already played a major symbolic role in the poem: it is the orienting body in the pilgrim's dark wood, it is the "sweet light" nostalgically wished for in Hell, and it is the day's light to guide to the pilgrims in Purgatory. In Paradise the Sun is the planet associated with divine wisdom and provides the world with God's light and order. It is the visible heavenly body within time that most resembles Eternity.

Canto 10, like the opening of *Paradiso's* first canto, begins with proclamation. Its introduction to the Sun articulates the Christian doctrine of God as Trinity and the world's creation by divinity. The Christian trinity, the poet tells us, is the ultimate foundation of the revolving order of the Heavens that gives rise to order in our physical and sensory world. Anyone who studies this creation, he continues, cannot but taste of its Creator.

What aspect of Heaven's creation does Dante single out here? It is the two lofty wheels of Heaven: the equator and ecliptic and their intersection, the Aries/Libra axis. This is so great a work that the Creator himself never ceases to look upon it. (*Paradiso* 10:10-12).

As these invisible wheels, moving in opposite directions, carry the visible Sun and other planets through the sky they create effects on Earth. From the celestial equator is the 'primary motion', moving East to West, whereby each planet rises, culminates, sets, and anticulminates each day. Additionally every month, or season, or year, the Sun, Moon, and other planets also move according to their own velocities. This is the 'secondary motion', along the ecliptic, that moves West to East. Dante tells us the world and our lives would be greatly compromised if the angle of the ecliptic from the equator were greater or lesser from each other than they are.

One is reminded of the depiction of the 'soul of the cosmos' from Plato's *Timaeus*, a commentary of which was available in the Medieval Latin West. According to this dialogue, the Demiurge set up specific number ratios to fashion these two circles that he joined in the shape of the Greek letter Chi. The celestial equator was the Circle of the Same (closer to pure Being); the Circle of the Other (closer to the realm of appearance) carried the planets along the ecliptic. Later Christians recognized this as the cross and the first letter of 'Christ'.[7]

The equatorial wheel is the superior wheel for it is closer to God and more closely patterns itself after divinity. In fact, in the opening lines to Canto 6, Justinian noted that when Aeneas fled Troy for Italy – West to East – the path of the Roman Eagle of Universal Empire had gone *counter* to the course of heaven.

If we keep track of the Sun's movement by season (along the circle of the ecliptic), we find its movement gives us our seasons of varying amounts of light and of predictable changes in rate of increasing light or darkness. This divinely inspired motion and order contrasts with the ever-changing weather patterns within our earthly seasons.* Once again the perfection is in Heaven, the imperfection is on Earth. The Sun becomes the keeper of both small and large reckonings of time, of day and of year.

In this way, according to John Sinclair, the Sun imprints on the earth "the goodness of Heaven and 'measuring time for us', so that the ultimate mysteries of the Godhead are in one context with the common order of the world, the daily sounding of the hours of prayer and the coming of the spring."[8]

When Dante and Beatrice enter the Sun they are entering a place without shadow and which is beyond our usual senses. This Sphere's brightness surpasses that of the visible Sun, the brightest object in the universe. Beatrice now asks Dante to give thanks to the Sun itself and in his adoration he momentarily forgets her – *che Beatrice eclissò ne l'oblio* – she has been eclipsed (line 58-60). Beatrice takes it well, as we see from the following stanza. Signaling his stronger perception and understanding, Dante is now able to look directly at this Sun's light without Beatrice as intermediary.

---

* At the beginning of *Inferno* 24, when "the Sun renews its rays beneath Aquarius", a farmer mistakes early morning frost for a new layer of snow. The sky, and particularly the location of the Sun, gives certainty: changing conditions on Earth easily confuse the farmer and the rest of us.

In this Heaven light eclipses light without traces of shadow anywhere. On Earth, a solar eclipse occurs at a New Moon when the luminaries are also close in ecliptical latitude; the Moon obscures all or part of the Sun. As the Moon gets in the way of the Sun's light, the Earth darkens as it falls into the Moon's shadow. In a lunar eclipse, occurring at a Full Moon under similar conditions, all or part of the Moon darkens as the Earth's shadow obscures the Sun's light reflecting on the Moon. Either eclipse is a darkening and an ominous portent; however, in Paradise, there is no shadow but only dazzling light.

In the Sphere of Venus the lights of the redeemed souls moved in circular form, singing; in the sphere of the Sun the same occurs yet more extravagantly. Singing and dancing, twelve bright stars (redeemed souls) encircle Beatrice and Dante as if forming a crown above them. Like an old Broadway or Hollywood musical, the action (if you could call it 'action') is punctuated and accentuated by music and dance numbers that occur episodically.

Let's ponder the Sun's astrological symbolism and once again we rely on Guido Bonatti. He cites the Sun's role as director of the heavens, the Sun's brilliance, and an association with wisdom and kingly dignity. Dante will save many of the virtuous rulers for the sphere of Jupiter; on the sphere of the Sun we meet those whose wisdom and devotion made them the guides of others. These were the Church's royalty.

> As [the Sun] signifies light and splendor, and beauty, and faith. And he even signifies a great kingdom, and all other lay dignities, both of magnates and others. And this, because he is posited in the middle of the others (just like a king), and the others stand next to him – certain ones on one side, certain ones on the other side (namely the superiors to his right, the inferiors to his left). And he has power in all planets, because he burns them all up. Moreover, his motion is practically uniform, and is not varied or altered, but always keeps the same similar advancements annually. And his motion is most noble above the motions of the other planets, nor does he go retrograde like others go retrograde…[9]

One of the lights approaches Dante and Beatrice, introducing first his teacher, Albertus Magnus, and then himself as Thomas Aquinas. When Aquinas introduces ten others in his circle, there are some surprises.

Along with other theologians we find one codifier of church law, two historians, an ancient authority on angelic realms, an encyclopedist, and Boethius the philosopher from late antiquity, who we discussed earlier and will do so again. Not one but many fields of learning constitute the knowledge and wisdom necessary for the good of the Church and the world.

Among the theologians is Siger of Brabant, glowing immediately to the left of Aquinas. Siger was a theological rival of Thomas and some of his teachings had been declared heretical. In Paradise, however, their doctrinal disputes are not in opposition but part of a greater harmony at the service of directing humanity correctly. The most surprising member of the circle of wisdom is the Hebrew King Solomon, cast as the most beautiful of the lights.

Like the celestial equator and ecliptic moving in opposite directions, we see the great teachers of the Church – and the examples of Francis and Dominic below – appearing to move in different directions but, from a larger perspective, being completely in harmony.

Francis and Dominic

Next we hear about two individuals who strove to renew the Church during their lifetimes. In Canto 11 Aquinas tells that God had sent two princes (*due principi*) to keep the church on the true path – implying that it had lost its way. Dante depicts both men as providentially installed to found the mendicant monastic orders to enable the Church to reform itself. Unfortunately, according to the poet, both orders have declined in more recent times. This appears to be the way of the world, from individuals to epochs.

Cantos 11 and 12 provide stories of the lives of Francis and Dominic respectively who were contemporaries, they may have met once, and both were canonized shortly after their deaths. The pilgrim does not see or talk with either of them but their lives are presented by others. In Canto 11 Thomas Aquinas, the Dominican, gives the story of Francis. In Canto 12 Bonaventure, the great Franciscan leader and theologian, gives the story of Dominic. By Dante's time, the orders founded by these two saints were rivals. Yet, their stories are complementary and in harmony, in spite of the differences between the two men and the orders they founded. This is reflected in the symmetry of these presentations about them.

We begin the first half of the symmetry with Francis. Thomas Aquinas begins Francis' personal life story by depicting his birthplace as symbolically being East, or *Oriente*. (*Paradiso* 11.49-54.) Francis represents the Eastern part of the known world and is associated with the rising sun. Likened to the order of angels called *seraphim*, renowned for ardent love, Francis was a lifelong companion of Lady Poverty. Although there is much of the troubadour in the depiction of Francis, he is also presented as a man of great strength and fearlessness. Aquinas finishes his discourse about Francis by noting the decline of the Dominicans – Aquinas' own order.

Canto 12 begins in grand style as from one circle of lights another circle appears around it, the second taking its motion and song from the first. The group's motion stops when a new light begins to speak. This is the Franciscan Bonaventure who tells the life story of Dominic, the founder of the Dominican order that is an order of preachers. Bonaventure's presentation of Dominic is full of metaphors of battle and militancy. If Aquinas casts Francis as brave lover, Bonaventure casts Dominic as brave warrior.

Bonaventure gives the birthplace for Dominic as symbolically being West near where the Sun goes below the horizon. (*Paradiso* 12: 46-51). Spain, at the extremity of the West, is symmetrical to Francis', whose birth was referenced to the Ganges, the extremity of the East.

We might think of this as a clever poetic device until we remember how Dante used India in the east and Spain and Morocco in the west, thought to be 180° apart, to help tell time in Purgatory. The introductions bring us back to the horizon axis and its extremities. Remember that this axis connects East and West, and its meridian is the vertical line that connects Hell, Purgatory, and Heaven.

Dominic is like the high angelic order of the *cherubim*, the holders of wisdom. He is depicted as brilliant, kind to companions in faith but fierce to his adversaries – the enemies of the Church. He burst forth like a mighty torrent, making combat with and crushing the defenders of heresy.

Bonaventure concludes by deploring the decline in his own Franciscan order. The symmetry to Aquinas continues as we look at the people accompanying Bonaventure. Bonaventure's circle of lights is a mixture of people similar to the first group, including a variety of theologians, a historian and grammarian, and one purportedly very good preacher. To Bonaventure's right are two of Francis' early followers. Just as Aquinas had his rival Siger to his left, Bonaventure has the prophetic Joachim of Fiore to his left, a man whose followers Bonaventure condemned.

The biographies of Francis and Dominic allow the pilgrim to learn complementary correct paths and provide personal examples to follow. Francis embraced the poverty voluntarily and lovingly that the exiled Dante will soon experience involuntarily. Dominic fought for truth fiercely and fearlessly. In the upcoming sphere the pilgrim hears that he will follow Dominic's example as well.

At the opening of Canto 13, the poet asks the reader to imagine the most prominent stars in the sky, including both Dippers and the North Star, and arrange them in two dancing circles around a center – Dante and Beatrice. From previously being guides to look up to in Purgatory, now the stars in Paradise have become transparent playthings of the creative imagination – and later they will disappear altogether in Canto 30, when Dante and Beatrice are at the rim of the highest Heaven.

Aquinas speaks again. He had previously noted Dante's silent surprise when Solomon was introduced as the wisest man without a rival. Aquinas first tells of light streaming from the triune God down through creation directly by God and indirectly through the angelic realms and stars and planets accounting for the imperfection of Earthly realm. Only two people were created directly by God and only these two, Adam and Jesus Christ, contained perfection (*Paradiso* 13:52-87).

Thomas addresses the pilgrim's question about Solomon. It was this king, he explains, who had asked God for the wisdom appropriate to a king – to govern well. The best wisdom may not be found among those given to metaphysical or theological speculation but that which is active and brings about positive effects in the outer world. Coming from Thomas the great medieval philosopher, this has a slight ironic quality.

The next canto, *Paradiso* 14, begins with a humbler metaphor, depicting two dancing circles of light as water moving rhythmically from center to rim and back again in a container. It is now Solomon's turn to speak and he speaks of the Final Judgment, at which time Heaven's spirits of light will regain their fleshy selves from their lives on earth.

His words are cause of even greater joy among the lights of the Sun. The doctrine of the resurrection of the body becomes increasingly important as we proceed upward in the *Paradiso*.

For this Sphere's finale, Dante depicts a *third* circle, one even brighter, now encompassing the other two – and presumably moving in the same direction. Dante follows with praise to the Holy Spirit (*Paradiso* 14.67-78). These three circles together may represent the Trinity whose evocation began the Sun's cantos and has been the subject of much of its lights' song. It also brings to mind the previously mentioned Joachim, whose historical speculations included a prophesized Third Age of the Holy Spirit.[10]

Later in the *Paradiso* we will see a new picture of the universe: the spheres of the stars and planets move around a central Light as concentric rings. On the Sphere of the Sun, the poet is giving us a prelude of this but in a world and a time that is more accessible to us.

Time and Telling Time

Before moving upward to the Sphere of Mars, we must pause to look at a metaphor from the end of Canto 10. Similar to the moving gears of a clock that summons the faithful to their morning prayers, the great lights dance and sing. Their dancing movements imitate the pulling and thrusting of the movements of a mechanical clock. Together they chime with a sweetness and harmony never seen on Earth. These tercets have an obvious romantic and even sexual dimension, but it is the mechanical dimension, the *clock image*, I find most worthy for us to consider here.

According to Hollander's commentary on these lines, this is the first mention in literature of a mechanical clock.[11] These large devices, installed upon towers, had appeared only a few decades beforehand and Dante may have seen one during a visit to Milan during the time he was writing the *Divine Comedy*. They were first used like mechanized bells to summon the community to prayer like a sundial but usable on cloudy days and at night.*

It is maybe a little sad that the mechanical clocks eventually replaced the more direct but imprecise ways of telling time using the

---

* The English 'clock' comes from the word for bell: In German a bell is 'eine Glocke'.

Sun's movements. The popular historian Daniel Boorstin celebrated the development of the mechanical clock as liberating us from being "slave to the Sun": the clock became "new proof of [humanity's] mastery over himself and his surroundings."[12] Yes, but we also lost something important, an experience that undergirds the Sun's daily rhythms that inform its symbolism in Dante's Purgatory and Paradise.

Dante's era did not generally tell time by the mechanical clock but more naturalistic means. There were water clocks, sandglasses, and, of course, sundials. Sundials inform much of the meaning of the Sun in the *Divine Comedy*.

At noon the Sun is at the meridian circle that runs due North and South from a specific location, and on a sundial the Sun's shadow would be the smallest and at the dial's center. At other times during the day you would measure time relative to the meridian by noting the changing shadows to the left and right. In Dante's time the shadow's position would tell the clergy and ordinary people the time for that hour's prayers, at least on clear days.

To use a sundial you would mark off segments on each side of the meridian marker to divide daylight into hours of the same length. There would be six hours before noon (*ante meridian*) and six hours after noon (*post meridian*) so that there are always twelve hours of daylight corresponding to twelve hours of darkness (they would mostly use water clocks to keep time when it was dark).

These segments, to the left and right, would form *unequal hours* (or, to an astrologer, planetary hours). In the Northern hemisphere hours would be longer in the spring and summer and shorter in the autumn and winter. These seasonal considerations would vary with the Sun's yearly journey along the ecliptic. A sundial would account for this secondary motion. They would also need to account for a location's latitude, so that the more extreme the latitude the greater variation we find in the length of hours.

This is akin to how modern astrologers constructed their astrological charts before the development of the personal computer. Using the time of birth or other event and correcting for a location's longitude, the astrologer determines solar time based on the Sun's relative location – as opposed to time based on time zones. This helps determine the right ascension of a location's meridian; this is converted to ecliptical coordinates and the astrological Midheaven. Then the astrologer adds the place's latitude to determine the Ascendant for the individual or event at this particular time.

The Sun's position along the equator and ecliptic from a particular location allows one to know what time of day it is and what day of year it is. In Dante's view, the Sun's perfect movement along these two circles orchestrates these earth's rhythms. The Sun is the maestro of the cosmos. A sundial, far more than a mechanical clock, epitomizes this perfection.

We are now ready to leave the Sphere of the Sun and move on to the Spheres of Mars, Jupiter, and Saturn. They bring us not greater refinement and higher abstraction but more concreteness, more emphasis on personal narrative, and a renewed interest in worldly affairs below.

The 'Outer Planets' and this World

Mars

If the *Paradiso* was a human body with the lower spheres at the feet and the Empyrean its head, the cantos of Mars are its heart. This is where historical, community, and personal dimensions of life come together, where the pilgrim receives his assignment from Heaven.

Beginning at Canto 14.82, pilgrim and guide ascend to the ruddy planet with a fiery smile that glows with astrological symbolism. Dante gives thanks and mentally makes a "burnt offering" (*olocausto*) to God, depicting the burning itself happening in his breast (14.87-93). Here on the Sphere of Mars, Dante sees a giant equilateral cross, formed as if from the stars of our Milky Way. Upon this huge cross Dante has a flashing vision of Christ, a symbol of martyrdom but also the human incarnation of divinity.

The lights on this cross – Mars' citizens – are numerous like tiny dust motes that float on the sunbeams glowing through a shuttered window. From the lights, he hears a song that is difficult to make out except for the words "arise" and "conquer". Here are the many saved souls of crusaders and martyrs, ones who, according to Dante, died fighting the good fight. They represent the perfection of courage or fortitude.

Canto 15 begins the encounter between pilgrim and ancestor. Like a shooting star blazing across the sky at night, one of the lights rushes joyfully toward Dante and Beatrice. He addresses Dante in Latin, "O sanguis meus…", "Oh blood of mine…" that is the greeting of Aeneas by his father Anchises from the *Aeneid*'s underworld. The glowing soul gives thanks to God that the gates of Heaven are open to the pilgrim now and will be after his death.

The light speaks in language that is difficult to make out, but finally his speech descends to something the pilgrim can understand. He begins not with a personal introduction but a statement of his ability to understand the book of the future in the mind of God, indicating that he knew well beforehand that this meeting would take place. Although he can read the pilgrim's mind well enough, he asks Dante to speak to him in a voice that is *"sicura, balda, e lieta"*, "confident, bold, and joyful" – happily Mars-like. Dante, bursting with joy, simply asks him who he is.

The light identifies himself as Cacciaguida (15.135). After identifying his (and the pilgrim's) family and telling a little of his own life, Cacciaguida briefly tells about his death. He was a follower of the Emperor Conrad who knighted him for a crusade (what historians call the Second Crusade) where he died, death taking him from the deceptions of this world on Earth to peace in Heaven (15.148).

Canto 16 opens with an admonition about family pride: a great and noble family background bestows nothing in itself but is like a garment that shrinks quickly and one must add to it daily, i.e. one must replenish family nobility with one's own. The pilgrim, overjoyed to be talking with a distant ancestor, addresses Cacciaguida using the honorific *voi* for 'you', attracting a quiet smile of warning from Beatrice.

Cacciaguida gives his birth year obliquely but significantly: from the "time *Ave* was first spoken" to the time of his mother's birth pangs, the planet Mars has come to "the Lion" 580 times (*Paradiso* 16.37-39). The year of the Annunciation (when *Ave* was spoken) would be 0 CE, according to Dante's knowledge. Mars has a sidereal cycle of 687 days. Multiplying 687 by 580 (550+30 times Mars has entered Leo) we get 1091.

Cacciaguida's mention of Mars in Leo should give us pause. Leo, the zodiacal sign of the Sun, dispenses a dignified and even regal countenance to Mars. Intriguingly, Mars entered Leo in the later days of May, 1265 when the poet was likely born. As Dante takes pains throughout these cantos to identify himself with his Mars-like crusading ancestor, it is likely that these lines link the poet with his noble ancestor astrologically. This will become useful in Appendix 2 when I suggest a plausible astrological chart for the poet.

Cacciaguida articulates the causes of Florence's decline. As Florence became larger and more prosperous, outsiders were let in and citizens' simpler ways became subject to luxury, conspicuous consumption, and corruption. Cacciaguida explains that all that is worldly is by nature subject to decay and even their great city is no exception. His words take us back to the discussion of Lady Fortune from *Inferno* 7 but now on a political level.

"E come 'l volger del ciel de la luna
cuopre e discuopre i liti sanza posa
così fa di Fiorenza la Fortuna"

"as the turning of the Heaven of the Moon
covers and uncovers the shore without rest
so does Fortune deal with Florence." (*Paradiso* 16.82-84)

Echoing Marco the Lombard in *Purgatory* 16, these are times when good leadership is needed and where it frequently falls short. Cacciaguida lists many families that were once noble but have declined; they could have made a difference but had been corrupted by pride and avarice.

In Canto 16, Mars is mentioned once directly and once indirectly, both referring to the same statue of Mars that had once adorned the city. Cacciaguida first speaks of the original and smaller Florence which went from the cathedral of John the Baptist on one side to the statue of Mars on the other (Line 47). Cacciaguida also points to a specific event later – a murder in 1215 that set prominent families against each other and exacerbated the Guelf/Ghibelline feud in Florence. This murder takes place upon a bridge under the same statue of Mars, referred to now as "*a quella pietra scema che guarda 'l ponte*" – "that wasted stone that guards the bridge" (16.145-146). These lines display the planet's influence at its best and at its worst. The statue was guardian of the old city that bred warriors like Cacciaguida; it was also the place of a revenge killing that divided the city and would shed blood for many decades.

At the beginning of Canto 17 the topic changes from city to citizen, for the pilgrim has a personal question. With Beatrice's encouragement, the pilgrim asks about the many confused dark prophecies, those grave words ("*parole gravi*"), he had heard about his future when he was touring Hell and Purgatory.

What follows (Canto 17:37-142 is) about the catastrophe that will befall the pilgrim and his family. Cacciaguida tells the pilgrim about his life in exile, noting that his first companions will be useless and not too bright, but later Dante will benefit from the generosity of good patrons. These patrons will include one who is marked by the sign of Mars. As a result of his journey through the afterlife, the pilgrim will fight to counter the moral and cultural decline in his world. Cacciaguida's prophecy unifies the particular life story of one person and the sweep of providential history. Up to the very end of the canticle, Canto 17 is the most dramatic moment in the *Paradiso*.

Now opening Canto 18, Cacciaguida silently rejoices in his own thoughts as one might whose mind mirrors the mind of God. Beatrice consoles the pilgrim who has now learned with certainty about his exile: he should consider that she, Beatrice, dwells with God who lightens the weight of every wrong. Dante then looks upon her; the sound of her voice and the look of her eyes dazzle him: divine revelation and bliss have overcome all traces of personal bitterness at Cacciaguida's prediction. This sweet interlude prepares us for the upcoming leap from the personal to the *trans*-personal. It is the nature of the jump from heavenly Mars to Jupiter, from the story of one man's struggles to the wider workings of divinity.

Jupiter and Justice, Worldly and Divine

Dante and Beatrice enter Jupiter slowly and deliberately and we will do that as well. Let's first consider astrology's Jupiter.

Traditionally Jupiter has qualities of warm and moist, fertile and life-supporting features. Between the orbits of Mars and Saturn, Jupiter is also temperate, befitting its placement between the excessive natures of both planets that surround it.

Modern astrologers tend to fall short giving Jupiter its symbolic due. Perhaps this is because modern astrology tends to overemphasize the modern planets Uranus, Neptune, and Pluto. This has led to the Great Benefic being reduced to vague notions of 'expansion' (in its many grammatical forms) and 'confidence'. Here in Paradise, beginning with the realm of Jupiter, we encounter dimensions of life and being that modern astrologers attribute to Uranus and Neptune (but not astrology's Pluto).

According to Guido Bonatti, Jupiter's professions include law "and judging people diligently and honestly." People with the nature of Jupiter can mediate well between contesting factions and bring about accord. He continues: "And [Jupiter] signifies the soul, life, happiness, and religion and truth, patience, and every good, beautiful, and valuable precept, and whatever pertains to honesty."[13] A well-disposed Jupiter brings good fame, friends, honor, and intellect; a poorly disposed Jupiter is inexperienced at doing well, tends toward sanctimonious pretense and toward social isolation and poor judgment.

The poet picks up many of these themes. Jupiter is a planet of public appearance and of correct and honest judgment. It is not the planet of ideology; at its best, Jupiter allows for the determination and articulation of truth for the greater good of society.

In the *Paradiso* and in astrology's traditional literature, Jupiter is the planet of justice. Justice, human and divine, is a central issue of the entire *Divine Comedy* and it is upon the sphere of Jupiter that we turn our attention directly to it.

What is Justice, worldly or divine? We know that there are just and unjust cities and nations, agreements, individuals. Ordinarily we think of societies and legal systems that treat their citizens relatively fairly and equitably as just. Just agreements give all sides their due; just people will not take advantage of others. Traditionally the field of justice is that of right relationships between individuals and between groups and individuals within them. (In Plato's *Republic* justice was extended to right relationships between parts of the individual's soul.) As we may remember from the inscription on the gates of Hell, divine justice rules over matters of salvation, over God's dispersal of damnation and mercy. In Dante's Jupiter, we take note of worldly manifestations of justice and go further into the ineffability of divine judgment. We are implored to transcend our ordinary understanding.

We now enter Jupiter's realm. The pilgrim looks on Beatrice whose eyes are so joyful and radiant that they outshine her glory of even a few moments ago. He now becomes aware that Heaven's circles have become wider. They are on a planet that is a sparkling radiant white, changed from ruddy Mars like a woman's blush quickly disappearing from her face

(Canto 18:64-66). Now emerge many holy creatures like birds eagerly rising from a river's edge.

What follows in Canto 18 is a fourteenth century poetic version of computer-enhanced special effects, for now the lights, an assembly singing and dancing, begin to form shapes of letters. From letters to whole words and finally the assembly displays this: *"Diligente iustitiam que iudicas terram"*, "Love justice you who judge the earth." The last letter of the last word, shaped like an ornate Gothic 'M', shines like silver overlaid with gold. Like sparks from a burning log, many lights fly up and then settle on the final letter, changing it into an Eagle that is depicted in profile. We previously traced the route of the Roman Eagle in Canto 6; now the Eagle's form represents divine justice itself.

> *"O dolce stella, quali e quante gemme*
> *me dimostraro che nostra giustizia*
> *effetto sia del ciel che tu ingemme!"*

> "O sweet star, how many and how bright the gems
> that showed me that our justice
> Is the effect of the heaven that you 'in-gem'!"
> (*Paradiso* 18.115-117)

This tercet notes the physical beauty of Jupiter in the night sky (note the repetition of *gemme* in rhyming position) and tells us that justice, an idea in the mind of God, affects our world through this Heaven.

Canto 18 ends with a condemnation of the Church's misuse of its authority. This is the first of many diatribes against the Church that we will witness high up in Heaven. Dante prays that Heaven's wrath will come down on those who use the Church for material gain, and he prays for those on Earth who are led astray by the Church's bad leadership. Here and above, as one's viewpoint becomes wider and understanding deeper, there is increasing alarm that the current Church has led humanity down the wrong path.

Although Jupiter's lights are seen as a whole, each light is also its own shining ruby that burns with piercing flame. Although the figure will say "I" it is also saying "we". True to form, the poet does not render the figure of the Eagle into a simple abstraction, but also emphasizes that these are individual souls speaking. All the lights speak together in one sound as one heat is felt from different coals (Canto 19:19-21).

Dante has a question which the Eagle had already read in his mind and has an answer for. The pilgrim's question is this: how is it just that somebody who has lived a virtuous life but not know Christ be excluded from Paradise?

The Eagle begins his response by noting that divine understanding is far beyond the understanding of any created being; it is like the difference between the complete spectrum of sunshine and a single ray of light. Every lesser nature (*minor natura*) is too small for the Goodness that is beyond limit. The Eagle emphasizes the depth and brilliance of divine justice, especially as compared to the limit of any person's understanding. It is like the open sea which is much more vast than the small surface that we can see from the seashore. If divine Justice comes from God and our sense of justice is derived from it, our sense of justice must be incorrect if it comes into conflict with its source.

> *"Or tu chi se', che vuo' sedere a scranna,*
> *per giudicar di lungi mille miglia*
> *con la veduta corta d'una spanna?"*

> "Who are you sitting on a bench judging from a thousand miles away when your eyesight is shorter than a span?"
>
> (Canto 19.79-81)

The modern secular reader might find this somewhat repugnant. The Eagle has proclaimed that our individual minds cannot fathom the essential truths of divinity. According to medieval Christian understanding, in this life we cannot reach a full knowledge of God: direct knowledge is only available to the saved in the afterlife. Consequently, questioning God's justice is an impious equating of our limited understanding with divine judgment.

This is not a flight into absurdity to Dante, for our earthly justice (like earthly goodness and intellect) reflects its ultimate source. Divine justice, embodied by the Eagle on the Sphere of Jupiter, accounts for our longing for justice and inspires us to fight for it.

For the remainder of Canto 19, the Eagle takes Dante back down to our worldly concerns. Echoing Cacciaguida's previous list of once-famous but declined families of Florence, the Eagle lists twelve unjust rulers who were contemporary with Dante in 1300. Various ills are associated with them: falsifying currency, pride, luxury and slothful ways, miserliness, cowardice, and the ever-present fault of avarice. In the name of justice, battling these qualities and the bad leaders who possess them is the good fight.

Canto 20 begins with the alternation between the Eagle consisting of many lights (like separate stars that appear in the night sky) and one Sun that the stars reflect. The song from the voices, separate and unified, slips and falls from the pilgrim's memory. Finally they speak clearly through the Eagle's beak and identify six lights that shine in the eye of the Eagle. The pupil of the Eagle's eye is King David. Of the remaining five inhabiting the Eagle's eyebrow, two are surprises and examples of the inscrutable nature of divine justice according to the poet's conception.

Roman Emperor Trajan was no particular friend of the new Christian religion but was otherwise considered a model ruler.* The second surprise is greater – a character in Virgil's *Aeneid* named Ripheus is among the redeemed. He was to have lived a thousand years before Christ. Virgil mentions Ripheus only in passing. He was an exemplary Trojan who was trapped when his city was taken by the Greeks: although he was "uniquely just among the Trojans/The soul of equity", the gods did not spare this good man.[14]

The Eagle explains that, centuries after his death and due to the prayers of Pope Gregory, Trajan was brought back into his body, educated and converted, and ascended Heaven upon his second death. Ripheus' righteousness was so impressive that God saw to it that he was baptized in Christ although there would be no Christ for many centuries. The story of Trajan follows a familiar medieval tale; that of Ripheus is likely the poet's invention.

The Jupiter cantos have, to this modern astrologer, more than a hint of Uranus and Neptune in them. When modern astrologers think of matters mystical or transpersonal, they especially think of these modern planets. Uranus is not the logical discursive mind of Mercury but the planet of genius, as if higher intellect has come down and taken root as intuitive, 'out of the box' thinking (and of distorted, crazy ungrounded thinking and bizarre eccentric behavior). Neptune is often aligned with the ineffable or metaphysical, mentally with the highly creative or deluded – and, at its worst, with escapist or addictive behavior or

---

* Trajan appears in *Purgatorio* 10 as a secular example of humility.

becoming victimized by others. Uranus and Neptune symbolize awareness beyond ordinary thought and a sense of oneness that allows us to see our 'mind-forged manacles' that have imprisoned us.

Of course Dante had no knowledge of any planetary bodies beyond Saturn. Yet his Jupiter of the *Paradiso* is abundantly transpersonal. The great glistening planet is, in the poet's hands, a preliminary display of divine mind; it is the following planet that demonstrates the practical means toward this great goal.

> ### Music and Paradise
> As the pilgrim has ascended the planetary spheres its music has become gradually more difficult to discern. Recall that in the hymn sung on Mars he could only make out the words "Arise" and "Conquer"; now on Jupiter he hears its hymn's sweetness and harmony although its notes have also become indistinct. This reminds me of much medieval polyphonic music that has great beauty but its complexity makes its words and even its melody hard to discern. At this time you might wonder how music will be rendered within the next sphere, on Saturn.

Saturn and the Great Contemplatives

When Dante and Beatrice ascend from Jupiter to Saturn they leave medieval astrology's Great Benefic and enter its Great Malefic. They move upwards from a sphere whose planet is bright and circles the night sky in a dignified stately way to one that is usually slower and dimmer in appearance. They ascend from a planet that is warm and moist to one that is cold and dry, from generosity to austerity, from the sanguine to the melancholy. Yet according to Dante's medieval cosmology Saturn is physically closer to God than Jupiter. What's a poet to do?

The pilgrim fixes his eyes upon Beatrice but now she does not smile. If she smiled now the pilgrim would be reduced to ashes as was Semele when the god Jupiter displayed his true blazing form; she must reduce the intensity of her appearance to the pilgrim. Beatrice announces that they have risen to the sphere of Saturn that is beneath the burning Lion's breast. (Implied here is that Leo's warmth helps temper the coldness of Saturn.*) Beatrice implores the pilgrim to remain focused. He is happy to obey her.

After Dante mentions – maybe wistfully – the mythical past Golden Age of Saturn, a golden ladder appears that spans a great length, extending above further than his eye can see all the way down to where they are. Upon its rungs are many splendors descending. Like birds flying around on a cold morning to warm themselves, these lights move in various ways.**

One of the lights moves next to Dante and Beatrice. The pilgrim is hesitant to speak with him, waiting for Beatrice's permission to speak. After explaining that he feels unworthy, Dante begins to question this light of Saturn. Here is a summary of their conversation (Canto 21.52-105) in dialogue form.

Q. What is the cause for you coming to me? And why is it silent here, when below I heard so much singing?

A. Your hearing is mortal like your sight. It is silent here for the same reason that Beatrice did not smile upon entering this region – you are not ready. I have come down here to welcome you, not because I love you more than anybody else here. Instead, I serve the Wisdom that governs the world.

Q. Why are you here to greet me instead of the many others?

While the pilgrim was speaking this light began moving around making of himself a center and began whirling around as if around a millwheel (Canto 21:79-81).

A. Divine light and power raise me far above myself and I can see into the Highest Essence, from which power is milked (*la somma essenza de quala è munta* 21.87). However, the most intelligent soul in Heaven could not answer your question, since God's eternal law

---

* You may remember Saturn's coldness mentioned at the beginning of *Purgatorio* 19.

** Hollander (2007, p.519) cites John Carroll's commentary on these lines (21.34-45) that discusses three kinds of motion, that, according to 12th century theologian Richard of St. Victor, correspond to three kinds of knowledge. *Straight* motion goes from senses to intellect; *oblique* motion, a mixture of straight and circular, blends reason and divine illumination; *circular* motion rotates around divine truth itself. These three motions correspond to motions (1) found on earth, (2) the motions of the planets, and (3) that of the fixed stars that parallel Dante's cosmology in the poem. I include this here because it associates cosmology and the human and divine. It also illustrates how detailed and rewarding Dante scholarship can be.

is hidden from our understanding. And when you get back to Earth do tell people not to be so presumptuous as to ask these kinds of questions.

Q. (Thoroughly chastened). Who are you?

Before giving his name as Peter Damian, he first tells where he entered the monastic life, where he began his life of serving God. So content was he that his food remained simple and he gladly endured heat and cold. He talks of his later years when, upon the Pope's request, he left his happy life of contemplation and reluctantly took up the office of a cardinal. By the present time the Church has become bloated with luxury, and his cloister that once gave a harvest to Heaven is now barren.

Those of you familiar with Saturn's symbolism are reading all this with a smile: the atmosphere here is endowed with both a traditional and modern psychological sense of Saturn. In addition to Saturn's symbolic characteristics of austerity and isolation, we find seriousness and restraint, silence and hesitation. The attitude that greets Dante seems a far cry from the tender affection that Cacciaguida bore for his descendant.

Peter Damian was an important church reformer from the eleventh century. He was then abbot of a Benedictine monastery. Pope Gregory VII selected Peter Damian and sought his help with church and monastic reforms. Throughout his lifetime Damian fiercely opposed the wealthy ways of the Church that became signs of the degeneracy of its spiritual calling.

Toward the end of Canto 21, more lights descend, whirling about, and gather around the old monk. Together they let out a thunderous deafening cry so loud that the pilgrim becomes frightened. (On Saturn we have a different polyphony than elsewhere.) Beatrice reassures her frightened student and reminds him that everything in Heaven is holy, including this cry of righteous zeal (*buon zelo*). Heaven's sword is always timely and will have its vengeance upon those who deserve it.

Hundreds of lights glowing like pearls come into view and Dante hesitates before speaking with the one who glows most brightly. Reading his thoughts, the light begins to speak to the pilgrim. He first identifies his place of activity, a mountain near Cassino. During his life he brought the Christian faith to an area strongly identified with its pagan roots and also helped convert those in the surrounding towns to Christianity. When this soul mentions a place called Cassino with a mountain, Dante's contemporaries can quickly identify this person as Benedict of Norcia, who is usually referred to as St. Benedict. He lived in the early sixth century.

It is difficult to overstate Benedict's historical importance. Living in the early sixth century when Christian monasticism was a new kind of contemplative lifestyle, he led by example and set up a set of rules for the monastic life. The 'Rule of St Benedict' promoted communal austerity and hard work without the spiritual athleticism and competitiveness that often accompanies the life of worldly renunciation. Instead, Benedictine rules strove to instill humility and obedience – two positive saturnine qualities. This allowed the monasteries to become a major factor in European life for the next thousand years, although over time further reform movements became necessary. In time everything declines if left on its own.

After listening to Benedict, Dante feels confident enough to engage with him. The pilgrim wants to see the great saint's face as it is and not veiled by light. (The pilgrim has not looked upon a saved soul's facial features since the Sphere of the Moon and only a smile on Mercury.) Benedict tells Dante that is too early for him to see them in their resurrected bodies; this will happen for him in the highest Heaven.

Like Dominic and Francis, the work of these two men helped the Church recover from its worldly success and helped maintain its purpose, the salvation of souls. These were not just great contemplatives but also highly political people in tune with the conditions and needs of their times. Both presage Bernard of Clairvaux whom we soon meet in the Empyrean.

The golden ladder that the souls descended, whose symbolism derives from Jacob's ladder (*Genesis* 28:11–19), goes from Saturn all the way up to the Empyrean. Jacob's ladder is the way up from the spheres of the planets to the higher realms of fixed stars and beyond. Dante and Beatrice now swiftly ascend the ladder.

Quickly, very quickly, pilgrim and guide have ascended to the stars themselves and the pilgrim sees that they are in the sign that follows Taurus (*io vidi 'l segno/ che segue il Tauro e fui dentro da esso*: Canto

> ### The Journey through the Planets – a Modern Version
> In the late 1940s astrologer Dane Rudhyar wrote a series of magazine articles correlating astrology's symbolism to stages of the spiritual life. His development of astrology's planets was first published in the 1960's as "The Illumined Road" within the larger *An Astrological Triptych*. Although I do not wish to compare Dante's poetry with Rudhyar's prose, Rudhyar's adaptation of celestial journey literature is interesting and insightful.
>
> Rudhyar supplants Dante's hierarchical model of the universe centered on God with one where the evolutionary goal is the "White City at the core of the Galaxy." This journey of spiritual integration into larger wholes begins with the seeker being a small Sun shooting out through astrology's planets into the vastness of the larger galactic system. The planets are phases of the journey; as with Dante, it's a Journey of Return.
>
> Here is Rudhyar's list of planetary phases (including one planet not yet discovered):
> Moon: Reorientation
> Mercury: Repolarization
> Venus: Revaluation
> Mars: Re-energization
> Jupiter: Reconversion
> Saturn: Re-incorporation
> Uranus: Transfiguration
> Neptune: Trans-substantiation
> Pluto: The Gate to Immortality
> The Proserpine Myth: The Resurrection and the Ascension

22.110-111). In a passage we will take up again at the beginning of Part Three, the poet praises this constellation (Gemini) that is the source of whatever talent he may have: when he was born the Sun resided here. Previously he had invoked the Muses and, at the beginning of the *Paradiso*, the poet invoked Apollo the god of prophecy: here he asks for inspiration from his own stars.

Beatrice then tells the pilgrim he should look under his feet and see how many heavens he has so far ascended. Dante looks back at the seven planetary spheres and at the very bottom, he sees the Earth itself; he smiles at seeing how mean or paltry it appears.

Closing Canto 22, Dante refers to the planets based on their parentage in ancient myth. Moon is daughter of Latona; Sun is son of Hyperion, circled by the son of Maia (Mercury) and the daughter of Dione (Venus). He sees Jupiter tempering the extremes of his father (Saturn) and son (Mars). He directly sees the planets' respective sizes and velocities and their positions relative to each other. This is similar to *The Dream of Scipio* where Scipio Africanus showed his grandson the planets and stars.

Citing mythical depictions highlights the illusory nature of what we have seen of Paradise and what is yet to come. The parental ties remind us of the true divine origin and purpose of the planetary spheres – they are all the offspring of God the creator.

Here are the wonderful last lines of Canto 22.

> "L' aiuola che ci fa tanto feroci,
> volgendom'io con li etterni Gemelli,
> tutta m' apparve da' colli a le foci;"

An aiuola is a small space; this word has been often translated as "little threshing floor," a place that functions here to separate the saved from the damned.[15] This small space or threshing-floor makes us fierce (*tanto feroci*), or, as we might say, drives us crazy. From the timeless constellation of Gemini the pilgrim sees all the inhabitable earth – from hills to shore, the mouths of rivers.

The pilgrim and the constellation Gemini are directly over the meridian of Jerusalem, midway between Spain and India. The Sun in Aries would be West of Jerusalem, possibly going over Italy. Dante and Beatrice must also be a significant height from the Sun – otherwise the Sun's beams would blot out the sight of the earth. The Sun must be like a flashlight that shines below. In Canto 27, after their stay on the Fixed Stars, Dante will again look down toward the planets and Earth and will see that Gemini and Aries moved to give a different sight of the Earth.

> "Poscia rivolsi li occhi a li occhi belli." (Canto 22.154)

The pilgrim's eyes now turn toward the beautiful eyes of Beatrice. Canto 22 ends by changing a large-scale vision to the briefest of intimate moments. This anticipates the next event and also the final ten cantos of the *Divine Comedy* – the final steps of the journey to God.

Beyond the Planets: Time into Timelessness

Stars, Apostles, and Angels

Dante and Beatrice have ascended from the planetary spheres to the fixed stars; they are now no longer in the Heavens of the irregularly moving planets but these heavenly bodies with a regular circular orbit. Dante the poet devotes Cantos 23-27 to this realm, more cantos than any other place in Paradise.

We also move from the Cardinal Virtues of Wisdom, Courage, Justice, and Temperance to the Theological Virtues of Faith, Hope, and Charity or Love. From this time to the end of the poem the encounters become more formal; the manner of presenting intriguing personalities and biographical sketches is cast far away. Paradoxically the poetry of the last ten cantos has an earthy concreteness to it, and it contains some of *Divine Comedy*'s greatest verse.

Highest Heaven Descending

Canto 23 begins with Beatrice who seems like a bird eagerly waiting for dawn to feed her young chicks. The sky begins to light up. This cannot be dawn for Heaven has no horizon. Instead the sky lights up *from above*, and what descends from there is like the brightest of lights surrounded by stars.

What follows is an episode of otherworldly drama and a singular example of literary chutzpah. The entire heavenly host, including Jesus and Mary, descend from above to greet Dante and Beatrice. Why?

Ascending to the fixed stars from the planetary spheres is a huge leap, but from the highest Heavens it is simply arriving closer to home. The pilgrim has been promoted from the wheel of the ecliptic, where the planets move in their complex motions, to the celestial equator that contains the regular orderly motion that we perceive as diurnal motion. One is also physically closer to God. In this canto we glimpse those who are physically closest to God (the angels and Adam) and to Jesus Christ (Mary and the apostles Peter, James, and John).

This assembly gives a glimpse or a prefiguring of what is to come in the final moments of union at the end of the poem. This brief foretaste contains the entire truth but only what is available to one not yet ready for its completeness. Between the Spheres of the Planets and the Empyrean, the intermediate realm of the Fixed Stars becomes the cosmic stage for this transition.

Like the Full Moon lighting up the night sky, Dante sees one Sun enkindling the many lights that surround it. Through this great light flows a shining substance (*lucente sustanza*) but Dante's eyes cannot tolerate its brightness. This bright substance is the form of the embodied Christ. The reference to "substance" reminds one of the Biblical story of the Transfiguration, when the apostles Peter, James, and John saw Christ shining like the Sun with raiment of glowing white.[16] This is an inverse transfiguration, here in Paradise the great light (Christ) is seen in *bodily* raiment. It is also a visual representation of the descent of grace that is required for the journey further above.

Reeling from a glimpse of Christ, the pilgrim's mind bursts forth like lightning from a cloud. Beatrice tells him that he is now able to see her as she really is and he should look upon the smile that was withheld from him on the sphere of Saturn. Beatrice also tells him to look around at the dazzling display of lights that is like a beautiful garden all in blossom.

Dante endeavors to see the splendor gathered around and above him, and what he sees is like a field of flowers as lit by the Sun through the clouds. However, he can no longer see the source of its light – Christ had ascended back to the highest Heaven.

Now able to see better, he glimpses the Virgin Mary, also embodied, outshining all the stars that surround her. Reminding the reader of the sweet sapphire of Venus that Dante and Virgil first see when they enter Purgatory, the poet calls Mary the being whose grace "ensapphires" the highest heaven. (Canto 23.101-102.) As Mary ascends back to the highest Heaven, Dante sees the stars reaching toward her with their tips as a baby reaches out to its mother after having drunk her milk, and all sing *Regina coeli*, "Queen of Heaven." It is noteworthy that the pilgrim, who cannot fix his gaze upon Christ, can see Mary – she is more accessible.

The Theological Virtues

Neither Dante nor any other poet could sustain the cosmic intensity achieved here. The following three cantos display a very different style.

The pilgrim is to be questioned about faith, hope, and love by the apostles Peter, James, and John respectively. He is given his final exam on his way to the final Paradise.

These encounters resemble the traditional university oral examination of the aspiring student or 'bachelor' (*baccialier*), and master (*maestro*); they have come down to us today as the thesis or dissertation defense. Importantly, these encounters also resemble a young squire or knight being tested for admission to the Emperor's court – particularly to the Emperor's military. Twice Dante addresses his inquirers as nobleman (*baron*) and once as commander or centurion (*primipilus*). Because the pilgrim is being tested for admission into the Empyrean, (the Celestial Court) and to take up arms for divine purposes, university and military metaphors apply equally.

In Purgatory the Theological Virtues were the stars above that were agents of protection during the pilgrims' nights upon the mountain. They became the purple-clad nymphs accompanying Beatrice's chariot in the Earthly Paradise. Although these virtues pervade Heaven, it is among the fixed stars that they become fully conscious and articulate. Recall that fixed stars do not move in their own particular motions but seemingly in a regular circular motion around the earth; their uniform and relatively perfect motions make them suitable symbols and stepping-stones to divinity which is beyond space and time.

Like the stars in the sky pointing to the divine nature, the virtues of faith, hope, and love make God available to those within earthly existence. They are stepping-stones to divinity, complemented by God's grace descending.

At the beginning of Canto 24, Christ and Mary have re-ascended and the remainder of the "saved ones" are arrayed around them, glowing. Beatrice asks them to examine this pilgrim so that he can partake in some of the dewdrops from the fountain of Heaven. In a scene reminiscent of the Sphere of the Sun in Canto 10, the blazing lights become like rings around fixed poles and wheel around, some almost motionless and another flying, like the wheels of a clock (Canto 24:10-15).* The

---

* Keep in mind the whirling motions of the lights of the fixed stars; we have encountered this motion on Venus as well as on Saturn and will encounter it further among the angels and in the poem's final image.

brightest among them circles around Beatrice three times; this is the apostle Peter. Beatrice asks Peter to test Dante's understanding of the virtue of *faith*.

Following scripture, Dante explains that faith is the substance of what is hoped for and the evidence of things unseen. Pleased, Peter asks his student whether he has faith in his purse – a resource to him – and Dante says that indeed he has. Peter, referring to faith as that gem upon which other virtues rest, asks Dante about the source of faith: the pilgrim dutifully cites scripture, miracles, and that Christianity became dominant without recourse to miracles.

Peter asks Dante for the content of his faith. He responds, "*Io credo in uno Dio/solo ed etterno, che tutto 'l ciel move, /non moto, con amore e con disio*". "I believe in one God/single and eternal, who moves all the heavens/ is unmoved, with love and desire" (Canto 24.130-133). These words recall the poem's first tercet at the beginning of Canto 1 and poem's final words at the end of Canto 33. As Dante's examination on faith concludes, Heaven bursts into song and Peter's light joyfully encircles Dante three times.

Canto 25 continues with a discussion of *hope*, doing so in a highly worldly and personal way. In its opening lines, the poet imagines his return to Florence lionized as the writer of the future *Divine Comedy*. He promises he will take the laurel crown to the font where he was once baptized. This is a rather personal statement made so high in Paradise.

Charles Singleton's commentary on this tercet calls its yearning "pathetic".[17] My opinion differs, however. Indeed these lines are full of *pathos*. Yet Dante appears to invoke hope not as an emotional escape but as a strengthening virtue; the opposite of hope is not realism but disempowering despair. These lines contain an affirmation of the need to continue.

A second light comes toward the visitors. Beatrice introduces the apostle James and asks him to discuss hope with the pilgrim. James tells Dante to lift up his head and be confident (*Leva la testa e fa che t'assicuri*. 25.34), for all that comes here becomes ripened in Heaven's radiance. To strengthen hope in himself and in others, Dante is asked to discuss the nature of hope and its sources for him.

Beatrice speaks and tells the apostle that nobody has more hope than this pilgrim here, and this is why he has come from "Egypt" to

"Jerusalem" during his earthly lifetime. Dante's definition emphasizes its origins as a gift of grace and also one's previous development. For hope to strengthen, we must have first strengthened in ourselves both faith and hope.

> "'Spene', diss'io, ''e uno attender certo
> de la gloria futura, il qual produce
> grazia divina e precedente merto.'"
>
> "'Hope,' I said, 'is the certain expectation
> of future glory, that is produced by
> divine grace and preceding merit.'" (Canto 25.67-69)

What is the "future glory" that Dante refers to? Dante quotes a line from the Bible that states that each in his homeland will be clad in a "double garment" (*doppia vesta*) and that this eventual home is the sweet life (*dolce vita*) (Canto 25:92-93). "Future glory" is the final resurrection of the body. Heaven bursts into joyful song.

Now appears another light but one so bright that if a star in the constellation Cancer had a light this bright the entire winter would be one endless day. Upon being introduced to this light, the apostle John, the pilgrim stares intensely: he had once heard that John also had ascended into Heaven with his body. Admonished for this wrong understanding, suddenly Dante cannot see and must now converse about love without his sight.

I have always found this moment's timing dramatic and telling. When we are without sight we must rely on other senses. We particularly rely on those bodily senses that tend to remain in the background but are at the root of much of our intuition and hidden thinking. To use modern language, Dante must rely on his 'felt sense' to discuss love.

Canto 26 opens with Dante reeling from his loss of sight but John tells him that his sight is not gone forever but can be restored by a glance from Beatrice. The pilgrim states, with unexpected equanimity, that Beatrice can restore sight now or later to these gates that she once entered with the fire with which he will always burn (Canto 26.13-15). Here Dante implies love's continuity from the youthful – and lustful – ardor of his youth to the more refined and sublimated love he feels in Heaven.

When asked about love the pilgrim first waxes philosophical. As one knows the good, love for the good is enkindled, so that the more there is knowledge of goodness the more there is love. Since God is the greatest good and the source of all goodness, all good things are reflections of the ultimate divine good.

John then asks Dante to become more personal, wanting to know what other cords bind him to God, so he can tell of the many teeth of which love bites (*con quanti denti questo amor ti morde*; Canto 26.51). Dante returns to the love of God – for creating the world and him, for the death of Christ and the resurrection to come, and for taking him from the sea of twisted love (*l'amore torto*) to love that is right. Using a metaphor the poet will bring up later in a different context, he states that he loves the leaves in the garden of the eternal Gardener according to the portion of goodness He has bestowed on them. The pilgrim professes love for the world's things only as they reflect quantities of God's goodness.

After all the expressions of *amore* in the *Divine Comedy*, this passage might leave the reader somewhat cold. Far up in Heaven, far from this Earth that makes us fierce, love is not a subjective feeling but a cosmic principle, indeed one that binds the universe together. According to this vision, our personal love, whether twisted or right, is but a drop in the ocean of this great binding force.

Heaven again bursts into song and, just as sleep is suddenly broken by a piercing light, the pilgrim's sight comes back. Now with the apostles he sees a fourth light and is introduced to Adam, the first human being created. In this last interview in the *Divine Comedy*, Adam detects Dante's many questions and the first man discourses about the timing of his creation and fall, the original language he spoke, and the reasons for God's anger with him. This exchange serves as a pleasant intellectual excursion: if you met the first man ever, what would you ask him?

Preparing for the Crystalline Sphere

Beginning Canto 27, the pilgrim, who is back with the apostles and drunk with joy, watches in stunned fashion as the atmosphere of Heaven and its citizens darken; the light of Peter changes countenance as would Jupiter if it exchanged plumage with Mars, i.e. turns red. Peter, the first Pope, engages in an angry and savage invective against Dante's contemporary papacy and in particular against Boniface VIII. As Beatrice blushes in shame and all of Heaven appears eclipsed to darkness, Peter indicts the current church for its greed and fraudulent ways. Although Peter predicts that providence will eventually come to the rescue, he also charges his new knight, the pilgrim Dante, to render his denunciation to those below – and don't make it pretty.

Then all the saints re-ascend into the yet unseen Empyrean. Think of a windless snowfall when the Sun "touches the horn" of Capricorn – *in reverse*. In this depiction of life beyond this world Dante takes an ordinary occurrence and turns it upside down and to make it extraordinary.

> **Earthly Time for the Last Time**
>
> The depiction of Dante's view of Earth (Canto 27.78-87) rewards close examination.[18] Since arriving to the constellation Gemini, they have travelled "*che fa dal mezzo al fine il primo clima*", "from the middle to the end of the first clime" (Canto 27.81). A 'clime' is the latitudinal band around the Earth. One half of the "first" clime encompasses the habitable globe between India and Spain.* If one half of this band is 180°, from the middle to the end is 90°. If the Sun's daily movement of this span is twelve hours long (corresponding to 180°), then they have been upon the Fixed Stars a total of six hours. The poet is using movement *above* the Sun to determine how much time that has elapsed.
>
> Previously he could see the inhabitable Earth from the Ganges to Morocco and Spain. Now he can see in the West the mad route taken by Ulysses. To the East he cannot see all the way to the Ganges but only as far as the shore of Asia Minor where Europa was abducted by the ancient god Jupiter, from the end of Book II in Ovid's *Metamorphosis*. Jupiter, lusting after her, changed himself into a bull. Europa began playing with the bull, eventually getting upon his back, whereupon Jupiter carried

---

* This returns to our discussion of the opening lines of *Purgatorio* 2 that considered "Spain" 90° East of Jerusalem and "India" 90° West of Jerusalem. Modern calculations put Jerusalem at between the two extremes of Dante's inhabitable earth but 35° of latitude on either side, not 90°.

> her off to the sea. Ulysses' folly to the West is complemented by Europa's folly to the East. There is a lot of folly down here.
>
> Where are Dante and Beatrice when pilgrim views the Eastern shore of Asia to the Western path of Ulysses? Six hours beforehand Dante was over Jerusalem and the Sun was probably near or over Italy; according to the poet's knowledge of geography, 90° W (six hours) would put the pilgrim over Spain and Morocco and the Sun over the Atlantic Ocean.
>
> This is the last specific time reference in the *Divine Comedy* and the last view of the Earth although it will soon return as an image. In the *Inferno* we have seen time reckoned by the position of the Moon and specific fixed stars; in the *Purgatorio* on the Earth's surface, we added the horizon, and we used the Sun and shadow to determine the time. In Canto 27 we use the diurnal heavenly movement around an unmoving Earth whose changing areas of visibility allow us to know the time. The moving shadow of a sundial would be the Earth itself.

Beatrice asks him to once again look downwards toward earth and Dante notes the time that has passed and how he sees this threshing floor or small patch of earth, *di questa aiuola*.

The pilgrim looks again toward Beatrice; this time no art of any kind could possibly depict her smiling face. As she looks back upon him, both are cast from Gemini to the swiftest heaven (*ciel velocissimo* Canto 27.99).

Our pilgrim and his guide have arrived at the ninth heaven which is generally called the *Primum Mobile* or First Motion. Commentators usually refer to it as the 'Crystalline Sphere'. This is not exactly a sphere although later we find that it does have a surface that can reflect Light from above. This area – if you want to call it that – has no parts. We are in a different reality from the bounded fixed stars that Dante divided into the zodiac's signs and constellations.

The Crystalline Sphere is enclosed by God's light and love that, in turn, encloses the other circles of Heaven, from the Fixed Stars down to the Moon. This very high Heaven has no location other than the mind of God from whom love enkindles its motion and from whom power rains down to the lower Heavens and downwards further to us.

Here is the origin of time, Beatrice says, that has its unseen roots in a single flower pot (Using the Hollander translation of *testo* that Musa translates as 'vase'), yet its leaves (*fronde*) are in all the others (Canto 27:118-120). The fixed stars and planetary spheres are like flowerpots whose foliage also descends. (Grandgent calls this a "grotesque metaphor".) Since we recently were called to witness a saintly snowfall falling upwards, we should not be surprised by a flower vase that is upside down.

Like a composer who uses one or two seemingly ornamental notes to change to a new motif, Beatrice uses this metaphor of flowerpots to pivot back to earthly affairs. She condemns our tendency toward greed (*cupidigia*) that is so deep in our waters that we cannot see above the waves, and she returns to the gardening motif: our will may blossom but the ceaseless rain makes its fruit go to rot. In this vein Beatrice says that once-innocent children are prone to all kinds of corruption and evil as they become older. The current sad state of affairs, due to lack of true leadership in the world, is from a bad job of cultivation from the top.

This sad condition will be reversed only when the month of January is un-wintered (Canto 27:142-144). Recall from our discussion of the time of the *Divine Comedy*'s journey that these lines may allude to the old Julian calendar that began to move backwards, or, according to Richard Kay and others, to the precession of the equinoxes.[19] Regardless of reference, Beatrice is talking of something that will happen inevitably but *in a long time*. Only then will the ship of earthly conditions reverse and "after the flower true fruit will come" (*e vero frutto verrà dopo 'l fiore.*)

The Universe Upside Down – Or Is It?

All this brings us to Canto 28 and the Crystalline Sphere and a reversal that is not metaphorical but cosmological. Here we're not concerned with snow falling upwards or flowers bearing fruit downwards but with a new image of the whole universe, one that reverses our conception of it – a Great Switcheroo.

Imagine that we're in a place, if you can call it a place, from where you could see all the galaxies moving away from each other as they are purported to do after the Big Bang. This is similar to what Dante's readers are about to experience.

Dante looks to Beatrice's beautiful eyes (*belli occhi*), those same eyes that once had caught him as a youth, where in the Earthly Paradise he saw a griffin that represented the dual nature of Christ. This time he sees a different reflection in her eyes. Like when seeing a flame's image in a mirror, he turns around to look at its source and sees a blazing point of light.

This point is so bright that the faintest star in our sky would seem as bright as the Moon. Around this infinitesimally small but piercingly bright light is a ring like a halo, whirling around the center at incredibly fast speed; around this is another blazing ring and around the second one is another and then another until there are nine. These concentric wheels all move in the same direction; as they become more distant from the central light their speeds become less swift. That ring of fire nearest to the light has the clearest flame and, Beatrice adds, it is directly moved by flaming love (*l' affocato amore*, 28:45) for the light in the center depicts God.

The pilgrim is confused: this is not the universe he knows. Although the circles moving around God most fast are those closest to divinity, the heavenly spheres nearer the Earth (like the Moon and Mercury) are faster and those further away and therefore those closer to God (like Saturn) are slower.

Does this vision of a point of light surrounded by blazing circles show us the *true* universe? If so, maybe our material universe is an illusion based on coarse appearance, a shallow version of its true picture. This would be a Neoplatonic point of view.

Perhaps this new universe that Dante sees is instead an abstraction or idealization of the *real sensory* universe. This vision is an image projected from Even Further Above for Dante's education. The view that our cosmos is essentially physical and manifests directly and truthfully to our sense perceptions is Aristotelian. In my view, Dante puts the two approaches together.

In the *Divine Comedy*, our perceptible cosmos is a reflection of this vision that Dante beholds and which ultimately generates from the timeless Mind of God. *However*, this reflection that we receive on Earth is not falsity but as much truth as we limited mortals can comprehend. Because they also are God's creation, they cannot be false or even illusory, merely pale reflections of the ultimate.

We usually think that the privileged viewpoint we have determines that what appears to us is real. In the same way, we magnify our world's centrality; from Heaven's point of view, however, our world is just a small place. Dante posits a more-true God-perspective above our more limited Earth-perspective but also includes our limited perspective as real in its

> **Absolutely One and Relatively Two Motions**
>
> In the final cantos of the *Divine Comedy* the spheres that are closest to God and the furthest from Earth are faster; the closer the spheres are to Earth and the more distant from God, the slower they become. This violates apparent reality, for here we see the Moon always changing shape and we note that it takes almost thirty years for Saturn to return. Both Moon and Saturn are depicted along the ecliptic in their 'secondary motion'. Yet the vision of *Paradiso* 28 is of one motion only, the diurnal 'primary motion' of the celestial equator that we see set in motion by the Sphere of the Fixed Stars.
>
> How do we "save the appearances", to quote a famous Neoplatonic project, to account for the appearances of a fast Moon and slow Saturn reconciled with one Primary Motion? The answer would be to regard the secondary motion as containing increasing amounts of deviance from the primary motion further from God and closer to Earth, from Saturn to Moon.
>
> If it is astronomical noon and the Sun is conjunct my local meridian how much time does it take for the next astronomical noon? It would take 24 hours and just under four minutes (closer is 3.944). This is because as the Earth rotates on its axis it also has some of its yearly revolution around the Sun. From a geocentric point of view, it is because the Sun, as it moves along the diurnal motion and the celestial equator, is also carried slightly the other way on the wheel of the ecliptic. This would be a deviation from the primary motion. Therefore the Sun has an additional 3.944 minutes to make up before it returns to noon.
>
> Let's extend this to realms of Dante's Heaven. Below the perfect rotation of the Crystalline Sphere is that of the Fixed

> Stars; this rotation deviates from perfect motion by only the very minutest amount, due to what we would call the precession of the equinoxes. Further away, the Sphere of Saturn has a close to perfect motion but there is more deviation. This continues down through the various Spheres to the Moon that has the largest deviation from the diurnal motion.
>
> If you take the Sun's 3.944 minutes and multiply this by the number of days in a year, it would take very slightly more than one year for the Sun's deviation to add up to one additional degree on the celestial equator (or longitude on Earth). Likewise Jupiter would take 12 years, Saturn 29, and Moon about 28 days.
>
> We have thus replaced the two wheels from the Sphere of the Sun with one wheel and a completely unified and orderly sky – with deviations, like the rest of the created world.

own fashion. In *Paradiso* 28 our world of appearance is seen as real but only relatively so.

A very large question arises from this model: *Where is the Earth, where are we?* We have previously contemplated the Heavens from Earth's perspective. But where is the Earth in this new vision? It is missing. And the reader has no 'place' from which to see this vision. So we are missing in this model as well.

Two possibilities arise. Perhaps the Earth would be the unseen base below, either square like an obelisk (or the Buddhist *stupa*) or round like a cone. Regardless of its bottom, the Heaven would be like the circumpolar stars (North or South) in their night's journey above our horizon. This would be from Earth's point of view.

From Heaven's point of view, perhaps the Earth is just the furthest Sphere from God. It would move the most slowly if at all, because of the drag of sequential time and the four elements. We will ponder this further when we discuss the *Paradiso*'s final image.

Canto 28 has yet another surprise. With the central bright light and concentric spheres in the background, Beatrice pauses. Around the nine circles the pilgrim sees innumerable sparks shooting out; he realizes they are angels, not sparks. Now, at the boundary of space and time, we encounter assemblies of angels.

We have met angels before in the poem. In Canto 9 of the *Inferno*, an angel disdainfully opened lower Hell's walls for Dante and Virgil. In *Purgatorio* Canto 2 an angel guided the boat that ferried the dead toward the mountain of Purgatory. An angel also guarded the entrance to Purgatory proper, questioned the pilgrim, drew 7 "P's" on his forehead, and let in pilgrim and guide. At the end of each ledge on Purgatory, an angel flicked off the appropriate "P". At the beginning of *Purgatorio* 27, an angel told Dante that he must walk through the fire on his way out of Purgatory toward the Earthly Paradise. Yet in the *Paradiso* no angel has appeared except as part of the mass assembly descending in Canto 23; their first appearance on their own is here in *Paradiso* 28, not as discrete individuals but as gigantic assemblies that turn the celestial spheres.

It is difficult for the modern imagination to think of angels as medieval men and women thought of them. The origin of the concept is deep within the human imagination and angels are among the many classes of invisible beings, spiritual or worldly or evil, embedded in many cultures around the world.

According to medieval Christian doctrine and modern Catholicism, angels have different functions: (1) they are attendants of God, as we will see above in the Empyrean; (2) they are divine messengers, as was Gabriel when he announced to Mary that she was to bear the son of God; (3) they are personal guardians to help us do the right thing; and (4) they help God govern the world.[20] Dante's presentation of angels here in the *Paradiso* follows this last function. In the *Inferno* and *Purgatorio* angels are divine agents and at first they appear too brightly for Dante to see them. In the *Paradiso* they form divine celestial hierarchies that act on behalf of God on the world by managing the celestial spheres above.

Canto 28 then lists the angelic hierarchies that surround the central light of God – there is no mention of planets. The circles closest to God, the Crystalline Sphere and the Fixed Stars, correspond to the orders of Seraphim and Cherubim; the first triad is rounded out by the Thrones that govern what appears to us as the Sphere of Saturn.

We have met all three orders previously in the *Paradiso*. From Canto 9:61-63, Thrones help cast God's judgments down to us; this order seems a good fit with our ideas of Saturn. From Canto 11:37-39 Thomas Aquinas likens Francis of Assisi to seraphic ardor and Dominic to cherubic light.

Corresponding to these two great saints, the Seraphim correspond to love and the Cherubim to wisdom. Of these two topmost orders of angels, Beatrice remarks that the swiftness of their motion is due to their desire for greatest likeness to the point of light in the middle.

The second triad blossoms in an eternal spring, *primavera sempiterna*, and sets into motion the wheels that correspond to Jupiter, Mars, and Sun: Dominions, Virtues, and Powers. The three below, furthest from God and closest to Earth, are the Principalities, Archangels, and Angels and turn the spheres of Venus, Mercury, and Moon.*

These orders of angels *contemplate* God and they act upon the world – simultaneously, continuously. Like humans, angels have active and contemplative dimensions. They all gaze upward and command what lies below them. We will return to this idea soon.

Canto 29 begins with a pause which precedes a discussion on creation and the fall of the angels. We will start by considering how this pause is depicted. The pause endures for the time when the Sun and Moon are in Aries and Libra on the horizon and perfectly balanced opposite each other.

Twice daily – when either 0° Aries or when 0° Libra ascend – at that instant 0° Cancer and 0° Capricorn are on opposite sides at the meridian axis. To this ordinary event we add the very extraordinary coincidence of Sun and Moon opposing each other that would also be a lunar eclipse. It is not clear which luminary would ascend and which luminary would descend, nor is it clear who is in Aries and who is in Libra. This is a moment of definiteness and indeterminacy together.**

For how long are these two luminaries exactly in balance? It could only be the briefest of instants, for one planet will ascend and one will descend, creating imbalance, instantly. One may consider this unique instant to be indivisible, not made of parts with which to measure duration, but simply 'now'.

---

* These orders derive from *The Celestial Hierarchy*, an important medieval text purportedly by Dionysius the Areopagite of the first century but actually written several hundred years later. This work, a wonderful example of Christian Neoplatonic mysticism, appears to have no interest in our appearing world.

** See Cornish (2000) "Planets and Angels", pp.119-141 for an elaborate discussion of this image. My remarks are largely taken from her presentation.

> ### Who's Running the Show?
> This notion of invisible orders of angels directing the spheres is unusual to our modern understanding. It is a notion with an interesting history that also shows the synthetic flavor of medieval thinking.
>
> This concept may originate from Plato's *Timaeus*, positing that "gods" are distributed throughout the planetary spheres (40a-b) and from Book Lambda (or Book Twelve) of Aristotle's *Metaphysics*. According to the latter work, God is an intellectual substance who moves the cosmos but is itself unmoved. In turn, God is an object of desire or love from the "Intelligences" who correspond to the many motions that set the planetary spheres moving (*Metaphysics*: 1073a30-40). Later in antiquity Neoplatonic philosophers thought that invisible beings, intermediate between the gods and the humans, emanated from God or the One and gave rise to the planetary spheres who in turn organizes what is below. During the Christian era, correlating movers of celestial spheres with the angels from scripture was a natural development.[21] This move helped bring 'secular' natural philosophy and religion together into one truth.
>
> When we consider astral causation depicted in the *Divine Comedy*, we ask: are the planets or the angelic intelligences the causes of effects on Earth? In *Paradiso* 2:127-132, Beatrice presents the relationship of planets to angels as the hammer (planets) to the smith (angels).

According to ancient and medieval thinking, linear time came into being along with the stars and planets. This striking depiction of the Sun and Moon and horizon, Aries and Libra, presages much of what is to come in the canto, for we need to glimpse an order of time different from the usual sequence from past to present to future. The briefest moment of balance between Sun and Moon, Aries and Libra, symbolizes time that is not linear but instantaneous, on the boundary of now and eternity.

We are now ready to consider the origin of the world. Beatrice's presentation on Creation and the fall of the angels is an implied dialogue and I will briefly summarize her main points in this way (Canto 29:13-81). She gives us an interesting depiction with metaphysical and ethical implications.

Why did God create the world? Did he need all this company?

It's not as if God needed to increase his Goodness – that would be impossible – but so that his splendor can shine back to him in conscious existence.

What was God doing before He created the universe?

His eternity is beyond time, since time itself was created with the created world. Since there could be no 'before' and 'after' in eternity, the question cannot properly be asked, let alone answered.

In what order was the world created?

It was created all at once: pure form, pure matter, and form and matter combined. All three were created like a bow with three strings to shoot forth three arrows at the same time.

'Pure form' may refer to angelic existences, and 'form and matter together' to the celestial spheres that organize Earthly being, 'matter' to the unorganized raw stuff awaiting in-forming. The angels, at the summit of the cosmos, are pure act (and therefore not material); pure potential or matter is in the lowest part. Between pure potential and pure activity are the Heavens.[22]

For how long were the angels in existence before some of them fell?

The bad angels' fall was almost instantaneous. The time between creation and when the bad angels crashed into the Earth would have been less than the time it takes to count to twenty.

How did the good angels stay good and the bad angels fall?

The good angels stayed with God and applied themselves to their task of turning the wheels of the cosmos; they had the quality of humility (*modesti*) and acknowledged that their intelligence came not from themselves but from divine goodness. Consequently, God's grace and their own merit raised their vision to such a height that their will became firm and complete forever.

The bad angels, on the other hand, fell due to jealousy or presumption, resulting in Lucifer being eternally crushed beneath the weight of the universe. The bad angels did not acknowledge the divine external origin of their good quality but *took it for themselves* and therefore severed themselves from God. As modern people we could call this 'the birth of ego'. The fallen angels were cast, or cast themselves, as far as possible from their divine origins.

Do angels have memory?

No: angels have no need for our conventional sense of memory. The faculty of memory implies that an angel's current view is interrupted and retrieves a previous object. Since there can be no interruption, there can be no forgetting and no remembering. Nor should we assume that angels have will and understanding in the same way we do. Time for the angels is simultaneous not sequential.

To close Canto 29 Beatrice once again pivots into condemnation, this one bitterer than the last one. She condemns bad preaching and bad teaching: bad preachers and teachers would rather entertain and be funny than educate people in truth. Christ did not tell his followers to preach trifles but gave them a good foundation to spread the word. We will return to this denunciation in Part Three.

Is it unseemly of the poet to have Beatrice talk in this way so high in Paradise, so close to the highest Heaven? Is Dante the poet just getting carried away by his own negativity? Barbara Reynolds (2006) writes, "…the style of this diatribe …is out of keeping with Beatrice in any of her roles and in irreconcilable conflict with the idealized portrait of her that comes soon afterwards."[23] Reynolds' assessment conflicts with the intensely deliberate nature that characterizes the *Divine Comedy*, for clearly Dante knew exactly what he was doing by making Beatrice the mouthpiece of such venom.

Beatrice's words are in line with some of the dramatic tension that pervades the *Paradiso*. We are up in Heaven where people experience the bliss of the vision and love of God – and we are alarmed about matters down here on Earth. Making Beatrice the spokesperson of such invective also emphasizes divine love's complementary quality of justice. Divine wrath is the flip-side of the contemplative love and joy we see throughout Paradise. It also underscores that, like *Inferno* and *Purgatorio*, *Paradiso* is about *this* world; in Heaven our world is seen increasingly from the viewpoint of divinity and eternity. Contrasts do not become fuzzier but sharper.

Once again Beatrice asks the pilgrim to look upon the magnificent display of the created world: look upon the height and breadth of the Eternal Goodness from which one light separates itself among all these mirrors but remains one, as it always was (Canto 29: 142-145).

Very Grand Finale
Canto 30

In Canto 30 of the *Purgatorio*, the pilgrim encountered Beatrice in the Earthly Paradise and began his final act of contrition so he could enter Heaven. In Canto 30 of the *Paradiso* the pilgrim reaches the highest Heaven, or more accurately, this Heaven discloses itself to the pilgrim. This will conclude Beatrice's role in the poem.*

First the stars and planets, including Venus, vanish. Here is a paraphrase of the canto's first tercet.

> "Six thousand miles from here the sixth hour is burning and this world's shadow inclines to a level bed." (Canto 30.1-3)

"*The sixth hour*" is noontime, six hours since sunrise in the early spring; you may recall that this was the standard way of reckoning time in the West until the modern era's focus on AM and PM.

What is meant by *six thousand miles*? Our trusted commentators note that Dante, following the scientific tradition of his day, thought the Earth's circumference to be 20,400 miles[24] (it's actually 24,902). From sunrise to noon would be six hours in the spring and by one quarter of the Earth's rotation. Converting time to distance, from noon to sunrise would be one quarter of 20,400 miles – 5,100 miles, not 6,000 miles. Therefore 6,000 miles is about seven hours before noontime, thus an hour before sunrise.

But the time reference is to "six thousand miles from *here*": where is "here"? It cannot be in the Crystalline Sphere or the Empyrean: measured distances would be immense and not a paltry 6,000 miles. Instead, "here" is in Italy with the poet Dante who is writing these lines.

At this time the world's shadow inclines to a level bed. The poet alludes not to a particular location but to spherical Earth, as if he is standing outside the world looking at the angle of the shadow on the other side of the Earth. According to the cosmology and poetic conception of

---

* If you are wondering about a parallel from the *Inferno* you should look at Canto 31 – the 30th Canto of Hell itself. Here we meet the giants below the *Malebolge* and Virgil bargains for passage downwards and finally descends to the lowest Hell and finally to Lucifer. This forms a perfect inversion with Canto 30 and its entry to the Empyrean and the vision of God.

the *Paradiso*, the Earth is still and the Sun appears to move around it. This helps us visualize what the poet is imagining here.

If you cast a light upon a sphere such as our planet, directly across from the light is a diminishing shadow in the shape of a cone. Just before sunrise along a particular horizon, the sunlight would be slightly below the horizon and someone on the horizon would be in shadow. When the Sun has broken the horizon on the other side in the East, at sunrise, the edge of this shadow meets the horizon. Sun and shadow are level with each other. As the morning Sun continues to rise in the East, the cone's shadow correspondingly goes down on the other side in the West.

At sunrise, heavenly bodies that had previously illuminated the sky begin to go out as the Sun begins to brighten the sky. One by one Heaven shuts off its lights, even its loveliest one – Venus, the planet that "strengthens love". We said hello to her in *Purgatorio* 1 and now, at the end of the journey, we say goodbye. *The night's stars have faded because they no longer need to represent anything.* We are about to encounter the good and the true without their mediation.

Nature and Illusion and the Stars

Back to the Sphere of the Sun and the opening of *Paradiso* 13, the poet asks us to imagine a collection from the fifteen bright stars of the sky, the seven stars of the Wain (the Big Dipper), two stars in the Little Dipper and the Pole Star on the other end. Join all these stars together – all 24 – into a double constellation with the two circles of the Sun, all moving together in synchronized fashion (13:1-21). These stars are not in the night sky but in the imagination of poet and reader.

Throughout the *Divine Comedy* the stars in the sky have gone from naturalistic effect to symbols for the imagination and here, in the heights of Heaven they are cast aside, for we are now ready for unmediated truth.

In the *Inferno* stars were used simply as time references with only vague hints of any symbolic functions for them. In the *Purgatorio* the night stars were presented as they were in nature but allegorized as the Cardinal and Theological Virtues.

High in Heaven all the stars provided by nature can be disposed of because the imagination no longer requires them. This failure of the creative imagination anticipates entering the highest Heaven to glimpse truth without mediation.

Beatrice tells the pilgrim what is about to happen. They have now gone from the Crystalline Sphere to "the Heaven of pure light" (*al ciel ch'˚e pura luce*). Now comes an ecstatic tercet heightened by its chant-like repetition.

> "*luce intellettüal, piena d' amore*
> *amor di vero ben, pien di letizia*
> *letizia che trascende ogne dolzore.*"

> "light intellectual, full of love
> love of the true good, full of joy,
> joy that transcends all sweetness." (Canto 30.40-42)

Beatrice tells Dante that he will soon see both the *milizie* of Paradise (redeemed souls and angels), and the souls will be in their form at the Last Judgment – i.e., fully embodied. The resurrection of the body is the event that those of the Sun's Sphere rejoiced in with anticipation, what Dante had asked Benedict about on the Sphere of Saturn, and what he tried to see in the apostle John in the Fixed Stars. The pilgrim is given a sight that would have not yet occurred in time.

A light appears around Dante that takes the form of a river, and on both banks are flowers emitting sparks. All these things, Beatrice says, are but "shadowy prefaces" (*umbriferi prefazi*) of what they really are. When the pilgrim bends his eyes toward the river of light and begins to drink of it, suddenly the river becomes a circle, the flowers and sparks become the courts of Heaven (*le corti del ciel*, Canto 30:96), the redeemed souls and angels respectively. The Empyrean has now become visible to Dante.

Think back to the descending rivers depicted in *Inferno* and *Purgatorio* and the rivers of baptism in the Earthly Paradise. Also recall the perfect circles in which the planets move in Paradise, especially in the Sphere of the Sun. It is appropriate that at the entrance to Heaven, these images are combined so that rivers now transform into circles. The flowers and bees of nature become redeemed souls and angels.

There is a light above that makes the Creator visible to every creature who finds peace in beholding him (30:100-102). This is not yet the *luce intellettüal*, the "intellectual light" that Beatrice had just previously mentioned. Instead the word *lume* is used (like our word 'illuminate') and it is more like the light's radiance or reflection.²⁵ This light of divine radiance or *lumen* spreads itself in a vast circular shape, and comes as a ray reflecting from the surface of Crystalline Sphere. Even up to the last moment and the final vision of God we remain in a realm of reflection, although one most rarefied.

Evoking the sight of a hillside with grass and flowers reflected in a body of water, the poet begins to describe the vast assembly of Heaven's citizens arranged above and all around the light that reflects God. Think of a huge spacious arena, like the Roman Coliseum with which Dante was acquainted, but with thousands of tiers and vast space occupied by an innumerable expanse of the saved souls and the angels. Our usual sense of distance is suspended and the pilgrim experiences no conventional sense of near or far (Canto 30:118-123).

The Poet now gives the general configuration of this heaven: it is shaped like a rose. But it is not just a shape but has living dimensions, including the scent of a rose. Dante renders this vision of the Empyrean's Rose in as sensory a manner as possible.

Before going into further detail on the Rose, the poet ends Canto 30 in a surprising way. Beatrice points out an empty seat among the vast heavenly assembly. This seat is reserved for Henry VII of Luxemburg, a youth in 1300 at the time of the *Divine Comedy*'s narrative who as an adult emperor will attempt to help Italy before Italy is ready to be helped.*

As Canto 30 concludes, Beatrice launches into her last denunciation in Paradise. She rails against *la cieca cupidigia*, the corrupting greed that brings us so much suffering. She then prophesizes that a pope – this is Clement V, who had opposed Emperor Henry in the early 1300's – will be cast to the part of Hell reserved for the simonists, those who traded in or sold church offices (see *Inferno* Canto 19). (His kicking feet will replace those of Boniface VIII who dwells atop the upside-down baptismal font in this hell.) Once again we are brought back to the world's difficulties and even back to Hell – Heaven's bliss offers no refuge.

---

* During the writing of much of the *Divine Comedy*, Henry's cause was Dante's great political interest. He turned out to be one more Emperor who was defeated by the Italian city-states. When Henry died, Dante's dream of a unified empire was dashed.

Approaching God

As Canto 31 begins, another dramatic contrast awaits us. First we see the angels with faces of flame, wings of gold and all else purely white. Their flight back and forth from the center does not obstruct the pilgrim's view – angels seem to have no material substance, unlike the embodied saints, and could not obstruct one's view in Heaven.

Like stunned barbarians seeing ancient Rome's monuments for the first time, Dante rejoices that he had come from his wretchedness to Heaven, from time to eternity, "and from Florence to a people just and sane" (*e di Fiorenza in popol giusto e sano* 31:39). Most commentators and readers find this line to be drippingly sarcastic.

The pilgrim raptly surveys the souls in Heaven. Unlike the angels who have no physical form and therefore little that can be called individual, Dante sees the embodied saints distinctly. As the pilgrim's eye moves around the sacred assembly he turns to Beatrice to ask her questions and suddenly she is not there; instead he sees an old man. Soon this man will identify himself as the 12th century mystic and monastic leader Bernard of Clairvaux. Where is she, "*Ov'è ella*", he asks, puzzled. The old man explains that Beatrice has asked him to guide and instruct Dante toward the final vision of God. Bernard points out Beatrice in her rightful place among the blessed, in the third tier but beyond near or far. Beatrice's invective against the greediness of popes was her last teaching in the poem.

Anticipating Bernard's prayer to Mary that begins the *Divine Comedy's* final canto, Dante now pens a moving song of praise and prayer to Beatrice (Canto 31.79-90). Striking and subdued in their last moment of personal encounter, she looks at Dante, smiles, and then turns once again toward the eternal fountain (*poi si tornò a létterna fontana* Canto 31.93). Like the stars disappearing from the night sky, the narrative has also gone beyond both the personal and the symbolic presence of Beatrice.

Bernard instructs the pilgrim that, in order to prepare his sight to rise to the Holy Light (*raggio divino*), first he needs to allow his eyes to move once again through the divine assembly and then to look up toward Mary (Canto 31:97-102). As Mary's great devotee during his lifetime, Bernard will help him with this.

Raising his eyes toward Mary, the pilgrim finds a light that is most strongly reflected from God. Even within the Empyrean there are gradations of light and Mary, surrounded by more than a thousand angels in song and game, is at the Rose's topmost place closest to God. As Dante gazes upon Mary he notes Bernard's loving gaze and the pilgrim becomes even more ardent. Thus ends Canto 31.

Canto 32 down-shifts from the two previous cantos: much of it consists of Bernard pointing out the Empyrean's assembly and its seating plan. Canto 32 is also a measured windup for what follows in the next canto, the *Divine Comedy*'s final verses.

Bernard outlines the structure of this assembly of saints that are gathered within the Celestial Rose. There is both horizontal and vertical organization. Directly below Mary is Eve and directly below that are the women of the Hebrew Bible. These women are amongst those who believed in 'the Christ to come', the Hebrew saints. Opposite Mary (and close to her across the uppermost rose) is John the Baptist and below him are men important in the Christian Church – Francis, Benedict, and Augustine. These are on the Christian side of the Rose and there are only a few empty seats left on this side: the Final Judgment must be fairly soon, or the world and its inhabitants have become completely unredeemable.

Below both groups, surprisingly, are children who never had the opportunity to sin. In Paradise we don't just see adults and hear Hosannas but see the faces of children and the sounds of their voices. Children have hardly appeared in the *Divine Comedy* and now they appear in Paradise. The last time we encountered children their names were Anselmo and Gaddo from *Inferno* 33: they were in a tower being starved to death along with their father Ugolino. Even high in Paradise the poet reminds the reader of Hell and of the misery that innocent humans suffer.

Bernard addresses the differences in divine access among those in the Empyrean. Since God differentially bestows grace among individuals, divine justice and the assigned places in Paradise fit together perfectly like a ring and its finger (Canto 32:55-57). In a passage that refers back to Piccarda from the Sphere of the Moon in *Paradiso* 3, nobody in Paradise could want more than God has allotted to them. The ranking system of Paradise is based upon closeness or distance from God and reflects differences in ability to receive the divine light. We might also remember that in Paradise there is no 'real' closeness or distance, for we have cancelled our earthly conventions of time and space.

> ### Angels and the Redeemed, Angelic and Human Time
> Recall that Canto 29 tells that the bad angels fell because they took for themselves what had come from God. They made their eternal mistake exactly once. The good angels were redeemed because they humbly waited for God's fullness of grace. Then, having received it according to their capacity, they cannot fall back. These classes of angels do not experience progressive sequential time as we do.
>
> Christian redemption of humans is a more complex affair because for us time *flows*. Our time is linear, proceeding from the past through the present into the future.
>
> Over the course of our lifetimes, we can make the same mistakes over again but can become remorseful and eventually find redemption. During the course of our lifetimes, our spiritual life progresses and regresses and is usually fragile.
>
> We must regard all the humans in Paradise (except Mary) as once having lives with the same spiritual fragility that we have. All of them, however, at some point made the right decision and stayed with it. This implies that in spite of an evil past, true repentance and conversion in one's last moment may suffice for salvation – even if this is fulfilled only after centuries in Purgatory, for Purgatory also keeps human time. The last moment for human surrender – and God's grace – is equivalent to the good angels humbly waiting (an interval of an instant) for God while their proud comrades fell slowly (count to 20, Beatrice says) to create Hell.

As Canto 32 moves toward its conclusion, Bernard directs Dante once more to look upon Mary, for only her radiance can allow the pilgrim to attain his final vision. The remainder of Canto 32 sets the stage for what is to come. In a reprise of Canto 23, the angel Gabriel, who had once announced to Mary that she would bear the infant Christ, attends her joyfully, singing. Returning once more to the image of the pre-dawn sky, Dante likens Gabriel to the morning star that reflects the Sun that is Mary (Canto 32:106-108).

Bernard asks Dante to shift his gaze around the saints once again: he is training Dante's 'eyesight' to become accustomed to increasing intensities of light by looking on Mary, looking around the assembly that is not so bright, and then coming back to Mary.

Now it is time for the pilgrim to prepare for his journey's goal. He is to fix his eyes directly upon the *primo amore*, the Primal Love so he can penetrate the divine radiance as far as he is capable. Yet even now the pilgrim may think this accomplishment to be his own doing and thus fall back (think fallen angels). The pilgrim must gain Mary's grace so she will help make a vision of God possible for him; she will 'sponsor' him to the vision of God.

Paradiso 33 and *Divine Comedy* 100

The endpoint of the *Divine Comedy* is the direct vision of God and the resolution of the poem's major themes. This is not an amorphous or emotional depiction of 'mystical experience', but, like everything else in this poem, it is complex and precisely rendered. The poet brings together Christian philosophy with its cosmology and the literature of Christian contemplation. To call the result a poetic *tour de force* would understate its impact.

As Canto 33 opens Bernard addresses Mary in prayer. Like any standard prayer or supplication, Bernard's prayer to Mary begins by addressing her in praise. This prayer begins with paradox heaped upon paradox ("Virgin mother, daughter of your Son, humble and exalted…"), placing her nature beyond our ordinary experience. These are not paradoxes to be solved but divine mysteries to be pondered: they open up spaces in our minds for what lies ahead.

Bernard continues, addressing Mary's power and role. He first notes her part as the loving womb that carried humanity's redeemer. Yet her role is ongoing: for those still on the Earth she is the torch of charity whose kindness gives freely to those who ask – and even to those who do not ask.

Bernard then presents Dante to her as a pilgrim who has come up from the pit of Hell to this highest realm of Heaven. Bernard asks Mary to help Dante lift his eyes toward the ultimate salvation (*l'ultima salute*). Bernard also asks her to protect the pilgrim afterwards from his all too human reactions (*movimenti umani*) to this experience – this would be his tendency toward pride, as if he had engineered all this by his own merits alone.

The Queen of Heaven responds. Having first fixed her eyes upon Bernard, Mary now turns her gaze toward the eternal light (*l'etterno lume*) and looks penetratingly into its brightness. Bernard signals with a smile to the pilgrim that he should also look upwards. But Dante is already doing this. His sight rises higher and higher moving itself through the ray of the exalted light...

Suddenly the canto's tone changes: we are not with the pilgrim's experience but the fading recollections of the poet who is attempting to describe it afterwards. Canto 33:55-75 tells of the poet's incapacity to render or even remember the experience adequately to do justice to it. When we wake from a dream its content fades but its flavor endures. Like an imprint fading in the melting snow, sometimes we can watch as the dream's content melts away from us.

The pilgrim cannot avert his gaze he intensifies it further until he reaches the infinite goodness (*valore infinito*). For an instant the universe comes together.

Here is a contemporary rendering of these tercets by Jean Hollander (2007).

> "In its depth I saw contained
> by love into a single volume bound,
> the pages scattered through the universe:
>
> substances, accidents, and the interplay between them,
> as though they were conflated in such ways
> that what I tell is but a simple light." (*Paradiso* 33:85-90)

For the pilgrim and poet, these words tell that within variability and contingency there is simplicity and necessity. The poet's image is that of a book, whose pages are bound together into one volume by love. This contrasts with the previous lines about the Sibyl of Cumae, who in Virgil's *Aeneid* is a priestess and seer who will help guide Aeneas to the underworld. Her visions are written upon leaves in her rocky cavern; however, if the door turns and wind blows in the leaves her prophecies are scattered (*Aeneid* Book III: 518-531). The pilgrim's experience is as if the leaves that once held together in his mind have been scattered as if by the wind bursting into the Sibyl's cave. But now there is brief clarity, seeing the book that binds together the universe.

But why here do we read about 'substance' and 'accident'? Compared to the previous verses and the clear image of the book and its leaves, these notions seem dry as dust. According to Aristotelian thinking, a 'substance' is an independent object of perception and conception that can have different attributes over time. An 'accident' results from changing circumstances that qualify the object. When I go outside today I will wear a hat and jacket, for it is bitterly cold; when I reach my destination indoors I will become hat-less and jacket-less. I am the substance; my changing means of attire are accidents.

These notions of substance and accident are concepts that pervade our ordinary worldly experience even if we don't use them much today. Relating to our modern meaning of 'accident', variable qualities serve as contingent circumstances within an always-changing and seemingly-random world. *Contingency includes the seemingly gratuitous and wobbly Wheel of Fortune.* According to the poet, God and Paradise and all its citizens know better.

Now the poet must go even further into this mystery. First the pilgrim/poet must qualify his own testimony.

"Un punto solo m'`e maggior letargo
che venticinque secoli a la 'mpresa
che fé Nettuno ammitar l'ombra d'Argo."

"This point alone brings to me more forgetfulness
than the twenty-five centuries since that enterprise
when Neptune in wonder saw the shadow of the Argo."
(Paradiso 33:94-96)

These enigmatic lines transport us back to Ovid and the ancient world and its mythology. There are different interpretations for these lines and I supply the one that seems most straightforward and relevant.[26] The god Neptune is amazed when suddenly he sees the bottom of mankind's first ship that is sailing above his kingdom of the sea. We are also amazed. The poet gives a view so much greater than our ordinary understanding that is like all that would be forgotten in the following 2500 years. As all else in creation, the pilgrim/poet can only attain the vision and beatitude of which he is capable and his current wonderment is like a distant memory.

As the pilgrim gazes further at the divine light he feels his sight gaining strength and he is becoming further transformed on the spot: it cannot be otherwise for now he is to plumb the mysteries of his Christian cosmos and its final reconciliations.

Within the divine ray's essence there appears three circles (*giri*) having three colors but only one circumference. They seem like rainbows, one seemed to reflect another, and a third is equally breathed forth by the first two (lines 116-120). Struggling to find words for it, Dante attempts to convey the self-contained quality of this vision. Dante is presenting the counterintuitive but essential teaching of the Christian Trinity. To the poet this is not doctrine but how the universe hangs together.

Dante's eyes continues to gaze at these three circles and one, the circling (*circulazion*) that had appeared as a reflection of the first (symbolizing the second person of the Trinity) now displays something of our human likeness (*la nostra effige*). This insight deep into the heart of the mystery of the Incarnation – the divine becoming human – proves difficult to comprehend. The key to the nature of the universe, all substances and accidents, is somehow connected to a human likeness. Like a geometer trying in vain to square the circle the pilgrim cannot figure this out.

From the viewpoint of ancient and medieval thinking, the motions of the celestial realm are circular and therefore perfect. A square inherently contains directionality, opposition, and is therefore like our conditions on Earth. 'Squaring the circle' is like reconciling earthly and divine nature.

Finally the circles become wheels and we turn our attention to the dazzling but enigmatic last four lines of the *Divine Comedy*.

The Final Four Lines
Then, in a flash all became clear – but that moment vanished. In these lines the lofty but fleeting visions of Canto 33 have become a transformed life. Here are the final four lines and two translations of them that illustrate the difficulties these lines bring.

> "A l'alta fantasia qui mancò possa,
> mia già volgeva il mio disio e 'l velle
> sì come rota ch' igualmente è mossa,
> l'Amor che move il sole e l'altre stelle." (*Paradiso* 33:142-146)

> "Here my exalted vision lost its power.
> But now my will and my desire, like wheels revolving
> with an even motion, were turning with
> the Love that moves the sun and all the other stars."
> (Hollander, 2007)

> "Here my high imagining failed of power; but already my desire and
> the *velle* were turned, like a wheel moved evenly,
> By the Love that moves the sun and the other stars."
> (Durling, 2010)

Note that Hollander translates *velle* as "will" but Durling leaves the word in the Italian and contrast "my desire" and "the *velle*". Hollander translates rota as the plural "wheels"; Durling uses the singular. Some things remain to be explained.

Let's first take it from the top. The pilgrim/poet's vision (or "high imagining" or "fantasy", *l'alta fantasia*) has lost its power but now his desire (*disio*) and will (*velle*), are like a wheel – or wheels – (*rota*) revolving evenly, already being turned (*volgeva*) with the Love that moves the Sun and the other stars, "*l'amor che move il sole e l'altre stelle*".

Desire and will are no longer separate from God or at odds with one another but at harmony with itself and with God's love that turns the universe. According to these verses, the pilgrim/poet has achieved a moving coordination with eternity. The result, or fruition, of the pilgrim's journey is not God Himself but life in this world.

Immediately some questions present themselves: what is 'desire' and what is 'will', and what is the difference between them? What is the meaning of the simile of the wheel; such an image suggests the cosmology of Paradise, but in what way? And, echoing the two translations above, are we to take wheel as singular or plural?

Durling suggests that the poet left his conclusion intentionally vague: since in the narrative the poet's verse is limited by the failure of limited imagination to understand or depict the ultimate beatitude, the final words should defy tidy conceptuality.[27] Like the three beasts blocking the way in the "dark wood" and two world prophecies that we will discuss in Part Three, ambiguity may be intended here for dramatic or didactic purposes. This may give us fresh opportunities for new understanding, for we don't have to seek one right answer but see what different possibilities these lines suggest.

We begin with the relationship between "desire" (*disio*) and "will" (*velle*). In our normal discourse there is great overlap between our concepts of desire and will, yet they are not the same thing. How are they different from one another?

There are many forms of *disio* and desire's many variants (including love) throughout the *Divine Comedy*. It is a major motif in the poem and is a word frequently used by the poet. Desire has become distorted and perverted In Hell; in Purgatory desire is straightened out and set on its right course toward God; in Paradise the dynamic between desire and fulfillment pervades the pilgrim and the redeemed souls.*

For Dante and the tradition he inherited, desire's activity is omnipresent and protean. It ranges in quality and object. Its lowest level we share with animals as we pursue and protect our physical survival and ordinary sensory pleasures. Because humans are 'rational animals', desire includes a hunger for understanding; many previous uses of the word *disio* in the *Paradiso* relate to the pilgrim's desire to know more. At last is the fulfillment of all desire – God himself.

Desire is the most intimate feature of ourselves and gives us most of our sense of who we are. Our desiring minds are continuously engaged, for even our negativity is from frustrated desire. Dante's final tercet stresses the personal nature of desire with the words *il mio disio*.

Velle or "will" has a different semantic field. *Velle* is not an ordinary word in Italian but a technical term derived from Latin, meaning to wish, desire, or will. Its only prior use in the poem was *Paradiso* 4:25 where Beatrice locates two different questions in the pilgrim's mind in his "*velle*". A look at the minds of the citizens of Paradise suggests a possible contrast between *velle* and *disio*. Let's briefly glimpse will, knowledge, and justice in the *Paradiso* as attunement with God.

---

* See Pertile, Lino (1995) "*Paradiso*: A Drama of Desire" for a strong articulation for desire and all its forms as a principle of dramatic unity in the third canticle.

In *Paradiso* 3:70-87, on the Sphere of the Moon, Piccarda addresses the pilgrim's concern that she and others might want a higher place in Heaven than they have. Piccarda tells that such a wish is impossible in Paradise since natural conformity to God's will (*la divina voglia*) is what their blessedness is. Recall the following line: "In his will is our peace". In Paradise's outskirts of the Moon, the will of the redeemed is perfectly harmonious with that of God.

Paradiso's middle cantos feature Dante's ancestor Cacciaguida. Not only does the pilgrim's upcoming exile appear clearly to Cacciaguida as a direct reflection of God's light, but Cacciaguida knew from the mind of God about Dante's visit and rejoices in it (*Paradiso* 15:55-60). Continuing onto the Sphere of Jupiter we have seen the Eagle as the direct spokesperson for Divine Justice from which Earthly Justice is derived and is a pale imitation.

In Paradise, knowledge, will, and a sense of justice are direct reflections of these qualities of divinity. If *disio* or desire is an ordinary personal experience, then *velle* is closer to an attunement with and reflection of the larger will that pervades the larger universe.

Velle brings together human and divine will and *disio* particularizes our own experiences of desire. As humans both activities are experienced within time. Because in eternity all time is simultaneous, 'divine will' will not have the same interaction between intention and object as it does for humans within time.

In Canto 33:143-144 both *disio* and *velle* are turned like a wheel (or wheels) evenly moving. What is the meaning of 'wheel'? What is the relationship, if any, between the wheels of cosmology and of the mind and life of the spiritually transformed person living in Dante and in our world?

As a self-contained shape without directionality or opposing parts, the circle was traditionally seen as the most perfect visible form. A wheel is an instrument of movement that is shaped like a circle; a wheel typically contains an outer rim, spokes, and a hub inside. Wheels depict the Heaven's motions as circles depict Heaven's forms. Wheels operate within sequential time; circles partake of eternal forms that do not change.

As we have seen, the Hollanders (2007) render rota into the plural "wheels". Although this is unusual there is some justification for it.

"Wheels" may suggest a mechanical clock as cited by their commentary on these lines.[28] At the end of *Paradiso* Canto 10 this was the image for the dancing circular array of twelve lights in the Sphere of the Sun; it also was used to depict the circular dancing of the apostles at the beginning of Canto 24.

We return to the order of the moving sky as interacting wheels that invisibly carry the planets and stars. The wheels of the equator and ecliptic opened Canto 10 to illustrate God's perfect creation. This conforms to the description in Plato's *Timaeus* of the World Soul made up of the Circle of the Same (celestial equator) and the Circle of the Other (ecliptic); together they form the Greek letter *Chi* that later Christians saw as the cross of Jesus and thus the Incarnation.

There are other possibilities for the plural "wheels". *Paradiso* 28 gives us the image of many concentric wheels moving around God that are governed by angelic realms. They move in one direction but at different speeds. Their activity is twofold. Here is the Durling translation.

> *"Questi ordini di sù tutti s'ammirano,*
> *e di giù vincon sì che verso Dio*
> *tutti tirati sono e tutti tirano."*

> "These orders all gaze upward and bind what is below, so that all are drawn, and all draw, toward God." (*Paradiso* 28:127-129)

Let's now consider another possible interpretation: one wheel but two motions. John Freccero (1986) writes that a wheel rotates around a fixed center and also advances in a particular direction. This gives us two movements: rotation and revolution.[29] In Plato's *Timaeus* there is discussion of celestial bodies that have both rotational and revolutionary motions – the planets and stars. Freccero quotes from a version of Plato's *Timaeus* by Chalcidius from the fourth century, a text that was available to Dante and his contemporaries. This passage describes both motions in ways that suggest spiritual dimensions.[30]

> "The one always going around itself in the same orbit and in the same place, always deliberating about the same things; the other of the sort which, always desiring to proceed forward, maintains a wheel-like movement around its object through the coercion of the same and unchanging nature (*intra obiectum eius rotabundus teneretur*)."

Going around itself in the same orbit, rotational motion is like our Earth rotating on its axis. The other motion is revolutionary, moving forward around an object. We have seen both motions in Paradise in Venus (Canto 8), Saturn (Canto 21) and particularly among the lights along the Fixed Stars (Canto 24).

According to Freccero, rotational motion corresponds to the soul's movement around God within one's own being. What, in practical terms, might this mean?

We can use our ordinary experience to help us understand this. How is a living soul "deliberating about the same things?" Usually it is deliberating about ME. As a living being our desires tend to be fixed on ourselves – as physical entities we preserve the body and the species and engage in all kinds of activities based our desires. Even our longing for knowledge and spiritual attainment is centered on ourselves. If this is transformed, what would be different?

The desires themselves would not change but their center would. Instead of a narrow concept of 'me' constituted by my appetites and desires, Dante's verses replace the self-referential 'me' with God. All our desires from 'lowest' to 'highest' would be centered not on me but constructed from Eternity. Thus all our experience, even the most personal and intimate, becomes sacred.

We now consider revolutionary motion around a fixed *external* center, like the Earth revolving around the Sun. According to Freccero, this corresponds to outer movement around a changeless nature of God. Again, on a personal level, what might this mean?

The ordinary center of the soul's revolution is the 'world' as it appears from the outside. This would include our natural and produced environments and even our bodies, especially when we become sick or are hurt in some way. Our 'world' includes our connections with others personally and through our culture and history. It includes all that appears to happen to us seemingly from the outside – our personal fortunes and misfortunes. Our ordinary focus continues to be on *me*, but its reference is from outside and events that happen to me. We may also say that our ordinary experience of this revolving wheel is the Wheel of Fortune.

If transformed, the revolving movement also replaces 'me' with God or Eternity; our ordinary orientation on personal fortune becomes the glory of God and the majesty of divine providence. Therefore the changing circumstances of our lives are aspects of divine knowledge and activity and are to be appreciated, even revered. This does not minimize the importance of what happens to us but gives it a different point of reference.

This is not the acquiescent piety associated with ancient Stoicism or the 'quietism' incorrectly associated with the religions from Asia but an active and reverential involvement with the world as it is. In Vajrayana Buddhism it is thought of as 'pure perception' or 'sacred outlook' and its content is 'sacred world'. In Dante's terms it is being moved – within oneself and in relation to our lived world – by "the Love that moves the Sun and the other stars."

Let's return to the 'wheels' and angels arranged concentrically from Canto 28-29. We need to contrast them with the two wheels that arrange our visible celestial world, those of the ecliptic and celestial equator.

Angels are not physical and they do not inhabit sequential time as we do. As humans we do not govern our world as angels do their planetary realms, but we are included within our world and are subject to it in many ways. Unlike the heavenly angels, even the most saintly human person can slide back into narrowness and worldliness. It is the difference between human redemptive time and angelic time that we discussed in the previous section.

The angelic realms themselves range from those closest to God, the seraphim and cherubim, to those farther away that govern the spheres of Mercury and the Moon. And the different planetary spheres contain a range of increasing deviation from the Primary Motion as they move from closest to God to farthest from God. Are not human beings simply lower down in the same continuity?

The concentric wheels and its angels give us a model for life of being focused 'above' but engaged in this world 'below' and the transformed human being can be the same – *but in human time*. Angels cannot be said to have memory as we do because they are not subject to linear time. They do not have minds like ours, with our oscillations of desire, frustration, and fulfillment. In order to help repair the world, the transformed human remains subject to time but has integrated his or her desires with the divine will. This allows humans an opportunity to do what angels cannot do – to repair this world of time.

We have noted that the picture of the universe as concentric spheres around God leaves no place for Earth. Here we could think of Earth as the slowest and most distant sphere and its 'angelic realm' that of human beings who must live within in time. But our world is much more than that. Cosmically this is the place of the Incarnation and historically it is the place of universal Empire and reform movements of the church exemplified by Francis and Dominic.

Closer to our experience on Earth is the symbolism of the invisible wheels of Heaven, the point of Aries that connects the two wheels, and the visible stars and planets that ride on them. Their motions account for the orderly movements of the skies of Heaven and allow us to locate and predict the movements of the planets and stars, the exemplars and keepers of sequential time that orders our lives.

Perhaps the celestial equator represents intellect and the ecliptic represents will, reflecting the priority of intellect over will in Thomist philosophy. My preference is to equate divine will with the celestial equator as that has the most regular motion in time; our changing desires are like the ecliptic. These two wheels go in opposite directions, for that is our experience of attempting to integrate the personal and the divine.

The ecliptic, Plato's Circle of the Other, may symbolize our changeable personal desire; the celestial equator, Plato's Circle of the Same, may symbolizes the will of God that reflects in the human will. Both wheels symbolize the imprint of eternity on the human soul. Their perfect interaction indicates that our flickering desires and will are both being turned by God's Love.

Connecting these wheels is the point of Aries that brings them together into one particularity, an Incarnation that can manifest fully on the Earth. When and where the point of Aries touches the horizon (the intersection of Heaven and Earth), the moment and location becomes most auspicious and Incarnation is complete. Only Adam and Christ, the only beings created directly by God (*Paradiso* 13:82-87) could be symbolized by the Point of Aries. The rest of us are like the ever-changing angles to the center point of the universe. We could even say we are all 360° of the astrological Ascendant. This image depicts the transformed human being who combines vast vision and worldly resourcefulness whose purpose it is to repair our world.

Here is one more possibility. Of the two wheels, it seems that we are not the loftier wheel of the celestial equator but the more complex wheel of the ecliptic that we divide into the twelve signs of the zodiac. In this way the vicissitudes of fortune are a personal occasions for providence (represented by the celestial equator) to manifest, represented by the appearing sky of the stars and planets that is itself a time-bound reflection of Eternity.

With all these possibilities we end our tour of Dante's Paradise.

Notes
1. Cornish, Alison (2000), pp.88-92
2. Stahl (1990), pp.136-139
3. See Durling/Martinez (2010), p.97. For a fascinating contrast, note Hollander (2007), pp.101-102 for another commentary on the same lines.
4. Ciardi (1961), p.45
5. *Convivio* Book II Chapters 13 and 14.
6. Durling (2010), p.178
7. Durling/Martinez (2010), p.216
8. Sinclair, p.158
9. Bonatti, Treatise 3 Chapter 4. From Dykes (2007), p.164
10. See Hollander (2007), pp.345-346
11. Hollander, p.251
12. Boorstin, p.36
13. Bonatti, Book I, Treatise 3, Chapter 2. Translation Dykes, B. Vol. 1, pp.156-157
14. Virgil's *Aeneid*. Trans. Fitzgerald, Book II, 560-564
15. See Durling/Martinez (2010), p.456
16. Sinclair, p.340
17. Singleton (1975), p.398
18. There are many detailed commentaries on these lines; most complete is Moore (1903), pp.62-71
19. Durling/Martinez (2010), p.556
20. *Catholic Encyclopedia* http://www.newadvent.org/cathen/01476d.htm
21. See Kay (1994), p.141 and Copleston (1993) pp.229-230
22. Durling/Martinez (2010), p.590
23. Reynolds, B. (2006) p.394
24. *Convivio* III.v.11, referenced in Singleton (1975) and Hollander (2007)
25. See Hollander (2007) commentary on these lines, p.751
26. See Hollander (2007), pp. 837-839 for a fuller range of possible interpretations and allusions.
27. Durling/Martinez (2010), p.741
28. Hollander (2007), p.843
29. Freccero, J. "The Final Image", in *Dante: The Poetics of Conversion* (1986) pp.254-257
30. Freccero, J. (1986) p.252

Part Three

Astrology: Art and Nature

Stars in Heaven, Diviners in Hell

Astrology, its art and its science, is not ancillary but is central to the *Divine Comedy*. Its role in the poem is complex and provocative. So far we have seen that the universe from the bottommost Earth to the peak of Heaven provides the physical background of the journey from fortune to providence and beyond into eternity itself. Part Three will tell you how astrology contributes to our theme. We will explore the poem's many approaches to astrology and will need to ask ourselves what astrology is. How does astrology relate to divination and prophecy, magic and nature?

This section examines the poem's famous condemnation of diviners and magicians in *Inferno* 20 and ponders astrology's links to divination and magic. I also note material elsewhere in the poem that expands on the 'evil' depicted in this canto. Part Three continues with a discussion of astrology and nature – human nature and cosmic nature. At issue is how the poet articulates the role of the stars and planets with the structure of the human body and soul and the structure of the universe. As we move from divination and magic to nature we will also move from sources in ancient literature to those that provide the philosophical background for the poem.

Before diving into *Inferno* 20 we begin with the *Divine Comedy*'s positive use of astrological factors within the poet's depiction of himself. On several occasions Dante cites the stars being the source of his advantage and genius and he never blames them for his difficulties in life. This helps us understand that Dante's treatment of astrology is more complex than what we may gather solely from *Inferno* 20.

Astrology's Positive Environment

Think back to the scorched sands within the Mars-like seventh circle whose inhabitants had committed acts of violence during their lives. We are returning to *Inferno* 15 and the encounter between Dante and Brunetto Latini. Previously Dante had witnessed the eternal fates of the suicides, bloodthirsty tyrants, and here he finds himself with the "sodomites". A plain of burning sand is pelted by fiery rain with people running around, avoiding the flames. Dante and Virgil are above the burning track looking down upon them. One scorched man below – Dante's former mentor and once-exiled writer Brunetto Latini – tugs at Dante's garment and marvels at who he sees above him.

After their recognition scene, Latini asks Dante how he is down here in Hell as a living person, what fortune or destiny, *Qual fortuna o destino*, had brought him there. After Dante replies that he was rescued from having lost his way in the bright life above, Latini's reply begins with these lines:

"Ed elli a me: 'Se tu segui tua stella,
non puoi fallire a glorïoso porto,
se ben m'accorsi ne la vita bella'."

"And he to me: by following your star
you cannot fail to reach a glorious port,
if I discerned well in the good life." (*Inferno* 15: 55-57)

It is not immediately clear how "star", *stella*, is meant. In the second line there's mention of a "glorious port". Is this a normal use of the seafaring metaphor to describe life purpose, or is it an indirect evocation of life purpose as disclosed by an astrological chart? I am inclined toward his port being the heavens, based on the upcoming *"il cielo e te così benigno,"* of line 59 – "the heaven that favors you".

Consider the words, "discerned well" (*ben m'accorsi*) from line 57. How might Brunetto Latini have "discerned well" Dante's positive life path? He could have sized up Dante's character through personal acquaintance or the young man's reputation – or he could have constructed and interpreted a natal chart for him. Latini, a highly educated man whose written works included much astronomy, could have easily devised and used an astrological chart for the younger Dante.

Yet Latini tells that his well-favored former student is not necessarily favored by fortune, at least not soon. He follows with some prophecy, warning Dante about the bad people who will attempt to take advantage of his many good qualities.

Let's move further down into Dante's Hell, deeper below to the *Malebolge* and where we hear more about the poet's favorable stars. In

Canto 26 Dante and Virgil are climbing down into the areas of the "Evil Counselors" and they are soon to encounter Ulysses and Guido da Montefeltro. But the poet, grieving over what he saw in this *bolgia*, tells us that he must restrain himself or he will overreach and misuse his poetic gifts. What are the sources of these gifts?

sì che, se stella bona o miglior cosa (Inferno 26: 23)

"*Se stella bona*" refers to his good star; "*miglior cosa*" is "something better" and is probably God's grace.[1] In light of his forthcoming introduction to the proud adventurer Ulysses, the poet wishes to restrain pride in his abilities that come from (1) his good star, or (2) God. Neither his star nor God's grace were his doing and therefore he should be grateful, not proud. In true Christian fashion, God's grace is always better than the favor of stars – it's more direct. (In Hell God can only be noted indirectly, so divine grace is rendered here as "something better".)

Finally emerging from Hell, we find reference to Dante's lucky stars in his famous meeting with Beatrice in the Earthly Paradise. The evocation of Dante's good stars is now turned against the spiritually slacking pilgrim. Beatrice is making the case about the pilgrim's lapsed moral and spiritual life after she had died. Speaking to those around her who beg her to be gentler, Beatrice tells them that this man had been favored by *both* the stars and God's grace. She refers to the stars in this way:

"Non pur per ovra de le rote magne
che drizzan ciascun seme ad alcun fine
secondo che le stelle son compagne," (Purgatorio 30:109-111)

M. S Merwin (2000) translates these lines thus:

"Not only through the working of the great
wheels which direct each seed toward some end
depending on what stars accompany it"

The cause and the purpose of Dante's gifts and his other advantages in life are set by the great wheels and their accompanying stars. The influence of Heaven and God's other graces descended upon him like rain flows from high clouds. Dante could have fulfilled great purposes but instead he squandered his gifts and caused himself such harm that he needs heavenly intervention to bail him out (Canto 30:112-141).

High up in Paradise beyond the planets is a passage that should be well-known to astrologers. Toward the end of *Paradiso* 22 the pilgrim finds himself amidst these fortunate heavenly bodies, the stars of Gemini. Here begins Dante's famous praise and invocation of these stars.

> "O glorïose stelle, o lume pregno
> di gram virtù, dal quale io riconosco
> tutto, qual che si sia, il mio ingegno"
> (*Paradiso* 22:-112-114)

> "O glorious stars, O pregnant light
> with great power, with my talent
> all, whatever it may be, its source for me..."

The pilgrim marvels: the stars Gemini, where the Sun resided when he was first born, is where now he finds himself. He asks their help: accomplishing the daunting work of the poem's final verses will require the strength of those stars that gave him his native talent. He invokes the stars of Gemini for poetic inspiration as he had done previously the Muses and Apollo.

From these passages, the *Divine Comedy* appears to be a friendly field for astrology, yet diviners and magicians – and two very famous thirteenth-century astrologers – are consigned to Hell for their work. *Inferno* 20 and the Fourth *bolgia* are now our destination.

The Twisted Realm of *Inferno* 20

Those depicted in this canto inappropriately (although not incorrectly) predicted the future through forms of divination – including reading the stars. Some used charms and potions to practice magic. They are all placed in one of the *Malebolge*, the "evil pits" within the Eighth Circle of Hell which has been reserved for people who have committed acts of fraud during their lifetimes. Dante depicts fraud as the use of an honest appearance or trusted position to disguise a baser reality that takes advantage of others.

You may recall from Canto 17 that Dante and Virgil ride the multiform Geryon downward to the ditches, the nine *Malebolge* that form Hell's eighth circle. Geryon, with an honest face and splendid garment but a reptilian body, is a bestial symbol of fraud. Those in the fourth *bolgia* had also exploited the difference between appearance and reality. Further down in the *Malebolge* we will see the course of evil among the fraudulent, as their motivations for fraud become increasingly malevolent.

Inferno 20 is a strange canto even by the *Inferno's* standards and this comes out right away in its poetic form. Here is how Durling translates the canto's first lines: "Of a strange new punishment for the twentieth song (*canto*) in this first canticle (*de la prima canzon*), which is of those submerged" (20:1-3). If these lines were subject to a modern editor they would have a very quick death, for they are poetically flat and contribute nothing to the narrative. Indeed the entire canto is dry of metaphor and poetic ornamentation. Much of its verse, especially Virgil's depiction of the founding of his hometown Mantua, is choppy and flat.[2] Even the last word of this canto is a colloquialism that Dante had once rejected as unfit for poetic use. The style of Canto 20 is plainness over elegance, the ordinary over the sensational. This helps set up a contrast to the kind of language used to defraud others.

The pilgrim sees this *bolgia's* inhabitants from a distance. The place consists of a large curving track where people walk and weep silently. Seeing the individuals more closely, the pilgrim finds that all their heads are twisted backwards so their faces were on the same side as their shoulders and backs. They are depicted walking backward, since, as Virgil says, seeing forward was denied them (*'l veder dinanzi era lor tolto* 20:15).

Dante weeps. How could not one pity the sight of a person's tears going into the crack of his or her buttocks? (This is the first of many graphic descriptions of physical distortions suffered by the inmates here.) Virgil reprimands his student for his pitying attitude and the impiety of implicitly questioning God's judgment in this matter. Virgil asks his student to raise his head and then begins to point out some of the people kept here.

The first five inmates are from the epic poetry of classical antiquity and, except for the woman, they are cast as diviners. What is striking is the discrepancy between their stories as told by Dante and their sources in Roman epic. We need to explore this discrepancy. We are not indulging in literary citation for its own sake but demonstrating a fascinating pattern that is unique to this canto. Virgil's depictions of the diviners will appear in italics.

Meet the Diviners

Virgil first points out Amphiaraus: *his shoulders are now his chest because he tried to look too far forward. Amphiaraus is depicted mockingly as somebody before whom the ground opened up and swallowed him with others taunting him, asking where he is rushing to away from battle. He wanted to see too far ahead and now looks behind and walks backward.* (Canto 20:31-38).

Dante's source for this story is Statius' *Thebiad*, an epic from the second century that is largely unknown to modern readers. This work traces the legend of the battle for Thebes that fulfilled Oedipus' curse that his two sons Etiocles and Polyneices would kill one another. Statius casts Amphiaraus, one of the men besieging Thebes, quite differently than Dante did.

According to the *Thebiad*, Amphiaraus was a warrior and a priest gifted with prophetic abilities. Through examining omens and the behavior of birds, Amphiaraus had seen portents of disaster for those who would attempt to recapture Thebes. He was quite reluctant to enter this war and joined the campaign unwillingly: he had gone into hiding but his wife was bribed into revealing his location. Then, having joined the besieging forces, he unsuccessfully attempted to restrain his comrades.

In battle the seer fought bravely and well but things began to move according to prediction. At the last moment, Apollo, who had previously guided Amphiaraus' chariot, appeared by his side and revealed to him that he was to become a priest and prophet in the Underworld. (This was a very high honor.) Soon the earth below Amphiaraus opened and he with his chariot plunged downward.[3]

Statius' story of Amphiaraus shows how drastically Dante has revised ancient epic source. The *Divine Comedy*'s poet turned a tragic and noble figure from antiquity into a coward for attempting to avoid his own prediction and for a fool for having made one. Yet the poet has also acknowledged the correctness of the seer's prediction.

Virgil points then out Tiresias. *Upon striking two mating serpents with his staff, Tiresias changed from a man to a woman and later, upon seeing the same snakes mating and striking them again, changed back to a man* (Canto 20:39-45).

Tiresias was antiquity's well-known blind seer. The poet presents him as an intentional shape-shifter which was incorrect. His being of both genders preceded his gifts as a soothsayer.

The origin of Tiresias' blindness and his gift of prophecy are found in Ovid's *Metamorphoses* Book 3 (lines 316-38) and also in Statius' *Thebiad*. Both tell that Jupiter and his wife Juno had been arguing about the former's large sexual appetite. The great god insisted that women achieve greater sexual pleasure than men, which compels men to compensate with quantity through their wanderings. To referee the matter they called on Tiresias, who had experienced being both genders, to give an answer. Tiresias replied that Jupiter was right, that indeed the woman experiences greater sexual pleasure than men by ten to one. In anger Juno struck Tiresias blind; to compensate for this calamity, Jupiter gave Tiresias prophetic abilities. According to Statius' account, Tiresias' particular gift of prophecy was from raising souls from Hades, since the dead are more reliable in prophecy than the living (*Thebiad* Book 3:1630-1635). We will discuss the matter of dead people and prophecy later in Part Three.

Virgil points out Arruns next, seen with back to Tiresias' belly. *Arruns had lived inside a cave above the fields where peasants below work the lands; from his cave he could see the sea and the stars at a very wide angle* (Canto 20:46-51).[4]

Arruns is more unknown to the modern reader even than Amphiaraus. The source is from the second century Roman poet Lucan, whose patron was the Emperor Nero. Lucan wrote the *Pharsalia* or *Civil War* about the Roman Civil War a century earlier. This poem is an overheated but entertaining piece of literature that should be more available to modern readers.

At the beginning of Lucan's epic, Julius Caesar was aiming to cross the Rubicon and take his armies directly to Rome; in response, Caesar's enemy Pompey and the Senate fled the city. At this time there were unsettling omens: odd movements of lightning, earthquakes, strange happenings with the entrails of sacrificed animals and the flights of birds, and many deformed births. There were also celestial omens – new constellations appeared, an ugly comet crossed the sky, some stars were visible in the daytime, there were powerful lunar and solar eclipses. None of this was good.

The leaders who remained in Rome consulted with the Etruscan diviner Arruns. As an intervention to counteract the dire outcomes he had foreseen from the omens, the seer ordered ritual burning and burial of ill-omened objects and purification rites conducted around the city walls.

Dante's facts vary wildly with Lucan's. According to the ancient epic, Arruns had practiced his craft not in a cave but within his city's walls. Nor, according to Lucan, was Arruns' divination from the sky: this was the role of Nigidius Figulus, a historical neo-Pythagorean philosopher who was renowned for his learning and his astrological and divinatory work. (*Pharsalia* Book 1:584-638)

In Lucan's account Figulus was the diviner who saw strange and terrible events to come. From this poem we can also tell that in first century Rome astrology had become widely used, at least by political and literary elites.

> "If the cold baleful planet Saturn were kindling his black fires the Midheaven, a flood like that of Deucalion would have been pouring from Aquarius and the entire land would have been hidden in the spreading expanse of water. If the Sun were now passing over the Nemean Lion (Leo) and goading him to fury with his rays conflagrations would be streaming all over the world, and the ether would have been kindled into flames by his chariot. <But> these heavenly bodies are inactive and their flames are still. What great [terror] is being prepared by Mars? He is setting fire to the Scorpion and making it threaten [war] and he is burning up its claws. Yes, and gentle Jupiter keeps low [below the horizon], Venus's benignant planet is dim, swift Mercury is stationary in his orbit, and Mars is in sole possession of the sky." (*Pharsalia* 1:651-663)[5]

Figulus had cast a chart modern astrologers would call an 'interrogation' or a 'horary' chart. This is one of astrology's most divinatory methods, by which one examines the moment of the asking of a question of concern. These lines argue not only for the use of interrogations in the ancient world but also for the sophistication of astrological lore and the Roman poet's ability to present it coherently.

Having done injury to tales from the *Thebiad* and the *Pharsalia*, the poet then moves to Virgil's own *Aeneid*. Here the medieval poet has Virgil repudiating his own work. We also find this canto's first mention of magical practice.

Virgil points out Manto who is the first woman mentioned in Canto 20. Manto is pictured in physically ignoble fashion: *her hair flows backwards falling around her breasts that fall on the same side as her "hairy parts"* (Canto 20:52-58).

In a tedious digression Virgil retells the story of the founding of his native city Mantua. Manto was the daughter of Tiresias mentioned above. After Tiresias died and Thebes was enslaved, Manto wandered around the world.

Virgil then goes through a description of the mountains and the river in the area of Mantua.* Where the river descends to the swamp, Manto, the "cruel virgin" (*la vergine cruda*) found a dry spot and lived alone with only her servants with her. *There she practiced her (unspecified) magic arts until she died. Later the city was built over Manto's dead bones. Although it was named for her there were no spells or incantations, no magic, in Mantua's origins.* Virgil says that anybody who tells you otherwise than this story is not telling the truth. Listening to this story, the pilgrim responds to affirm the truth of his guide's report (Canto 20:59-102).

Once again *Inferno* 20 varies with its ancient sources. In Statius' *Thebiad*, Manto is her father's assistant and it is unclear whether she has prophetic powers. According to Virgil's *Aeneid*, it was *Ocnus not Manto* who founded Mantua, although it was named for Ocnus' "sibylline" mother Manto (*Aeneid* Book 10.272-277).

Another inconsistency emerges, now between the *Divine Comedy* and itself. In *Purgatorio* 22 Virgil lists well-known ancient figures that are among Hell's "virtuous pagans". Surprisingly, Manto, referred to as the daughter of Tiresias, is among them. This is not the poet being sloppy, for he is never sloppy, but sometimes deliberately confusing.

Dante asks his guide to identify some others here who are among the damned. Virgil begins with another name from the *Aeneid*, a character named Euryplyus whose beard falls onto his shoulders. *This man was allegedly a soothsayer during the time of the Trojan War. Along with the better-known Calchas, Euryplyus advised of an auspicious time for the Greeks to sail to Troy.* Virgil refers to this man's appearance in *l'alta mia tragedia* – "my high tragedy" (Canto 20:106-114).

---

* Boitani (1998) explains it thus: "Dante has redesigned the founding of Virgil's heroic birthplace in such a way that geographical genealogy takes precedence over heroic genealogy (which is suppressed to some degree by making Manto a virgin), the quotidian realities of landscape over the exalted exploits of heroes." (p.283)

Calchas was indeed the soothsayer who told the Greeks when to sail for Troy. In *Aeneid* Book 2 Euryplyus' name comes up. In a dramatic scene Aeneas is retelling the story of the last moments of the Trojan War. In this version, the defeated Greeks were attempting to find a proper time to sail back home. Euryplyus brought back from the oracles a command that another human sacrifice was necessary for them to go home. The Greeks picked a man named Sinon to be sacrificial victim, but Sinon escaped from the Greeks on the day of his sacrifice and soon was captured by the Trojans (*Aeneid* 2:146-174). Was Euryplyus an augur or just a bringer of bad news? One cannot tell from the text.

There is a far larger problem, however. Anybody familiar with the *Aeneid* knows that *the entire story is a fabrication*. Sinon's testimony to the Trojans is intended to dupe them into believing that the Greeks had indeed sailed away and left the 'Trojan Horse' behind. When the naïve Trojans let the wooden horse into their city and began to celebrate their victory, Sinon freed the Greeks hiding within it; the soldiers opened the gates to the remainder of the Greek forces and the rest is epic history. (We meet Sinon in the *Inferno* among the "falsifiers" in the bottommost *bolgia*.)

Lies, Damn Lies, but Mostly Bullshit

We have seen that *Inferno* 20 mangles its sources in ancient epic poetry. Elsewhere in the *Divine Comedy* Dante renovates existing structures and situations from ancient epic but he does not alter the facts needlessly: here he distorts and twists his sources gratuitously, rendering the facts backwards like the shape of fourth *bolgia*'s inmates.

Here is an incomplete answer. Dante the medieval poet is attempting to draw a clear line separating his Christian culture from the divinatory and ritual practices of the ancient world. In a Christian universe there is no place for seers who read divine communications from bird flights, bird entrails, or heavenly or earthly portents, nor is there a place for bargaining with divinity through ritual and sacrifice. Dante was breaking with the pagan excesses of his past and illuminating important differences between his Christian culture and its Roman background.

This explanation is incomplete because it does not account for Dante twisting the facts in *Inferno* 20 with such vigor and so arbitrarily.

The poet could have easily identified Figulus as Rome's astrologer and Calchas as the Greeks' diviner but chose to do otherwise. And it is this randomness and seemingly-careless disregard for the facts that gives us our answer: it arises from an *unconcern* with matters of truth or falsity.

This is not simple lying. When one lies, the liar implicitly acknowledges the truth he or she is deviating from, and there is always a motive for presenting a substitute for the truth. This is different from the unconcern for truth we see in *Inferno* 20, one that is also practiced by many contemporary politicians and their consultants, the media, 'opinion leaders' of all kinds – and even by a one or two psychics and astrologers. This unconcern with truth often accompanies an image of its bearer being knowledgeable and wise and we're acquainted with its practice as engaging in bullshit.*

Bullshit occurs when large ideas meet a small mind that is more interested in making an impression than the truth or falsity of what he or she is presenting. In Canto 20 the poet quite deliberately indulges in bullshit. Is this another example of imitation in the *Inferno*? If so it would be imitation not by the pilgrim's behavior but Virgil's words and the tone of the canto.

Through the vehicle of this canto's style and depictions, the poet tells us that this *bolgia*'s inmates were involved not in lies but in bullshit through which they conveyed a false sense of having special knowledge and ability. In life they would have made the facts fit their patterns of belief, deliver what their customers or clients or patrons want to hear, and present themselves to others as knowing or wise. Perhaps they appeared to have a special direct pipeline to reality. This canto's poetics of plainness also contrasts with the elevated appearance of many manifestations of bullshit.

Ironically we find more about this high in Paradise amidst the lofty discourse of *Paradiso* 29. From the rather arcane topic of whether angels have memory, Beatrice launches into a bitter and mocking diatribe against their contemporary preachers and teachers (*Paradiso* 29:82-126).

---

* For a stimulating discussion of this topic I heartily recommend a short classic: Frankfurt, H.G. *On Bullshit* (2005) Princeton University Press. The depiction here summarizes Frankfurt's analysis. This definition is from pp.33-34 of that work.

People who know better, she says, attempt to entertain and show off more than to convey Christian teachings correctly. They distort the truth by making things up when it serves them, for they are more interested in getting a good laugh from their audience and bolstering their own swelling pride than in conveying truth. Christ did not, Beatrice says, tell his first congregation to preach chatter or gossip to the world.

Later we will see that the condemnation of diviners and magicians is from more than just bullshit and fits into a larger picture of the scope and extent of evil. For this we will explore some of the lower layers of the *Malebolge*.

Games of "Magic Fraud"

We return to *Inferno* 20. At lines 115-117 Virgil points out a well-known historical figure from the first half of Dante's previous century, Michael Scot. Michael Scot is cast as the one with "skinny flanks" who could play well the game of "magic fraud" (*le magiche frode*) (lines 115-117). The reference to Scot's lean flanks is not clear; the accusation of magic fraud is clearer.

The historical Michael Scot was born late in the twelfth century, was educated at Paris and Oxford and he learned his Arabic in Toledo. He was a scholar, translating works of Aristotle from Arabic into Latin. Dante would have known him as an advisor to the court of Frederick II and he was the Emperor's astrologer – or one of them. Michael Scot wrote books about astrology, alchemy, and the magical arts, hence his fame as a magician.

Then, in line 118 we read, "*Vedi Guido Bonatti*", "See Guido Bonatti". That's all. I wish the great poet wrote more about one of his sources who he nonetheless consigned to Hell. As we saw in Part Two, Bonatti's writings informed much of Dante's astrological imagery in the *Divine Comedy*.

Bonatti is the best-known astrologer of the medieval era and was also famous in his own time. During his lifetime he was the astrological advisor to several prominent Guibellines, particularly the reputedly cruel Ezzelino da Romano (*Inferno* 12) and the crafty Guido da Montefeltro (*Inferno* 27). He notably advised his patrons about the best times to go into battle and what strategies to use – based on astrological technique.

From different eras of the thirteenth century, Michael Scot and Guido Bonatti were famous astrological (or magical) consultants linked with important political and military figures.

The remainder of Canto 20's sad parade is lower down the social ladder and, like Bonatti, is given only brief mention. Virgil first points out a man called *Asdente* or "toothless". Asdente was from Parma and was celebrated for his predictive work. In the *Convivio* Dante mentions him as a person far more notorious than noble.[6] Now, Virgil states, he repents too late that he left behind his honest work as a cobbler. Last in line are the "miserable ones" (*triste*), women who left their spindle and thread for the activities of divination and sorcery, for casting spells with herbs and images (10:121-123). These women also left behind their legitimate work for more glamorous activities.

This concludes the line-up from *Inferno* 20. Let's now take a general look at divination, prophecy, and magic and their applications to the *Divine Comedy*.

Telling and Shaping the Future: Divination and Magic

Currently the relationship between astrology and divination is a matter of interest among many astrologers. First we will look at exactly what we mean by 'divination' and by its sibling 'prophecy'. Prophecy has a prominent role throughout the *Divine Comedy*. Then we will leave Dante for a short while and look at magic and its relationship to astrology.

Divination and Astrology

Divination is an important feature of astrology although it is not the only feature. What follows are some general outlines of divination and its relationship to astrology.

One does not practice divination by consulting a weather map to find tomorrow's weather or a company's quarterly report to decide whether to invest in that company, for these sources of information are commonly available. In divination the sources of information are hidden or *occult*. A diviner tends to be an outsider in his or her own particular culture but is called on for formal occasions or in times of emergency.

Like the practice of magic, divination has its likely origins in religious ritual. In its many manifestations divination is the activity of seeking information from patterns seen in seemingly random events.

It is one way in which humans have worked with uncertainty in their lives. Divinatory practices have a sequence that begins with an initial situation or problem and ends with an interpretation by a diviner.

Often the divinatory process begins with a *situational context*: the king wants to go to war; there is anxiety about the year's crop yield; someone is concerned about a matter of love or career or health, or about a missing item from the household. It might be the occasion for founding a city or the coronation of a new king. (The word 'inauguration' is from the word 'augur', a person who watched the flights of birds for good or bad signs from the Gods.[7]) One does not practice divination for a matter that one can control or on a frivolous matter, but to clarify when there is an urgent matter of uncertain outcome.

This process may also begin unbidden with *omens*: external events are disturbing – 'ominous' – and call for clarification. In ancient literature, the winds become still and do not allow the Greek ships to sail to Troy; when Oedipus was king of Thebes there was a plague. These events called for Calchas and Tiresias respectively. In ancient times unexplained calamities like epidemics or drought were thought to carry some kind of communication that required explanation. Today even people with no personal interest in divination wonder if a surprising event is 'a sign' of something, perhaps a warning to be attended to. In many religious traditions the birth of the religion's founder occasioned unusual positive events we would call 'miraculous': in the case of Buddha and Jesus Christ, diviners were called in to interpret the situation. These occurrences would be considered not ominous but favorable and auspicious.

A diviner may be consulted when there is already a background situation from which omens appear: in Lucan's rendition of the Roman Civil War, there were comets, solar and lunar eclipses and terrestrial events like many deformed births and extreme weather patterns. The diviner may turn *magus* and recommend remedial action, as in Lucan's work.

Having been brought onto the scene, a qualified diviner then *looks at something specific* for information. In ancient times, he or she may look at the flight patterns or songs of birds or at the entrails of a sacrificed animal. In geomancy one finds specific markings on the Earth or as an art in which a pattern is created by tossing soil or rocks or mechanically generating patterns that could be interpreted. In modern times one might answer a question by throwing coins or sticks to use an *I Ching*, or by turning over cards from a Tarot deck. An astrologer may cast a chart to help explain an ominous event from the event itself or for the time of asking a specific question – a 'horary' chart.

What do all these activities have in common? One requirement seems to be an event's apparent accidental quality; Liz Greene calls it "randomization".[8] For divination to occur one cannot know in advance about upcoming bird flights or what a calf's liver will look like, what sides of coins turn up, what cards will be uncovered, or know the exact configuration of the heavens. There needs to be some kind of causal gap for an event to attain divinatory status.

Having received the appropriate information, the diviner then applies a *procedure* or 'art' to the information rendered. Some expertise is required and is usually personally transmitted from master to student. The ancient diviner may be acquainted with the range of bird songs or flights or vulnerabilities in the liver of a sacrificed animal. A modern practitioner of *I Ching* or Tarot would have to learn the meanings of the different hexagrams or cards that may come up. People take astrology classes for the same reason.

The process concludes with an *interpretation*. This step requires some kind of leap that synthesizes the information at hand, including all relevant background and foreground factors, with an intuitive leap which comes from the divinatory art itself. This often occurs abruptly and what emerges seems not to come from the diviner but from elsewhere, almost like a revelation. The diviner applies the full interpretation to the area of uncertainty and he or she may recommend remedial action.

A valid divinatory interpretation seems to require both 'objective' procedural and 'subjective' intuitive processes. The success of any divination technique lies in striking a balance between the two: if one favors intuition over procedure, the result often transparently reflects the practitioner's preconceptions and is untrustworthy. If one favors procedure over intuition the results are usually artificial, tangential, and also untrustworthy.

Is the art of astrology an art of divination? Historically it has been packaged as such. Cicero's *On Divination* from the first century BCE is a notable source of information about divinatory practices in Rome. In his famous diatribe against the validity of augury, Cicero classified astrology as one of many divinatory practices. According to the account from Book I of that work, astrology came late onto the Roman divination scene and was not native but imported from the 'Chaldeans'. It is not clear that his account is historically reliable but it is clear that his agenda was strongly political.[9] Yet, by classifying astrology as a species of divination, Cicero may be right after all.

Based on almanacs, ephemerides, or tables, astrologers have long used the configurations of the sky from a specific location at a specific time to form a figure or 'chart'. This may be the chart of a public event like the crowning of a king or emperor, or the founding of a city. In Greek this was called a *katarche* that means 'according to a beginning' and was also the first stage of a ritual.

As we have seen, a *horary* chart is based upon the moment of asking a question. We have seen this with Lucan's depiction of Nigidius Figulus reading the skies. Horary astrology was common in the medieval and early modern eras, and its exemplars are Guido Bonatti from the thirteenth century and William Lilly from the seventeenth. Horary astrology continues to be practiced by many astrologers today, including me.

The work of Geoffrey Cornelius, particularly his book *The Moment of Astrology* (2003), stresses the divinatory nature of *all* astrological practice including natal and predictive astrology. According to the divinatory model associated with Cornelius and others, astrology cannot work without the astrologer to divine and interpret. Cornelius' work is particularly groundbreaking in its depiction of the intuitive nature of astrological interpretation.

In my view, astrologers are diviners yet this is not all of what makes astrology special. The art of reading the skies carries with it something else – the sky itself. This brings us into the realm of 'natural astrology'.

Astrology posits that the wheels of the sky and the positions of stars and planets – are situationally, psychologically and spiritually significant. We can look at the configurations of the sky not just as the source of omens, bidden and unbidden, but also as *a revealer of cosmic pattern*. Astrology developed a specific body of knowledge that allowed future events to be discerned objectively and, in their own fashion, scientifically. To the ancient and medieval mind, the orderly beauty of stellar configurations implied that the universe contains patterns that have been worked out beforehand. The night sky visually renders the universe's essential harmony amidst the chaos of our own lives; this gives astrology it a unique power as a predictive and divinatory art. This field of 'natural astrology' posits direct relationships between the stars and planets and our lives down here, even if there are no astrological charts or astrologers to interpret them.

Prophecy and Dead People

The *Divine Comedy* contains much about the personal and global future. For centuries amused readers have noted the specificity of its personal predictions and the opacity of its global predictions. When the pilgrim Dante hears about his upcoming exile or his gracious hosts he will meet, we all know the poet was writing these predictions after these events have occurred. Dante's poem also contains forecasts of better things to come that have defied centuries of commentators. The *Divine Comedy*'s excursions into the future are not just narrative device but have a strong place within the multilayered fabric of the poem.

To understand prophecy and how Dante used prophecy in the *Divine Comedy*, we will look at some of its general features that would have been known to the poet. Again we find ourselves first within ancient religious and literary traditions. We begin with the ancient practice of oracles.

In ancient Greece and Rome, oracles were located in specific usually remote places. In answer to a question, a god would appear to a medium (usually a woman) who assumed a mantic frenzy and whose usually incoherent words were interpreted by a priest or official augur. In some ways this resembles modern 'channeling' although the modern practice appears less dramatic.

In ancient Rome the most prominent interpreters were women assigned to specific holy places: they were called Sibyls, and in the *Aeneid* Book 6 the Sibyl guides Aeneas in his journey to the underworld. We find a whole range of prophetic work in both ancient and modern worlds.

Generally commentators use the word 'prophecy' for the *Divine Comedy*'s depictions of the future and I will keep to that convention. A Greek lexicon tells us that the adjective 'prophetic', means 'oracular', and that a 'prophet' is an 'interpreter of the will of the god'.[10] The word 'prophecy', therefore, has come to us as an immediate access to 'occult' knowledge that proceeds from divinity itself. Let's begin with an interesting ancient convention for prophecy that returns us to the strange world of ancient epic.

Within the great amounts of divination and prophecy in the epic tradition, no words of the future are more reliable than from those who have died and now reside in the Underworld. We see this as early as Homer: in Book 11 of the *Odyssey*, Ulysses goes down to Hades to consult with the dead seer Tiresias to learn how finally to return home. In Virgil's *Aeneid* Book 5, after another catastrophe occurred to those seeking their new home in Italy, Aeneas' father Anchises appears to his despairing son in a dream. Anchises tells his son to go into the Underworld and speak with him directly to hear about the destiny of his race (*Aeneid* 5:801-821). (*Aeneid* 6, the tale of Aeneas' subsequent journey to meet with his father in the Underworld, contains some of the template for the *Inferno* 1300 years later.)

In Statius' *Thebiad* Jupiter gives Tiresias the ability to tell the future based on communicating with souls in the Underworld. In Book 3, Tiresias summons Laius, the father of Oedipus, from the Underworld, to tell of the outcome of the war between Laius' grandsons Etiocles and Polyneices. Laius says that for all of his aggression, Polyneices will never seize the kingdom of Thebes from Etiocles. What he doesn't say is that the two brothers will kill each other (*Thebiad*: Book 4:636-645).

More sensationalistic and grisly is Book 6 of Lucan's *Pharsalia*. Erictho, one of the three Furies, is summoned to gain information about the future for Pompey and Caesar who are at war.* Erictho chooses a dead body and by sorcery restores the person to semi-life, and she asks him about the future. After telling of the expansion of Rome's Civil War even into the Underworld, the once-dead person tells of the future catastrophes of Rome and of Pompey himself. Erichto then restores the ghastly being to death (*Pharsalia* 6:589-830).

---

* There is an allusion to this story in *Inferno* 9:22-30. At that time Virgil and Dante are stuck outside the walls of Dis and Dante asks his guide if any souls from uppermost Hell have ever gone down below. Virgil replies that Erictho had summoned his own spirit and was forced to go to the circle of the traitors to bring up another spirit who was cast down there.

Not only did the poet leave this convention intact but he used it throughout the *Divine Comedy*, for indeed many of the souls there – all dead, of course – accurately tell Dante of his future. From Hell to Paradise they do so in different circumstances and with increasing clarity.

Those in Hell who tell the pilgrim about his future tell the truth partly and obscurely and all have their reasons. We see this first in *Inferno* 6 among the gluttons. Pounded by thick smelly rain, Ciacco tells the pilgrim about *the vicissitudes of the conflict between Black and White Guelfs in Florence*. Ciacco's concern is the great pride and subsequent downfall of the Florentines. Their conversation is friendly; Ciacco seems motivated by a desire for the pilgrim Dante to speak well of him upon returning to the Earth's surface.

From *Inferno* 10, Farinata's prophecy from his fiery tomb is better known and more dramatic. Recall Farinata, the Ghibelline lord whose forces once conquered Guelf-dominated Florence. After their subsequent defeat, Farinata's family had been banished and to date hadn't been allowed to Florence even after a general amnesty. The pilgrim chides him that his family had not yet learned the art of returning from exile. The damned heretic then makes this famous comeback.

"Ma non cinquanta volte fia raccesa
la faccia de la donna che qui regge,
che tu saprai quanto quell' arte pesa."

"Not fifty times will be rekindled
the face of the queen who reigns here,
that you will learn how this art is difficult."* (*Inferno* 10: 79-81)

Farinata's motive seems to be a simple case of one-upmanship. One may also detect some sympathy for the evil destiny that will befall this pilgrim presently touring Hell.

The next prophecy is made in Canto 15 among the "sodomites", within the famous exchange between Dante and his former mentor Brunetto Latini. In keeping to the general tone of their conversation, Latini's depiction of the future lays it on pretty thickly: *the rabble that*

---

* You will notice that the circlings of the Moon – not the Sun – give the time reference for Farinata's dark prophecy in Hell. (Ulysses also uses the Moon's movements to give the duration of his mad voyage at the end of *Inferno* 26.)

had polluted the good blood of the Florentines continues to do their evil and will victimize Dante because of his good deeds. Since Dante's destiny is so honorable he should be able to rise above these beasts who seek to devour him (*Inferno* 15:61-78).

More malevolent is the prophecy of Vanni Fucci at the end of *Inferno* 24. Dante and Virgil are visiting the *bolgia* of the thieves, whose fate is to be oppressed by huge serpents who periodically take over their bodies. Vanni Fucci would rather remain unknown but is identified anyway by one of his fellow inmates. The sinner retaliates for being "outed": in rapid-fire style he tells Dante about *the coming vicissitudes of the White and Black Guelfs in Pistoia and Florence that ends with a victory of the Blacks over the Whites* (recall that Dante is a White Guelf). Then in the canto's final line he states that he says this to make the touring poet more miserable.

Thus, the prophecies in Hell are all fairly general and are made with ulterior motives, such as Farinata's one-upmanship and Vanni Fucci's desire to spread around his misery. Now, we move to the *Purgatorio* that also contains personal prophecy but its atmosphere is more positive and the interactions more comradely. There are four to consider.

In *Purgatorio* 8 it is just before dark on their first overnight and Dante and Virgil are just below the mountain's ledge, in the Valley of the Princes. The snake in the grass has been chased away and the four stars representing the Cardinal Virtues have been replaced by three representing the Theological Virtues. A new shade now approaches Dante and his guide and identifies himself as Currado of the Malaspina family. After Dante praises this family's good reputation, Currado stops him and states that *before the Sun returns to its present sign Aries seven times he will have more personal proof of the goodness of this family* (*Purgatorio* 8:133-139).*

In *Purgatorio* 11, Dante and Virgil are upon the ledge of the once-proud whose inhabitants carry immense boulders on their backs. Oderisi, the former illuminated manuscript maker, points out Provenzano Salvani, once a successful leader in Siena who is atoning for his pride in position and accomplishment. Salvani had just had recently died, and Dante

---

* Now that they are in Purgatory it is the Sun and not the Moon that gives the time references.

Astrology, Art and Nature   191

wonders why he had begun on the mountain of Purgatory so quickly. Oderisi replies that to help a friend Salvani had made a difficult public gesture of humility but – *not much time will pass when Dante's neighbors will force a similar circumstance upon him*: Dante himself will have his own opportunity to be publicly humiliated (Canto 11:139-141).

Higher upon the Mountain and closer to the Earthly Paradise, *Purgatorio* 24 depicts the penance of the now-emaciated former gluttons. Bonagiunta, a poet from the city of Lucca and once a critic of Dante's school of poetry, begins a conversation with the pilgrim by noting that *in the future a woman from Lucca will make the town pleasing to him* although others may revile the city. (We may wonder how she will do this.) Later, Bonagiunta says, the meaning of his words will be clearer (Canto 24:43-48).

Upon meeting his old friend Forese Donati, the pilgrim hears a more direct but guarded prediction of things to come. Forese begins with his own family: *much blame will fall on his brother Corso Donati*. You may recall that Corso Donati was the leader of the Black Guelfs who took control of Florence in 1301 that was the occasion of Dante's banishment from the city. Forese also says that *his brother Corso will be dragged along by the beast who will lead him into Hell*. This alludes to Corso Donati's conspiracy with the pope but also his death from being dragged by a horse. Then, however, Forese tells his old friend Dante, "Not very far have these wheels to turn…" (*Non hanno molto a volger quelle ruote*, Canto 24:88), and then he looks toward the sky but cuts himself off.

Note that Forese is using even a grander scale than the circling Sun to reckon time: he cites the movements of the entire sky itself. Telling the pilgrim that his obscure words will become clearer later, he departs.

Obscure Prophecies of World Deliverance

We now consider some of the most puzzling passages in the entire poem. They are both prophetic and are symmetrical to one another: one is from the first canto of the *Inferno* and the other from the last canto of the *Purgatorio*. The first is delivered by his first guide Virgil, the second by his second guide Beatrice.

We return to Dante in the dark wood where he had just met Virgil. Dante had been driven back from the Sun's rays first by the leopard, then by the lion, and thirdly by the she-wolf. Dante expresses great fear of the wolf in particular. Virgil describes this vicious beast with the greedy insatiable nature. The she-wolf will mate with many others until a hound (*veltre*) will give her a painful death. This person will feed on wisdom, love, and power and *e sua nazion sarà tra feltro e feltro*, "and his birth will be (note future tense) *between "feltro" and "feltro"*. (*Inferno* 1:105) It is unclear whether these "feltros" should be capitalized.

We do not know what the poet means by any of this. One possibility lies with the fact that between the cities of Feltre and Montefeltro is Verona; this was the residence of Cangrande della Scala who was Dante's patron and to whom he had dedicated the *Paradiso*. "Hound" also may be a pun on the name Cangrande. There's a problem though – these verses imply that such a person had not yet been born and Cangrande would have been nine years old in 1300.

Another possibility is of an astrological kind: the Dioscuri, the Roman deities that were Castor and Pollux of the constellation Gemini, were often depicted wearing felt caps.[11] If so it could not refer to Dante: although 'a Gemini', the poet was thirty-five years old at the time of the *Divine Comedy*'s narrative. Nor do we know the role the sign Gemini may have in this prophecy. All these possibilities have their problems; the poet has left centuries of readers and commentators in an interpretative muddle.

Moving to the end of *Purgatorio*, the poem's next world prophecy muddles matters even further. Now we have gone from the dark wood to the luminous Earthly Paradise and from Virgil to Beatrice – who is never mistaken. Beatrice and the pilgrim have just witnessed the pageant showing the various downfalls of the Church in history, culminating in the harlot (the Church) being dragged off by the monster (the French monarchy) into the forest. Beatrice notes the pilgrim's bewilderment and gives this prophecy: somebody will come who will be the appropriate secular leader, for the stars are already near that promise the time for this.

> *"nel quale un cinquecento diece e cinque,*
> *messo di Dio, anciderà la fuia*
> *con quel gigante che con lei delinque"*
>
> "When five hundred ten and five
> sent by God, will slay the harlot
> and the monster who sins with her." (*Purgatorio* 33:43-45)
>
> Beatrice then says that her words may be obscure (she is correct). She does say that she is reading the stars (instead of the mind of God directly) for the timing of things to become better. It is unknown what stars she is referring to or the meanings of these three numbers 500, 10, and 5. We see the use of numbers for prophetic reasons in the Biblical Book of Revelations. Using Roman numerals, these three numbers may instead point to a name or designation: five hundred, ten, and five spell out DXV and may relate to the word DUX, the word for 'leader'.[12] If so it is a rather convoluted way of indicating nothing. We know from the use of ancient oracles that unprocessed prophecy is often opaque and here the poet appears to be lining up with that tradition.
>
> At the end of Paradiso 27, ending a diatribe against the waywardness of their world, Beatrice tells that things will get better when January will be "unwintered". Then, she says, rays from the lofty circles (the ecliptic and equator) will shine forth: *raggeran sì questi cerchi superni*. The resulting storm will turn the ships to their opposite sides so they can run their true courses and good fruit will result (*Paradiso* 27:144-148).
>
> This prophecy does not tell us how – other than through providence – the tempest will turn things around to the right way. We may also note glancing allusions to both the twisted bodies of the diviners from *Inferno* 20 and the shipwreck of Ulysses in *Inferno* 26 that we will soon discuss. (Note that divine intervention is seen written in the circles of Heaven.)

We are now ready for the final personal prophecy in the *Divine Comedy*, spoken to the pilgrim by his ancestor Cacciaguida upon the Sphere of Mars in Canto 17 of the *Paradisio*. It is a high point in the

Divine Comedy's narrative, the *Paradiso*'s midpoint, and an example of a really good prophecy – or a prediction. It is also the poem's great example of fortune completed and transcended by providence, illustrating the right relationship between the two.

The poet has carefully prepared the reader for this encounter. From Cacciaguida's first words to his descendent, the poet means for us to think of the relationship of Aeneas to his father Anchises from Book 6 of *The Aeneid* and Aeneas' journey into the Underworld. Anchises predicts the future of Aeneas' descendants: they will be the Romans who will govern the world.

Dante has a request of his ancestor, but before making his request, the pilgrim first acknowledges his ancestor's ability to tell the future infallibly, with the ability to see contingencies (*contingenti*) before they appear (Canto 17:16-18). Dante asks his ancestor about the dark words he has heard elsewhere on his journey through the afterlife. He wants to know about this more precisely for "an arrow that one expects will come more slowly" (lines 25-27).

Cacciaguida tells the pilgrim that he will be banished from his city, not from any fault of his own, but from the treachery of others. It is not the loss of public reputation that will first hurt from exile but separation from his loved ones. In his new life in exile, he will learn the salty taste of another's bread (Florentines didn't put salt in their bread) and how hard it is to go up and down the stairs belonging to someone else (*Paradiso* 17.46-60). Dante first will fall in with some companions who turn out to be neither good nor very bright people. They will eventually turn on him and he will become a party only of himself.

Afterwards, Cacciaguida says, Dante will find better people and more gracious hosts, including one who is currently but a child. Dante's future Veronese host Cangrande is described as so impressed upon by this mighty star Mars that his deeds later will gain him fame.

Cacciaguida guides his descendent through his future trials. He first advises the pilgrim not to despise his many enemies for his life (and fame?) will outlast theirs. Dante remarks that on his tour of the afterlife he had seen many things that could clearly make others uncomfortable; he may make even more enemies. Dante encourages himself and steels his own courage: if he is a timid friend to the truth, then his name will not survive long into the future (*Paradiso* 17.106-120).

Cacciaguida now glows with greater brightness as he renders Heaven's mandate to his descendent: upon the pilgrim's return to the world of the living, he is to speak truthfully of what he has seen; if this will be difficult for some people maybe it should be. He will inevitably make powerful enemies along the way. The bitter taste of the pilgrim's words will eventually become vital nourishment for others.

The purpose of this forecast is not to enable the pilgrim to wrest some advantage or even to help him position himself toward less misery but to show him his place in God's world and disclose God's intention. In Heaven prophecy is straightforward, appropriate, and guiding.

Those of us who have practiced astrological prediction will recognize Cacciaguida's words to the pilgrim as predictive and counseling work at its absolute best. Even though the pilgrim's coming misfortunes conform to the workings of providence, they do not lose their meaning and importance. Dante's forthcoming catastrophe is part of God's grand plan of political and spiritual redemption.

So far we have examined various ways to know the future. We now turn to means whereby we influence the future. This is the activity of magic that we also saw condemned in *Inferno* 20 but is a pervasive motif in past cultures and in our own. This will also serve to move toward the *Divine Comedy*'s rendition of nature and super-nature that are the means by which divine providence would govern the world.

What is 'Magic'?
Consider the many ways the word 'magic' appears in popular culture and our daily discourse. The word may mean an event that is inexplicably wonderful ('that was a magical first date'), occult forms of spiritual or medical practice, and even forms of entertainment in which the customer is paying to be tricked.

Attempting to define the wide semantic field for 'magic' has its challenges. Most difficult is the topic of cultural relativism, that practices that might be ordinary in one place or time carry qualities of 'magic' in another. The following discussion is meant to establish a basic understanding of magic specific to Dante's European culture and to modern astrological practice.

The logic and boundaries of what we call 'magic' overlap with divination. Divination and magic both utilize hidden or occult principles:

if *everybody* can access certain knowledge, or perform a particular action for its desired effect, this cannot be considered divinatory or magical. Just as divination requires a diviner who has special abilities, magic requires a magician or *magus*. Like diviners, people who practice magic are generally considered outsiders, seen as having special abilities that set them apart from others. The fundamental difference between divination and magic is that the former seeks knowledge and the latter seeks to change outside circumstances.

Magic lies somewhere between what we call religion and what we call science, yet in practice there is overlap between them. (This is also said about astrology.) In order to highlight distinctions between magic and both religion and science, I need to be somewhat restrictive in how I define magic.

I exclude from the concept of magic conventional religious rites such as sacrifices and offerings to the ancient gods or the Christian ceremony of the Eucharist wherein (in the Catholic doctrine) a priest transforms bread and wine into the body and blood of Christ. These practices and practitioners are within the mainstreams of their respective cultures.

I also exclude from magic individual ritual practices that are *solely* for spiritual development and transformation. In late antiquity and in the Renaissance these activities were practiced among those of the cultural elite and are usually named *theurgy* ('God-working') whose motive was uniting the practitioner with divinity. Like magic, theurgical practice may also use charms, rituals, and invocations but its purpose is primarily to change the practitioner.

Clearly it is possible to do theurgical practice and magical practice at the same time and this is particularly the case with alchemy. Spanning from the medieval era into the modern era, it is not always clear whether alchemy transformed the being of the practitioner or the substances in the outer world; if the former it is theurgical, and if the latter it is magical.*

Since magical practices are to bring about specific effects, what is

---

* From India, theurigical practice was called *sadhana*, from a word that means 'accomplishment'. Buddhist tantra distinguishes two kinds of accomplishments or *siddhis*: 'absolute *siddhi*' is spiritual enlightenment and 'relative *siddhi*' is the ability to bring about various effects upon ones world. The latter would be considered magical.

the boundary between healing by magic and by science? Perhaps this question is as old as Asclepius and Hippocrates who respectively represent magical and scientific healing traditions within ancient Greek culture. Healing practices that involve praying to deities (or invoking planets) are more on the side of magic, for they employ the healer's personal qualities to bring about otherworldly intervention for the purpose of healing. On the other hand, medical techniques could be practiced by anybody with the requisite education and experience. (Today we have an analogous situation with people who are called 'medical intuitives', whose interpretative work is much closer to Asklepian divination than the more conventional Hippocratic science.)

There are different perspectives on the relationship between magical practice and science. Lynn Thorndike's monumental *History of Magic and Experimental Science* (1923-1958) finds the boundary between magical and scientific investigation porous and conjectures that magical practice provided much of the impetus toward the empirical investigation of the world that has become our tradition of science.

I take a position closer to R. Kieckefer (1994) according to whom medieval magical practices were based on principles that were not scientific (or pseudo-scientific), nor were they irrational, but contained a rationality of their own. This rationality may have been unconventional but was nonetheless consistent and provided validity to its own activities.

Let's begin with the most popularized form of magic. Some of what we call magic, and especially that which is found in literature from Merlin to *MacBeth* to Harry Potter, is 'ceremonial magic'. Ceremonial magic uses rites that may include ritual gestures, substances, and incantations to invoke unseen forces or beings.

Ancient ceremonial practice often called upon *daimones* who were lesser deities; they could be associated with the planets, with particular places, or even with abstractions like love or war. You would do so to attain worldly advantage: to subdue your opponents, gain favor with a desired person, or to gain power or to stay healthy and be protected from harm. One may use ceremonial magic to create a talisman or image or to empower a gem to assist you in your daily life. In the medieval world one also invokes invisible conscious entities to help create the specific effects sought for. The beings invoked may be either good or evil.

It is not a large jump from '*daimones*' to *demons*, powerful evil spirits who try to tempt and trick people. This we call demonic magic and in the eyes of some, *all* ceremonial magic is demonic magic. Summoning evil spirits, even Lucifer himself, brings magic into the realm of 'sorcery'. Although they are not depicted as practicing ceremonial magic, the "miserable ones" that the poet refers to at the end of *Inferno* 20 are an unfortunate foreshadowing of the persecutions of witches centuries later – those targeted tended to be lower-class women.

Reflecting the concepts of their times, Dante's major philosophical sources (including Albert the Great and Thomas Aquinas) accepted as real those evil beings one could invoke through ceremonial magic.[13] Aquinas warned that astrologers were vulnerable to temptation by evil spirits. In the background was a view in which hidden forces for good and evil battled for the souls of humanity.

This was not Dante's belief. To the poet of The *Divine Comedy*, the notion that the world is inhabited by powerful evil beings was foreign and even unchristian. Dante is consistent with the view from Neoplatonic and Christian philosophy that Being = Good and that God is Absolute Being, therefore evil can only be a *privation* of being. In the *Divine Comedy*, evil may be pervasive and seductive but is fundamentally impotent. One needs look no further than the *Divine Comedy*'s vacuous devils and Lucifer, frozen silent and powerless in Hell.*

Another species of magic that is called 'natural magic' is more positively depicted. It does not require invoking beings but instead

---

* At the bottom of Hell Lucifer is encased in ice, senseless and immobile, the furthest from God and the Heavens, a symbol of absolute negation. The devils of the *Divine Comedy* have but minor roles as tormentors of the condemned and guardians of the various areas of hell. Twice in the poem a devil comes to claim the soul of a person who had recently died: a "black Cherubim" claimed Guido da Montefeltro in *Inferno* 27 – the devil got him – and that of son Buonconte Montefeltro in *Purgatorio* 5 – the devil lost him. In *Inferno* 33, Dante encounters the soul of the treacherous Alberigo encased in Cocytus' ice but in 1300 he hadn't been dead yet – his soul had gone into the ice and his body above was inhabited by a devil (*Inferno* 33:121-135). Nowhere in Dante do devils influence the living; Alberigo's soul had already died when he mortally sinned, we could say the sin itself had existentially killed him. Conjuring evil spirits to do harm is metaphysically impossible and antithetical to the spirit of the *Divine Comedy*.

invokes occult forces that are already in nature. The herbs and images of the "wretched ones" from *Inferno* 20 are probably substances in natural magic. Both Albert and Thomas Aquinas looked upon practices of natural magic with greater favor, as long as they did not evoke spirits as does ceremonial magic. In practice, natural magical procedures and remedies could be difficult to distinguish from conventional healing practices and medicines.

How was natural magic considered to work? In ancient times and in the Renaissance, natural magic was accounted for by the concept of world spirit or *pneuma* that invisibly held the world together. Today we might call this 'subtle energy' or borrow from the Chinese the concept of *ch'i*. In this way entities physically distant from one another can operate together. These practices may be used for worldly ends or as spiritual practice or in combination.[14]

How do these occult forces bind the universe together? They could do so based on *similarity*, by which things which resemble each other may have an effect on each other. Natural magical practice based on this is usually called *sympathetic magic*. The most primitive level of sympathetic magic might be fashioning an effigy that looks like a particular person; the magician would work with this object in a prescribed ritualistic way to cause an effect – sometimes an evil effect – on the person whose image it depicts. One may also use an object once owned by a person to influence that person. One could fashion an object with sympathetic power, e.g. by making a potion with herbs governed by Venus to attract somebody to you: one would use literally an 'aphrodisiac'.

The Neoplatonic vision of the universe was also used to account for natural magical practice. From the rather worldly *Picatrix* and later from the more devotional and cosmological *Corpus Hermeticum* and the more theurigical Kaballah, an item of nature could become empowered to be made more spiritual as a step up the ladder of creation. From these traditions it is possible that matter could become en-souled, and, taken to its limit, the human soul can return to divinity.

Here's how this could happen in ordinary life. For help with an endeavor we might call mercurial, one might contact 'Mercury' by performing a rite on Wednesday at sunrise (day and hour of Mercury), or when the planet itself would become visible on the horizon, or attired in clothes and colors associated with Mercury or with a statue of the ancient deity. A particular gem or talisman might invoke the presence of Mercury.

The person may invoke energies embodied in the planet and the planet's attributes and this follows the tenor of modern astrology. Less abstract was the Renaissance sage Marsilio Ficino who posited planetary *daimones* that were not angelic in a Christian sense but instruments of spirit or *pneuma* in a more Neoplatonic style. Ficino advocated invoking their energies to aid physical or psychological health. Others might be more ambitious, attempting through magical practice to unify with cosmic consciousness or divine nature through the intermediary of 'Mercury'.

If 'Mercury' is a conscious entity that is associated with the planet, this may be close to demonic magic and could be condemned as idolatrous or even devil-worship in medieval Europe. (Ficino's students and successors were less inhibited about this kind of magic than their more cautious master.) In the *Divine Comedy*, planetary *daimones* are not demons but the classes of angels; however, they are not worshipped or invoked but are the bureaucracy of providence.

To what extent is modern astrological practice magical? Only a few modern astrologers practice ceremonial magic as part of their work; planets are generally not designated as conscious entities to be invoked but more like 'archetypal energies' to be embodied. Yet as Nick Campion (2009) asserts, "If magic is the deliberate attempt to change the future then all astrology which moves beyond a simple prediction into any sort of action is magical."[15]

Electional astrology has kinship with magical practice as horary astrology does with divination. Electional astrology is used to find the most promising time for planned activity that might be buying a house, having a promotion interview or starting a new job or beginning a wedding or a retreat.

When astrologers thus try to synchronize a planned activity with the configurations of the heavens, are they not practicing a form of sympathetic magic? A modern electional astrologer does not invoke planetary deities but seeks a resemblance between the activity and the

---

* In traditional Indian astrology or *Jyotish* there is a clear understanding that planets and gods are indistinguishable, so that the practitioner consciously invokes a deity along with a planet.

heavens that would correspond to that activity being successful.* Some modern astrologers design rituals to accompany astrological elections and thereby bring elements of ceremonial magic into their work. I would consider modern electional astrology a form of natural magic.

Thorndike (1929) gives us a story about Guido Bonatti that has often been cited. When working for Guido de Montefeltro and his city (Forli) was under siege, the political leader and his astrologer summoned the townspeople together. Allegedly based on the changing configurations of heaven, the told the townspeople to stage a mock withdrawal from their city but return later when the invaders were celebrating their victory inside the city. This stratagem worked.[16]

If we look at the consulting work of modern astrologers there are other features that may be a weak form of natural magic, attempting to change the future by offering to a client a better way to encounter it. A timid client has a dignified angular Mars: the astrologer is likely to suggest methods of forceful activity and to explore his or her experiences with anger. An overweight client has transiting Saturn on his or her Ascendant and is thinking about going on a diet; this person's astrologer is very likely to commend such an endeavor as long as the client does not think of it as a condition of oppression to be endured. One could say that these are forms of sympathetic magic that bring planet and activity together although tamely.

More consciously magical are astrologers who recommend that their clients use certain talismans or wear certain kinds of clothing or gems or listen to specific kinds of music: they are intentionally using features of natural magic in their daily lives.

Whereas diviners might present themselves as all-knowing for their access to occult sources of knowledge, magicians may be cast as having 'magical powers' because of their skill in utilizing occult sources of power. In medieval times and today, people who practice magic may utilize a theatricality and personal grandiosity that can result in deception. Like diviners, Dante would also considered *magi* vulnerable to bullshit.

Diviners and Magicians: The Bottom Line

We need to dive further into the *Malebolge* to find the trajectory of evil from the diviners and magicians into evil's greater abysses. Dante's placement of diviners and magicians in Hell will become even clearer.

Canto 20's diviners are not in Hell for having made erroneous predictions. Asdente was famously accurate in his work. Amphiaraus' dire predictions were correct – unfortunately for him. One cannot tell about Euryplyus since the source is on the other side of trustworthy. I am not qualified to judge the accuracy of Tiresias' judgment about which gender experiences greater sexual pleasure.

To their fiercest modern critics, divination and magic are considered self-indulgent and exploitative of gullible people, not as greatly evil. From Canto 20 all we've established is a pretense of knowledge or power and an activity of bullshitting. As we go further down we find something more fundamental to an overall portrait of evil that applies to the diviners and magicians.

In Dante's conception, the diviners and magicians share one key aspect with those further below: they leapt over the boundaries of what we, as limited beings in this life, could know and could do. Following his culture, Dante articulated that we all have our proper places and that attempting to go beyond them could be disruptive of the social and natural order. Not until the 'age of exploration' and early Italian Renaissance was this basic assumption broken down.

We now stop at the eighth *bolgia* and Cantos 26 and 27 that are devoted to what are usually called the "Evil Counselors". They intentionally used their cleverness to 'con' others into actions that caused harm to them or others. They are eternally trapped in the kind of fire that once consumed their hearts and prompted their evil activity.

Unlike the diviners and magicians above who are silent, in Cantos 26 and 27 we hear directly from two of the *Inferno*'s most unforgettable characters. Ulysses of the Trojan Horse and the Italian strategist Guido da Montefeltro have major speaking roles in the *Inferno*.

Ulysses and his wartime companion Diomedes are encased in fire together. Virgil, not Dante, is the interlocutor for the celebrated meeting with the shade of Ulysses in Canto 26. Virgil asks both about the manner of their deaths and hears from Ulysses about his final voyage. This is one of the more memorable and famous moments of the *Inferno*, taking us beyond this *bolgia* toward a general depiction of the poet's conception of evil.

Speaking with effort from a tongue of flame, Ulysses tells that even when finally reunited with his home and family he could not stay there.

His identity as husband to his wife, son to his father and father to his son were insufficient for him – he wanted adventure, the pursuit of even more experience and knowledge. Ulysses assembled his remaining crew and they headed east and finally passed through the Pillars of Hercules that, to the medieval mind, was a visual sign to go no further. In a short rousing speech to his crew he played on their pride, inspiring them to go with him further into the unknown.

They headed south on their *folle volo*, their mad voyage, for five times the Moon would be rekindled – five New Moons. Then in the distance they saw a mountain that seemed higher than any before seen. The crew rejoiced but a storm arose from the land and the ship was immersed in a whirlpool, the ocean closed up over them and they were lost. The mountain was the mountain of Purgatory.

This proud epic character's tale casts a shadow over the poem and stands as an example of willful pride taking one beyond the natural conditions of this God-created world. Looking back to the diviners and magicians, we see that their activity also stretched their knowledge and ability beyond what Dante's time considered to be rightfully theirs – beyond nature as ordained by providence.

> **Ulysses and the Astrologers**
>
> Cultural acceptance of astrology and social acceptance of astrologers are issues of importance – and confusion – to those who practice the art of astrology. Many of us have seen astrology ridiculed by the media and our work discounted by those who we think should know better. We have also seen that we astrologers provide an important service to those who seek us out and that their lives are better for having us in them. We sense that our work, as misunderstood as it is, does serve the larger culture.
>
> Considering that diviners and magicians were traditionally given outsider status, the current isolation of astrologers and their art from social conventionality should be no surprise. It creates much personal and collective confusion for astrologers and I have written about this previously.[17] Is this outsider status to be decried or to be embraced? The figure of Ulysses may carry a lesson for us.

> Dante's Ulysses is one who has deliberately cut himself from social bonds to pursue greater knowledge and activity and is thus condemned by the medieval poet. Dante's version of Ulysses risked social isolation and his salvation for his personal pursuits that, however noble they may seem, ultimately would not serve anybody but himself. The poet has reduced the grandeur of the epic hero to sterile grandiosity.
>
> There are alternatives that we find in subsequent depictions of Ulysses. Alfred Lord Tennyson's well-known poem 'Ulysses' uses Dante's story and creates from it a more positive version of the character, stressing his defiant heroism in the face of the burden of social convention and advancing age. Yet a closer reading of Tennyson's poem finds that it also sees Ulysses as problematic.
>
> A better alternative comes from the twentieth century in the character of Leopold Bloom from the Ulysses of James Joyce. The main character, also patterned after the Homeric hero, does not deliberately isolate himself from mainstream society; as a Jew in early twentieth century Dublin, he is already isolated. Yet Bloom participates actively in his city; he is helpful to many people who look down on him and is continuously seeking intelligent connection with others. Joyce's character with his many flaws is the wisest and most creative person we meet on that June day in Dublin that Joyce depicts.
>
> Although Dante condemns Ulysses as an outsider and Tennyson accentuates its heroism, Joyce's Ulysses – an outsider without resentment – is perhaps a more useful model for today's diviners and magicians and astrologers.

If Ulysses is like the proud Farinata of *Inferno* 10, Guido da Montefeltro is more like Farinata's tomb-mate, the agitated and timorous Calvacanti. Montefeltro displays the pathos of the conman who gets conned himself. Montefeltro was famous as a military and political strategist for the side of the Ghibellines (and for his astrologer Guido Bonatti). Later in life he made his peace with the Church, retired to become a Franciscan monk, and appeared to have repented his previous evil ways. Soon, however,

Pope Boniface visited his monastery wanting his advice: the Pope desired to defeat a city (modern Palestrina, near Rome) and subdue its ruling family against whom the Pope had a grudge. After the Pope insisted that he could absolve Montefelto of any sins incurred by his activity for him, the old counselor gave the Pope this immortal piece of evil advice:

"*Lunga promessa con l'attender corto*"

"A long promise and a short keeping of it." (*Inferno* 27:110)

Boniface, duly following this advice, sent out an offer of amnesty to the occupiers of Palestrina. Once it was accepted his troops entered and destroyed the city.

Upon Montefeltro's death Francis of Assisi came for him but so did a "black cherubim". This man, this devil claimed, had given fraudulent counsel (*'l consiglio frodolente*). Nor had he sufficiently repented, for how could he have repented his sins and not have repented them at the same time? The devil took Montefeltro down to Hell, joking that perhaps the condemned man did not know that the devil himself was a logician.

As a shrewd strategist, Montefeltro had conned many a military and political foe but also toward the end of his life had attempted to con a naïve public through his retirement to a monastery and even God through his thin repentance. But his sin of conmanship was turned on him: he had been taken in by Boniface's promises.

Diviners are not down so far in Hell as these two famous *consiglieri*, for the judgments and activities of diviners are not malevolent in intent. The twisted inmates of the Fourth *bolgia* merely wanted to impress their patrons and make a good name for themselves. Down further we have gone from exploitation to malice.

We have one more place to go to in Hell and this brings us to the place of Nature – human and celestial – in the *Divine Comedy* and its relationship to the poem's astrology.

Sickened Nature

Undergirding the *Divine Comedy*'s conceptualization is an admiration of nature – cosmic and terrestrial, physical and metaphysical. This is illustrated vividly further down in Hell. We leave the evil counselors, we skip the sowers of discord, and we arrive at the lowest of the *Malebolge* and come to the middle of Canto 29. Here we find one of the most pathetic scenes in the *Inferno*, the Hell of the "falsifiers".

The poet evokes scenes of a hospital during an outbreak of malaria but much worse – diseased bodies are strewn about next to and on top of one another, the entire scene emitting a foul stench. Here, the poet tells us, *infallibil giustizia/punisce i falsador*: [God's] infallible justice/punishes the falsifiers. We will meet several people and three different classes of "falsifiers" in Canto 29 and 30, but our interest here is in the first group.

Among the many diseased souls Dante and Virgil first happen onto two leaning against each other whose scaly skin, itching intensely, causes them to scratch at their skin violently. The first soul does not give his name, although commentators recognize him as Griffilino from Arezzo; he was burned as a heretic in 1272 when Dante was six or seven.

But Griffolino is in Hell for his practice of alchemy. His companion now speaks, identifying himself as Capocchio, who had also falsified metals through alchemy: in the final lines he asks Dante to remember him *com'io fui di natura buona scimia*, "how good an ape I was of nature". (The Italian *scimia* means 'monkey' with the same range of meanings as our English 'ape'.)*

In the *Divine Comedy* alchemists do not make noble metals from base metals but rather produce metals that give the *appearance* of being noble but are not. Alchemy is cast not as transmuting but counterfeiting; it is not magical but a method of fabrication. (This view also appears in Chaucer's *Canterbury Tales*.)

Following the poet's structure of Hell, the vilest form of "simple fraud" is that of falsifying – metals like our alchemists made, impersonating others, or what we would call perjured testimony. By falsifying the truth

---

* The conversation of Griffolino and Capocchio with Dante is remarkable for its charm and light humor within an utterly bleak environment. Griffolino talks about how he joked that he could take himself into the air and how this proved to be his undoing when he could not teach this skill to a gullible nobleman. Both men ridiculed the Sienese and their extravagant ways. Even in the last line Capocchio alludes to his reputation during his lifetime as an expert mimic. Neither one displays ill-humor at their eternal fates. Their lighthearted conversation is short-lived, however; in the next canto the rabid impersonator Gianni Schicchi attacks Capocchio.

they have also degraded reality, the condition of things as they are; their eternal fates are to be a body – a human body its natural capacities for life, health, and activity – in the most degraded and diseased forms the poet can imagine.

In Hell, the diviners and magicians had twisted and distorted nature to make a good impression of themselves on others – and in *Inferno* 20 they are therefore physically twisted and distorted. The falsifiers of *Inferno* 29 and 30 had subverted nature and its divine essence; in Hell, therefore, they themselves have become the degraded Nature.

Underlying this condemnation of the falsifiers is the poet's assumption about the world – about worldly reality – that is both metaphysical and theological. This world is not illusory nor is it inferior, but quite real and imbued with divinely-rendered positive qualities. Nature itself, hierarchically arranged, is sacred, to the extent that it receives God's glory. We are brought back to the opening lines of the *Paradiso*, that God's glory pervades all of creation; the entire universe reflects divinity but differently in different parts.

The poet uses a concept of nature that includes Heaven and Earth within one cosmological scheme. Therefore reading the stars – *astrology* – is reading nature. In my view, there is nothing fundamentally incompatible between understanding the theory of astrological interpretation that is based on divination alongside a cosmological account of astrology's content. Ultimately such a mixed approach may be required.* We move toward Dante's negative account of astrology as divination to his positive account of astrology as nature.

---

* Geoffrey Cornelius (2003) draws many distinctions between divinatory and natural astrology. Having mentioned differences between logical exclusivity in modern rational thinking and the inclusiveness of the symbolic imagination he states, "…it would be self-defeating for the divinatory understanding of astrology to deny the validity of an objective and scientific natural astrology. The divinatory approach, remember, is sustained in multiple interpretations but this does not work in reverse. Modern scientific and rationalistic paradigms of astrology cannot handle levels [e.g. literal and symbolic] and they disallow any suggestion of astrology being founded in a divinatory or even a genuinely symbolic approach." (p.252) Clearly there are opportunities for many different approaches to astrology.

Human Nature, Freedom, and Vocation

Our examination begins with human nature, what we call 'psychology', the study of the soul. Aristotle's *De Anima* was the foundational text for medieval discussions of the soul, and Dante would have been very familiar with it. According to Aristotle, soul is the actualization of a body that is capable of being alive, and therefore soul and body are inextricably fused in this life. Bound up with the body as its formal principle, the soul is organized in different ways. In its lowest embodiment, soul accounts for life and growth; it governs bodily movement and sensation; in its highest manifestation, the human soul reasons and makes choices and appears to operate incorporeally.

Medieval philosophy, interested in matters of redemption and eternal life, added to Aristotle a stronger distinction between a body/soul combination that is subject to death and an immortal soul that outlasts the body's death. It is the immortal soul that inclines us toward God in this life and may experience God directly in the afterlife.

What is the relationship between the different concepts of soul, the human faculty of will, the fact of human freedom, and the role of the stars and planets? These are important questions for astrologers today as they were in Dante's time.

We will begin to answer this by looking at *Purgatorio* 16 and Marco the Lombard's discussion of astral causation and free will. In the following cantos Virgil adds a discussion of love and will that helps clarify what is meant by both. We move ahead to *Purgatorio* 25, where Statius expounds on the origins of our individual "lower" and "higher" faculties in the stars and in God respectively; his subject is the body and soul before and after one's lifetime. Finally in *Paradiso* 8 Charles Martel discusses the role of "circling nature" and our lives' vocations.

Through the Fog Darkly

We begin with *Purgatorio* 16, the 50th canto of the poem's 100 cantos. At the beginning of this canto, Dante and Virgil have entered the black smoke of that part of Purgatory that purifies anger; Dante must hold onto Virgil like a blind person being guided through an unfamiliar area. Around them they hear souls together singing *Agnus Dei* 'Lamb of God'. One of the souls approaches the two visitors, asking them who they are.

The soul is Marco the Lombard, who was a courtier and person of some political importance in the generation before Dante. He is a somewhat difficult character whose distain for the increasingly corrupt ways of the world anticipates the equally critical but more appealing Cacciaguida on the sphere of Mars in Heaven. Dante gives one of the more important discussions in the poem to a minor historical character and one of the many unfinished redemptive projects the poet places on the terraces of Purgatory.

The pilgrim asks Marco to explain the cause of all the wickedness of the world, for some put the blame on heaven and some on earth (16:61-63). Addressing only the former misconception, Marco sighs a heavy "uhi!" (This must be Italian for "oy veh".) The world is blind, he exclaims, and so must be his questioner. According to Marco, everybody alive blames Heaven (the stars and planets) for their problems, thinking that Heaven makes everything happen by necessity. If that were so, Marco exclaims, there would be no justice, no consequent joy for goodness and misery for evil.

Marco is saying nothing special: if the good or evil we do is a result of stellar necessity then there would be no point in praise or blame. This reasoning can also extend to those who insist that their genetic inheritance, brain chemistry, dysfunctional family background, or ethnic group's previous history of oppression excuses their bad behavior. Few social thinkers or astrologers – medieval or modern – would assert otherwise.

At the same time Marco concedes a causal relationship between the Heavens and our "lower" physical or instinctual natures, as opposed to the rational soul that is free from stellar causation.

"Lo cielo i vostri movimenti inizia;
non dico tutti, ma, posto ch'i' 'l dica,
lume v'è dato a bene e a malizia,
e libero voler...."

"The heavens initiate your movements,
not all of them, but if I did,
you still have light to distinguish between good and evil
and a free will..."
(Purgatorio 16:73-75)

The heavens begin the movements of our "lower" faculties of soul which accounts for our basic processes of living and our instinctual emotional life. In our liberty, Marco states, we are subject to a greater power (*maggior forza*) and a better nature (*miglior natura*), and stars and planets have no say in the matter. The greater power is God; the greater nature is our human activity of intellect. Humans as rational animals share intellect with the incorporeal angels but share physical and instinctual life with animals. What makes us human is our free will, our ability to choose alternatives.

If we can withstand our first conflicts with the fixed heavens (i.e. childhood and adolescence) then, with proper preparation, we can prevail over our many inclinations. At the beginning of our lives, Marco says, our emotions change quickly and we're automatically drawn toward what delights us. Without restraint we are typically ensnared and we follow our impulses naively.

Marco tells that our free will can become stronger or weaker based on social and cultural influences. Our ability to choose wisely between alternatives must be nurtured and maintained by a society with good laws and good individuals to exemplify and enforce them. It is from a lack of good leadership, Marco tells Dante, that there is so much evil in the world. Having finished, Marco then goes back into the darkness and Dante and Virgil move on.

The depiction of 'free will' in *Purgatorio* 16 is rather general and serves to assert human responsibility and not allow astral or any other causation to excuse bad behavior. Marco the Lombard asserts that free will – as yet undefined – subjects us to a greater power than the stars. The following two cantos that feature Virgil add to this by bringing in the topic of love and focusing on the individual.

Love and Will

In *Purgatorio* 17 Dante and Virgil have left the smoky realm of the angry and have begun to move toward the next ledge of Purgatory's Mountain. Night has descended and pilgrim and guide must stop their climb and rest. With some time on their hands, Virgil begins to discourse on the nature of love and will.

Virgil begins by stating that neither God nor any of his creation is without love and therefore love is natural and inherently positive in us.

When organized correctly and pursued well (by our rational faculties), love does not commit error. We miss the mark through three kinds of error that are purified on Purgatory. First, there is love that is tainted, and purifying this fault is accomplished on the ledges for the proud, the envious, and the angry. Those whose love falls short are purified here on the ledge for the lazy. Where love is excessive or unregulated, people must purify tendencies toward avarice, gluttony, and lust, and this occurs on the terraces above. We all have our various inclinations that may manifest as our burdens in Purgatory.

(There is an interesting possibility here for astrologers. The fact that we have faults that will someday require time in Purgatory is not astrologically determined, but our inclinations toward them – that would manifest among the various Seven Cardinal Sins – may be astrologically signified. These inclinations may come along with our basic character that can be astrologically accounted for.)

At the beginning of the next canto, Dante asks Virgil about the nature of this love that is the root of both good and evil activity. Virgil replies that from the start we naturally form objects in our minds and they can become what we love, what captures our soul. The resulting desire may turn into joy when fulfilled and this is natural and inherently good – but not every outcome is good (*Purgatorio* 18:37-39).

Why then, the pilgrim continues, do we attach praise and blame to activities based on love that is inherently good? Virgil replies that we have general objects of desire based on our conditions as corporeal human beings. (He is unclear to their origin, although they would be thought of as divinely created.) Praise and blame are based upon our having free human will, here defined as the activity of the rational soul to which the other appetites must conform. This allows us to choose between goods.

Although our basic desires arise in us from necessity, from the 'way we're built', we might say, we also have the ability to manage them. The great moral philosophers of antiquity, Virgil says, had recognized this power that we all have. Thereby we give praise and blame to ourselves and others for its use or lack of use; although our loves come to us by the necessity of our nature, the ability to manage how we use that love is ours.

Love and Appetite

Here is Thomas of Aquinas' definition of human will.

"The will is a rational appetite. Now every appetite is only of something good. The reason for this is that the appetite is nothing else than an inclination of a person desirous of a thing towards that thing. Now every inclination is to something like and suitable to the thing inclined. Since, therefore, everything, inasmuch as it is being and substance, is a good, it must needs be that every inclination is to something good. And hence it is that the Philosopher says (Ethic. I, 1) that 'the good is that which all desire'."

Summa Theologica II, Part One, q.8

A good is defined simply as any object of appetite. According to the medieval philosopher, all the goods of this world – wealth, physical pleasure, power, or even philosophical understanding – are limited. The greatest good or *summum bonum*, according to Thomas and his contemporaries, is for God Himself and this fulfillment is our greatest joy. However, full attainment of this is not possible in this life.

As stated above, will is defined as the appetite of the intellect that, under the sway of general ends, selects specific goals and the means toward them. From our sensitive and intellectual appetites there is a broad range of goods we can pursue. According to a doctrine that also finds support in the writings of Thomas of Aquinas, stellar causes cannot impact our choices from intellect.

You may notice that I substituted 'appetite' for 'love' to depict the traditional teaching. Usually moderns think of appetite and love very differently, appetite being largely stimulated from the outside and love more an internalized response, yet the medieval view largely thinks of love as quality of appetite.

By referring to love instead of appetite, Dante hints at the final vision of the poem, for at its end it is love that brings the cosmos and person together within one process. To the medieval mind 'love' was as much a matter of theology as psychology, for this word best described the relationship between God and

> humanity and is the third and greatest of the three theological virtues. Aristotle's final book of the *Metaphysics* describes the stars and planets in relationship with God as Prime Mover as an activity of love. In Dante's view our worldly romantic love is a lower-level (but readily available) copy of the most basic relationship between humans and God that is also mediated and expressed by the stars and planets and their angelic intelligences.
>
> Bringing together the discussions of Marco and Virgil in these cantos of the *Purgatorio*, the poet tells us that our inclinations are innately good and are set in motion by the planets and stars. Our will or intellectual faculty organizes what we want and how to go about getting what we want, and this is free from stellar causation.

Pre-life and Post-life

Let's look further at issues of bodily form and the intellectual soul through the prism of 'natural philosophy' or what we would call 'science', influenced by the biology of Aristotle and modified by Christian doctrine. We will look at pre-birth and post-mortem body/mind relationship, the means of stellar causation, and the hand of God.

Purgatorio 25 takes us to the upper terraces of Purgatory. Dante, Statius, and Virgil are climbing from the terrace of the gluttons toward the lustful. The pilgrim asks how souls in the afterlife can appear to suffer physically when they do not have physical bodies. How can former gluttons be hungry and thin when nobody needs to eat or drink in the afterlife?

Virgil replies by using general analogies but does not give a real answer, reminding me of a teacher trying to sound like he or she knows the answer to a question that was not anticipated. Virgil then asks Statius to respond. This shift of teachers is necessary because the topic becomes the relationship between body and soul and this is where natural philosophy (Virgil) leaves off and theology (Statius) takes over (*Purgatorio* 25:31-108).

Statius begins by describing how a person's bodily nature – or generic self – originates. "Perfected blood" descends from the heart to the male genitals, and then flows onto the female's blood contained in its natural vessel.* A fetus coagulates and begins to grow; the active power (*la virtute attiva*) first becomes a soul like a plant, then it takes a transitional form and seems like a sea sponge, and finally the fetus assumes an 'animal' soul with the shaping of its appropriate organs. Note the gradual development from vegetative to sensitive soul, not a replacement of one with the other; this view is associated not with Aquinas but his teacher Albertus Magnus.[18]

Statius then provides the Christian part of the story. Once the fashioning of the brain has been completed, God (*lo Motor primo*) rejoicing over Nature's art, breathes a new spirit (*e spira / spirito novo*), that combines with the active principle of the creature into a soul that animates a particular human being.

The artistry by Nature is from the heavenly bodies and the angelic intelligences that move them, but it is the First Mover who gives the creature its rational soul that creates one complete person. This reminds me of the studio of a Renaissance painter where the students create the landscape and rooms but the great artist himself fashions the bodies and faces of the central characters and thus gives the painting its vital nature. (The paint and canvas would be the material substratum of a human life.) The totality of who we are is from the 'Studio of God', the work executed by His students and the final figure painted in by the Maestro Himself.

Statius' last point – that the soul is not divided into the parts but is a particular unity – emphasizes that a person is *one* substance and not the sum of its faculties. The "lower" nature fashioned by the stars and the "higher" nature placed by the Artist are not necessarily at war with each other but can act together. If this is not what we see in our lives, the fault lies with ourselves, not with the stars or God. (Reintegrating these natures is the penitential work of Purgatory and restores one to an original innocence symbolized by the Earthly Paradise.)

So far what appears is a dualism between our physical/emotional nature and our intellectual nature, the latter having priority by virtue of being created directly by God. However, we must remember that Dante

---

* This assumes the ancient and medieval doctrine that the active and formal principle is male and the receiving or material principle is female.

> **Death and the Body**
> What happens to body and soul when we die? This is the thrust of the pilgrim's original question. At death, Statius concludes, the soul leaves its human flesh with its human and divine powers. The intellectual soul's powers of memory, understanding, and will are now greater than before. Like the air taking on colors to form a rainbow, the air surrounding the deceased soul (who arrives at one shore or another) takes on the form of the soul and becomes the soul's 'body' that has sensations, emotions, and is visible to others. This is the shade that has physical sufferings and other responses in the afterlife. The soul is the form that fashions the body according to its nature (*Purgatorio* 25: 79-108).

is still in Purgatory; these viewpoints must be considered provisional in light of knowledge to be gained above in Paradise.

Our Calling and the Stars

We now go to *Paradiso* 8. Dante and Beatrice have arrived on the Sphere of Venus. Recall that this canto opens by naming Venus as the planet once thought to rain down mad beams of love, an error that caused ancient people to pray to and make sacrifices to the goddess (*Paradiso* 8:1-6).

The pilgrim meets Charles Martel, the young King of Bohemia who had once visited Florence and befriended Dante. Recall that Martel had died young; his brother succeeded him and contributed to the political chaos of Dante's Italy. Dante asks his friend, *com' esser può di dolce seme amaro*, how from sweet seed do we get bitter fruit? (Canto 8:93) Martel's response, in the style of a philosophic dialogue with Dante, forms the remainder of Canto 8.

God (or the Good, *lo ben*), causes these wheels of Heaven, the instruments of God's providence, to revolve. From the divine mind all beings and their well-being are foreseen and have their actualization. Their origins are perfect because of the perfection of the divine maker and the angelic realms that move Heaven's spheres – but the result down here is not necessarily perfect.

Martel continues: since human beings are social creatures and society requires a diversity of callings or functions (*offici*) to flourish, the stars create different effects on Earth that are the inclinations and callings of different people. One may be born to be a politician, another to be a military leader, or a priest, or an inventor. Heaven's intention, not our families of origin, gives rise to our callings in life and the gifts that allow us to fulfill them.

> "*La circular natura, ch' è suggello*
> *a la cera mortal, fa ben sua arte,*
> *ma non distingue l'un da l'altro ostello.*"

> "Circling nature, stamping its seal
> on mortal wax, using her good art
> does not distinguish between families." (*Paradiso* 8:127-129)

The stars have endowed us well with our purposes in society; it cannot be otherwise, for that would imply that Heaven's products are inherently defective. But like seed attempting to grow in unsuitable soil, what is designed by Heaven can develop badly if forced into a development down here that is contrary to its purpose.

If the world paid more attention to the foundation laid by nature and built upon that, Charles Martel says, people could turn out differently and better. By forcing somebody into an unsuitable mold we depart from Heaven's purposes. This, he implies, accounts for the differences in quality between people, even from the same family.

How do we attend to what the Heavens have fashioned? We can look at the natural inclinations of people; perhaps we can also look at their astrological charts. Clearly the poet does not exclude such a possibility. In the astrology of Dante's time one could certainly seek information about vocation from a natal chart, as one might also find Dante's poetic gifts that have come from the stars.

Does the account of *Paradiso* 8 square with Marco the Lombard who insists that only our lower natures are subject to the heavens? Do these purportedly lower natures play a role determining our gifts and our places in society? Paradise has modified what was presented in Purgatory, for Charles Martel has expanded the realm of human nature that derives from the stars and planets.

We can go further. Are there corporeal manifestations of our individual natures and designated vocations? We need to consider the strong influence of body type and physical (or physiological) features on our individual natures and outcomes. The four temperaments were psychophysical groupings within ancient and medieval traditions: this classification divides people into the slim and dour but contemplative melancholic, the more fleshy and energetic sanguine person, the corpulent and introverted phlegmatic, and the more muscular and volatile choleric. Vocational and marriage preferences may follow closely upon these psychophysical features: cholerics give rise to athletes and melancholics to scholars and attractive and sociable sanguine types will seek the company of others like them. Modern astrologers tend to use the distribution of elements in a natal chart (planets in fire, earth, air, and water signs) for some of these purposes, although their interests tend to be exclusively psychological. From *Paradiso* 8 Dante's conception of stellar causation and individual inclination fits well into an astrologer's conceptions – to the extent that both body and mind are included.

Modern astrology, more psychologically minded than its predecessors, has extended this notion of diversity to individual personality. If we ask our parents and those with whom we grew up, many of our individual qualities – including the best features of ourselves – have been present from the beginning of our lives. Reinforced and supported by good examples from our culture, we gain maturity and self-mastery through developing those habits of virtue *that are most appropriate to our individual natures*. Astrology tells us that this information about our natures is written in the astrological chart; according to the *Divine Comedy*, it is caused by the stars and planets.

Freedom, Free Will, and Astrology

The identity of free will and rational soul, as Thomas Aquinas and Dante would have it, has been subject to much scrutiny. The issue has long legs in the history of western philosophy and strongly influences how astrologers do their work today.

What is this rational soul that makes us human? If will and rational soul are the same, we exercise freedom of will when we deliberate or make conscious choices between alternatives. Clearly this capacity varies from person to person and with regard to specific situations. Although ancient and medieval traditions tend to draw a strict boundary between the rational soul and what purportedly lies below, our modern understanding is somewhat different.

To the modern mind placing 'intellectual' or 'rational' together with 'appetite' seems contradictory, for we tend to consider 'appetite' very difficult to manage rationally. We have also seen that we need to widen our concept of appetite into any object of any desire. But can desire be 'rational' or 'intellectual'?

We need to let go of the modern science fiction idea presenting 'rationality' with images of people with pointed ears or bulging foreheads. Instead we're looking at something far closer to the modern concept of 'emotional intelligence'. This is a quality of personal objectivity that includes an ability to take the perspective of others and learn from them, to note and manage one's own mind and its many movements, and to find patterns within complex situations, particularly those that are interpersonally messy. These features of us are all 'rational'. We may contrast 'intellectual appetite' not only with blind habit and impulsiveness but with indulgent sentimentalism or 'idiot compassion'.

As we all know, even in the best of circumstances the range of rational souls is rather limited. Upon examination, many of our supposedly rational judgments and choices are effects of unconscious desires and fantasies or from habitual personal and cultural tendencies. As we know ourselves more completely, we see that what we think of as freely chosen is often the result of compulsion. Paradoxically this is one of the first fruits of our applying intelligence to our lives.

Even Thomas Aquinas, Dante's source on this matter, understood this. How many of us are truly rational and, for those who are, how often? According to Thomas, it is the non-rational parts of our being that are caused by stars and planets. This is how he depicts the non-rational parts of us and the resulting causation by planets and stars.

> "The majority of men follow their passions, which are movements of the sensitive appetite, in which movements heavenly bodies can cooperate: but few are wise enough to resist these passions. Consequently astrologers are able to foretell the truth in the majority of cases, especially in a general way. But not in particular

cases; for nothing prevents man's resisting his passions by his free will. Wherefore the astrologers themselves are wont to say that 'the wise man is stronger than the stars' [Ptolemy, Centiloquium, prop. 5], forasmuch as, to wit, he conquers his passions."
Summa Theologica I, q.115, a.4, ad 3

Here is an additional concern. When we note humans in contrast with other species we note not a clear line but a continuum between instinct and intellect. We see this among ourselves and other kinds of living being.

Those of us who have pets or observe animal behavior know how different animal types have behaviors 'hardwired' in different degrees. Some dogs appear to adapt more flexibly to changing circumstances and at times even appear to deliberate. Cats have less of this quality, and the behavior of rabbits, mice and reptiles seems almost wholly instinctual and pre-programmed. Only humans seem to be able to detect and judge their emotional and instinctual responses and to reflect on them.

What does all this mean for living the best kind of human life? Consider Plato's articulation of justice in the *Republic* as the harmony between our different tendencies and desires based on the hegemony of our rational nature. Aristotle depicted 'excellence' or virtue (from the word root implying power and authority) as choosing the mean between two extremes in attitude or behavior. By using reason we can delay or moderate the gratification of the senses and, without neglecting the needs of the organism, we can aim toward higher goods. Somebody whose rational will is in command – whose soul is well integrated – will display greater flexibility and precision in both attitude and behavior. These are laudable qualities yet all are based on self-interest, enlightened or otherwise.

Onto this template Aquinas and others grafted the doctrine that the peak of human existence, our *summum bonum* or ultimate good, is the desire for God and other goods are incomplete compared to this one. To pursue and obtain one's most complete good, the gift of God's grace must be added to our natural faculties. It is the rational soul that pursues the desire for God.

Four Cardinal Virtues

We have seen the four qualities of wisdom, fortitude, justice, and temperance as stars in the dawn sky in the *Purgatorio* and as purified qualities, infused by God's grace, in Heaven. This list has its origin in Plato's *Republic*, was elaborated on by Aristotle's *Nicomachean Ethics* and was further elaborated on by Thomas Aquinas.

The word virtue is from the Latin word meaning 'man' and connotes power or mastery, as in the expression 'by virtue of…' It is an ability to act according to one's purposes, its equivalent in Aristotle is *agate* or 'excellence', and virtue, as the reader might imagine, is in contrast with dispositions and behavior resulting from our impulses and blind habits.

The word cardinal is from the Latin word for the 'hinge' of a door that allows the door to turn; other good human qualities require the cardinal virtues to function properly. Here they are:

Prudence or practical wisdom is applying right reason to an action. It is the understanding of moral responsibilities, such as loving one's neighbor as oneself, and the ability to apply one's moral responsibilities to specific situations. We might call prudence a kind of 'objectivity' toward oneself and others. (Recall that Hell's inmates have "lost the good of the intellect", focusing narrowly on oneself and one's short term gratifications or meaningless victories.)

Fortitude is the ability to work with difficulties we may encounter when it comes to doing the right thing. In particular it is the ability not to be deflected by fear or the opposite, overconfidence and rashness.

Justice brings one beyond our narrow interest in self and directs our relationships with others and our social world. Its object is what is right for oneself and others and implies an equality with others of benefits and burdens. (The levels of Hell downward from the walls of Dis are according to degrees of injustice as articulated by Aristotle.)

Temperance works with difficulties brought about by temptations toward temporary pleasures and gratifications, for it

> is easy for one's purposes and activity to be sidetracked by desires for food, drink, sex, and other fine things in life. Following Aristotle, temperance is between the extremes of greedy impulsiveness and apathy or self-denial.

Now let's apply all this to astrology. The "lower" aspects of our nature engendered by planets and stars include body type, emotional disposition, and, at least in a general way, our vocational outlook. Traditional astrology, based on sources in ancient and medieval astrology, may depict an individual's possibilities for personality, relationship, fame, finances, and even length of life.

Modern astrology tends to focus more exclusively on issues of personality, yet in practice both traditional and modern astrologers work directly with an individual's range of choices and inclinations. In the words of Charles Martel, how do we build on what heavenly nature has endowed us? Clarifying an individual's life possibilities and range of choices is what makes interpreting an astrological chart useful: it turns out that it is our 'rational soul' that uses astrology.

What does this mean for human freedom and responsibility? Acting according to our innate endowment increases our range of freedom. From the modern astrological doctrine that the natal chart is the cosmos' blueprint for an individual, freedom consists of acting most closely to the universe's purpose for the individual, as articulated by his or her astrological chart. Our true freedom may increase with help from our environment and from developing positive habits of thinking and behavior, and a competent astrologer can help a person in this direction. Moving away from this blueprint diminishes freedom, causing poor decisions, consequent unhappiness and general lack of fulfillment in life. This is called an intellectualist or rational approach to human freedom, and many astrologers are intellectualists or rationalists in their attitude toward freedom.

There is another tradition of freedom we need to consider called 'voluntarism' that instead places an emphasis on the spontaneity of the human will. Indeed, most of us do not experience our will as some kind of (conscious or unconscious) calculation of means and ends but as a more fundamental experience of mind.

The Intellectualist Approach to Freedom

This attitude's ancestors include the Stoics, for whom freedom was an accommodating attitude of mind in the face of necessity that was not arbitrary but divinely ordained. It is no accident that astrology flourished when stoicism flourished.

Examples of the intellectualist approach after the medieval era are the seventeenth century Dutch philosopher Spinoza and John Stuart Mill from the nineteenth century. Spinoza's *Ethics* argued against an autonomous free will but asserted that human freedom results from an increase of knowledge (what we might call 'consciousness') beyond the immediate to the broader reaches of reality, culminating in an 'intellectual love of God' (or the universe as a totality). Of an entirely different temperament – and more influential for contemporary political philosophy – was Mill, whose philosophy of utilitarianism argued for a moral calculus based on coordinating personal and societal self-interest.

A little closer to our time, Marxism implies that freedom is the greater ability to act according to one's interest, cast in economic and political terms. Sigmund Freud asserted the same thing but from a psychological point of view, and his attitude is implicit in modern psychodynamic theory.

How do we account for these higher purposes for our lives? The medieval era replaced an ancient universe which was ordered by many gods with a universe ordered by one God. Yet both universes ordered themselves from divinity through the stars and planets. Most modern astrologers are more conceptual, relying on an abstracted 'universe' or a transpersonal 'soul' behind the planets and stars to do the ordering for the individual and the world.

The voluntarist approach points to problems encountered with the intellectualist or rationalist approach. According to adherents of a voluntarist conception of freedom, will as intellectual appetite simply operates within subtle causes and is therefore not truly free, for we are bounded by our preferences toward the various kinds of happiness.

Additionally, we all have the experience of calculating toward one course of action but performing another and the result is not what we had wished for. Are our bad choices from a weakened will or do they express a more fundamental kind of freedom, a freedom to choose even if we choose stupidly or wrongly? As self-destructive as we can be, we seem very protective of our freedom to make our own bad choices.

The kind of freedom implied here is fundamentally indeterminate, based not on natural inclinations toward certain goods but on a faculty independent of these inclinations and conditions. This concept is probably Judeo-Christian in origin but was developed further in the medieval era and has never ceased to be with us.

In the medieval era the name most associated with this teaching on will is Duns Scotus who was probably born in the same year as Dante. Scotus was educated and taught in Paris, Oxford, and Cologne. He died in the early 1300's. Medieval philosophy began to place greater emphasis on God's omnipotence and, deriving from that, on the essential freedom of the human will. Following the earlier speculations of Anselm of Canterbury, Scotus distinguished the will from an intellectual appetite or considerations of personal happiness, whether worldly or heavenly. At the level of theology, Scotus asserted that the highest good was not an ingrained love of God but the gratuitous love of God without conditions or consideration of resulting heavenly bliss.

According to a voluntarist approach, it is not the quality of one's calculations but *the good or evil will* that determines how we judge a person's actions. Because we can freely choose between alternatives of good and evil, we must take full responsibility for our choices. We are not let off the hook because of our astrology or any other kind of determining factors in our lives; we always have an ability to choose positive or negative paths playing the cards life has dealt us. We are alone responsible for choosing positive paths and are blamed for choosing negative ones.

None of this is new to astrologers. Modern astrologers tell us that a good or bad will cannot be astrologically determined or depicted. Although traditional astrology and some modern schools of spiritual astrology seem to judge the quality of a person's character from his or her astrological chart, most astrologers do not attempt to render this kind of judgment. Put differently, an astrologer cannot know how 'evolved' or 'unevolved' a person is. One may embody his or her chart in different ways that will lead him or her down different moral paths, and a competent astrologer will outline these possibilities to a client. We tend to leave it to our clients to make his or her ultimate choices.

> ### The 'Voluntarist' Approach to Freedom
> Thomas' philosophical successors, Duns Scotus and William of Ockham, gradually developed the doctrine of volunteerism, placing emphasis on the freedom of will – God's and ours – from the calculus of rational choice and self-interest.
>
> Later this was taken up by the eighteenth century philosopher Immanuel Kant, who posited that the realm of the moral was the good or bad will and that the autonomy of the will is a necessary condition for moral choice. It enabled Dostoyevsky's 'Underground Man' to enjoy his toothache because he could and to rebel against the limitations implied in the life of the reasonable. Closer to our contemporary era, modern existentialism posits the primacy and ungrounded essence of human freedom and our consequent responsibility for ourselves and our worlds.

Now that we have looked at astral causation from the point of view of its *effects* – i.e. our human bodies and minds – we now examine it from the point of view of *cause*, from divinity to the stars and planets to our existence on Earth. This will take us to *Paradiso* Canto 2 and Beatrice's famous (or infamous) explanation of the shadings on the Moon; her explanation describes how divinity operates through the stars and planets to our Earth. We also need to contemplate the many imperfections of God's perfect creations and for this we will note passages from *Paradiso* Cantos 1 and 13. We will also see that the poet has threaded Neo-Platonic and Aristotelian themes together. How do these viewpoints influence modern astrology?

Celestial Nature, Philosophers, and Astrology

Paradiso, Moon Spots and the Imperfections of Creation

Before launching into more cosmology in the *Paradiso*, I bring back *Inferno* 20 very briefly to look at how that canto ends. Again Virgil is in the speaking role:

> "Ma vienne omai, ché già tiene 'l confine
> d'amendue li emisperi e tocca l'onda
> sotto Sobilia Caino e le spine"

> "Now come along, [for] already holding the boundary
> of both hemispheres and touching the waves
> below Seville [is] Cain and the thorns" (124-126)

The Moon, 'Cain and the thorns' (*Caino e le spine*), is descending in the West (*Seville*). 'Cain and the thorns' refers to the medieval notion that the markings on the Moon are a picture of Cain from the Bible, who had killed his brother Abel and was exiled by God to the Moon to carry thorns on his back. Our interest is that the depiction itself is a folk story and (once again) is an error of fact. Yet like a composer who introduces a modest flourish early in a large work to bring it back later as a major theme, this casual reference to the Moon's markings in *Inferno* 20 reappears in *Paradiso* 2 as a matter of great importance.

In *Paradiso* 2 Dante and Beatrice have arrived at the sphere of the Moon; this planet's appearance is now *lucida, spessa, solida, e pulita* – shining, dense, solid, and without blemish (line 32). The pilgrim asks Beatrice about the Moon's famously dark spots and the common stories about the Moon and Cain. In response, Beatrice first notes that because we're dependent on our sense experience for knowledge we frequently get things wrong. She then asks Dante how *he* thinks the Moon's markings have come about. Conforming to medieval speculation and his previous position, the pilgrim tells Beatrice that they are from differences in the dense and thin matter on the Moon itself.

Beatrice presents different refutations for this hypothesis (Canto 2:64-108). For example, if the Moon had material that was thick and thin we would be able to see through parts of the Moon during a solar eclipse.

Then Beatrice describes the ongoing activity of the universe to her student pilgrim by providing a spiritual or metaphysical explanation for Moon spots (*Paradiso* 2.112-148). She does this by explaining how God's creative power diffuses downwards from the highest heavens through the planetary sphere further down to our material earth.

Beatrice begins her explanation by depicting the timeless and motionless Empyrean, the eternal now that is invisible and utterly simple. In this tenth Heaven God's light and love are unitary and undifferentiated but also immediate. This is the highest Heaven of divine repose or peace, *Dentro dal ciel de la divina pace*.

Beneath this highest heaven is the ninth heaven, the first motion or *Primum Mobile*. This Heaven is invisible and without parts but sets the Heavens in motion. This Heaven possesses the power (*virtute*) and the being or existence (*l'esser*) of all things contained in it. This is not just the source of the sky's clockwise diurnal motion but contains the essences and impetus toward existence of what manifests below (lines 112-114).

The next tercet (lines 115-117) depicts the realm of the Fixed Stars, lit with many different lights and dividing the unitary essence into many essences (*esser parte per diverse essenze*). We will also see that this is where the powers that correspond to the stars are differentiated and distributed.[19] (Dante's depiction of this realm seems to refer to the stars singly in their individual natures rather than as participants in their constellations or zodiacal signs.)

Beatrice continues (lines 118-120): beneath the Fixed Stars are the "other spheres", our familiar seven planets from Saturn to Moon. In different ways (according to their own natures) different planets receive diverse powers or essences from above and direct them below – according to their individual purposes. Durling (2010) suggests that this occurs due to the planets' changing positions relative to one another.[20] Through the planets, divine being and power is further differentiated and dispersed to what is below to give rise to earthly form and power.

In Dante's theologized cosmology, hierarchies of angels manage all these heavens of the stars and planets. As soul is distributed throughout our body and its faculties, the angelic intelligences bring their bounty (*bontate*) in various ways through the stars (2:133-138). From this joyous nature, like the joy that shines through an eye's pupil, a mixed power (*la virtù mista*) shines through each star and together they account for the markings on the Moon. As different lights shine differently downwards, they will render the Moon's surface brighter or darker. This is not a physical but a metaphysical explanation for the Moon's markings.

The process is a multistep diffusion from single divinity (pure actuality) to multiple powers or essences that help organize the matter below (potentiality).* This step-down sequence is not mechanical but intentional, ultimately from the divine will and managed by means of angelic intelligence. This is analogous to the radiance of light: the simple light of the higher heavens diffuses through the spheres to animate what is below, finally reaching the Earth itself. It radiates to make essences that help constitute things down here, moving from the general and the conceptual to the particular and the sensory. The stars and planets, therefore, reflecting from what is above, give rise to the diversity of things and the mixed effects of our world.

This sounds like a pretty smooth operation but our resulting world is wildly imperfect, messy and requiring ongoing renewal. How does the poet account for this? We begin by returning to *Paradiso* 1.

Dante and Beatrice have begun their bodily ascent to the first heavenly sphere, the Moon. How can they move upwards in this way, the pilgrim wonders. Everything resembles God in its own way, Beatrice says, although only humans and angels are able to see this footprint (lines 103-108). From the earthly elements that move in various directions to the angels who circle around God, all move toward different ports in the great sea of being. Humans are carried back toward God as the bowstring of providence aims us back toward God.

She continues by accounting for our world's many imperfections: we can depart from our divinely-ordained course like fire can move downwards in the form of lightning. In our case it is similar to when an artist cannot make their material yield to their intentions – perhaps

---

* There is a variety of opinions about the inherent tendency within earthly matter to take form. At one extreme, the light of the heavenly bodies contain the form that is imposed on passive matter. In the middle is Albert, the teacher of Thomas Aquinas, who, following Augustine, posited that matter has inherently a tendency toward form that is fulfilled by Heaven. Thomas of Aquinas conceded only that the Heavenly bodies communicate the "motion toward form" *motus ad forman* (Durling 2010, p.744)

when we become distracted by false pleasure, for example (lines 121-135).

We now move to *Paradiso* 13:53-84, on the Sphere of the Sun. Thomas of Aquinas further accounts for earthly imperfection in a divinely-wrought world. His presentation is less imagistic and more philosophical than that of Beatrice.

All creation, Thomas says, reflects the Idea that the Lord has brought about through Love (these three concepts are the aspects of Christianity's trinity). This unitary divine light radiates like light gathered by a mirror and shines downwards through the nine *sussistenze* or subsistances, the spheres of the fixed stars and planets. As the greatest potency descends to our level of earthly activity, what is produced is not immutable or perfect but *brevi contingenze*, 'brief contingencies'. They are the secondary creations of God, for they come about through the movements of the heavens (the changing configurations of the planets?). This is our world that consists of many different possibilities.

The poet returns us to the metaphor of seal and wax: beneath the Idea's imprint (form) and the wax (matter) there are variations of light. If the wax was perfectly prepared and heaven greatly powerful, then the full light of heaven would shine, but nature tends to diminish the results: the craft or artistry may be good but the artist brings an unsteady hand to the work; trees that bear the same fruit provide some that are better and some that are not so good. From the divine source, imperfections result from secondary creation through the angels and planetary spheres onto the coarser realm of our material realm down here. Only Adam and Jesus were directly created by God; the rest of us and the rest of creation are imperfect particulars from a perfect template. Therefore the world and all of us are prone to corruption and decay.

Providing for the world's periodic renewal, at the heart of the poem's purpose, is an ongoing activity of divine providence. Sometimes individuals seem born specifically for this purpose. Recall from *Paradiso* 11 and 12 how "two princes" (*due principi*), one associated with the west and one with the east, were ordained by God to protect and guide the church through its difficulties (*Paradiso* 11:34-36). Dominic and Francis appear to have been sent directly by God for this purpose. As presented by Cacciaguida on the sphere of Mars, the pilgrim's destiny is also to be an agent of renewal.

Some readers will find Dante's depiction of Heaven's dynamics rather quaint and medieval, yet modern astrologers may find the poet's presentation provocative and vaguely inspiring. Dante's cosmology, as outdated as it seems, is in many ways our world of traditional and modern astrology. To update the poet's vision we need to examine its metaphysics.

The *Divine Comedy*'s cosmology is *both* Aristotelian and Neoplatonic, reflecting the twin ancient sources of medieval philosophy. They are at work in Dante's depiction of the relationship between Heaven and Earth and his depiction of astrological causation in nature.

These twin towers of philosophy can be very helpful for astrology's understanding of itself. This includes the role of archetypes in astrology and the application of Aristotle's four causes to astrology. It is especially important that we consider the Neoplatonic legacy, for this legacy is the attitude behind the spirituality of Dante's cosmology and it is the backdrop of much modern astrology. We must first explore some of the metaphysics and theology of the ancient and Christian eras and then swiftly move to modern astrological thinking.

The Neoplatonic Thread, Then and Now
According to the Platonic enterprise, objective truth (also forming the basis for moral behavior) is available to human beings who work for it. In the fourth century BCE, Plato posited that for understanding to occur there must be objective nonphysical Ideas or Forms that are outside and prior to any particular object of sense experience. The contents of arithmetic and geometry, for example, exist timelessly while structuring all the world's particulars that are subject to change. An Idea or Form is a model for which diverse things and qualities are particular instances. (This is opposed to more relativist approaches whereby there are no objective truths in knowledge or ethics.)

Plato's doctrine of Forms expresses itself in a few dialogues (*Republic*, *Phaedo*, *Timaeus*) but not in a systematic manner; in one dialogue (*Parmenides*) Plato even supplies a refutation for the entire doctrine.

Plato's student Aristotle criticized Plato's Forms on a number of grounds, especially his teacher's assertion that a Form could exist outside a particular object and be known without reference to the object under investigation. Aristotle was more concerned with what we would call biology and less with the universal truths of mathematics.

Fast-forward five centuries to Late Antiquity: this was a time when different schools of philosophical thought were brought together in different ways and when the relationship between the transcendent and the natural had become a major concern. Plato's emphasis on dialectic was augmented by an appreciation for direct contemplation of reality. This was also the time when Christianity was ascendant in the Roman Empire.

In the 200's CE the Egyptian philosopher Plotinus presented Plato's doctrines in a systematic form and emphasized doctrines that have a religious or contemplative feel to them. He is considered the founder and greatest exponent of Neoplatonism.

Plotinus' writings were not translated from Greek into Latin until the 1490s so Dante would not have been directly familiar with them. Through the writings of Pseudo-Dionysus the Areopagite, Augustine, the Arab philosopher Avicenna, and the scholastic philosophy in the 1200's, the Neoplatonic stream was wide and deep in the medieval era and strongly influenced its philosophy and its art. The *Divine Comedy* is the crowning example of Neoplatonic influence in medieval poetry.

Because Plotinus has the most complete account of Neoplatonism and because of the philosopher's popularity among many modern astrologers, it's appropriate to present some of his template. His doctrines also provide some useful context for the cosmology in the *Paradiso* and its cosmology.

Using the metaphysics of Plato, Plotinus needed to account for our world of change within a context of intelligibility. For this he posited intermediary stages called hypostases (or 'foundations') between the Absolute (or God) and our fleeting visible world. The hypostases step downward in stages to account for all levels of being. These are like the upside down 'flower pots' we encountered as a metaphor in *Paradiso* 27.

Plotinus called the absolutely first principle of everything "the One" that is beyond description or determination or even considerations of unity that would contrast with multiplicity and thus provide two factors of single and multiple. This absolute level of reality is both immanent and transcendent. All things are contained within it but is transcendent because it is beyond all determinate things, beyond even being the cause of all determinate things, for the concept of causes requires a distinct cause and effect. Although considered self-sufficient and a fullness without limit, the One 'outflows' or emanates or radiates like light from the Sun.

The first stage from the One – although hardly a stage as an event in time – is the image of the One that is variously translated as 'Intelligence' or the 'Intellectual Principle', from the Greek *nous* that means 'mind'. In its relationship to the One, the Intellectual Principle is neither the same nor different than the One, but brings into being the principles of being and of thought. As the Intellectual Principle contemplates the generative power of the One we arrive at thinking, multiplicity and a basic subject-object duality. This is also the realm of Plato's Forms, each of which is undivided from the entire Intellectual Principle and therefore from the One. Yet these Forms or Ideas are the template for further creations as they extend further into particularity and materiality.

Plotinus' "Soul" is not the Aristotelian principle of life and form of a body. Rather, it contains the divinity and rationality above but orients itself further into multiplicity and externalization. It contains the imprints of the One and the Intellectual Principle but is oriented toward specific embodiment.

This is also Plato's "Soul of the Universe" from the *Timaeus*, the wheels of the celestial equator and ecliptic that give rise to order and harmony from Heaven to Earth. As the vehicle whereby the Intellectual Principle may manifest, the level of soul is a stellar realm of being that can carry Ideas downward. However, as soul identifies itself with its physical vehicle and surroundings it forgets its own divine origins – yet we aspire to return to our higher nature.

Our world of 'Nature' manifests all its variety and confusion – and intelligibility – in-formed from the higher realms of being. However, as Soul identifies with nature it takes on some of its characteristics and forgets its higher essence. Although we live much of our lives embedded in the necessities of the realm of nature we all contain a quality of soul that looks upward and desires to carry us upward, like the effortless upward movement of Dante and Beatrice in *Paradiso* 1. Our desire for beauty, goodness, and truth via their manifestations in the world may begin us on our journey.

Christian thinking was influenced by Platonism from the outset and many of the church fathers were steeped in its doctrine. Yet Christian thinkers had many problems with the Platonic and Neoplatonic legacy, all of which have something to do with the realm of the material.

First, the Neoplatonic view of the One was not Christianity's personal God but an utterly nonconceptual principle of unity. The Christian understanding was of a God who, as the saying went, knows how many hairs are on a man's head and when a sparrow falls to the ground. The Neoplatonic doctrine and temperament excludes this personal God who governs this world directly through divine providence.

Another problem is that of creation: according to *Genesis* it was God himself who personally created everything. This is very different from Neoplatonic theories in which the world manifests as a step-down process, not instantaneous and on the border of time and eternity as we saw in *Paradiso* 29. When you return to this canto's discussion of creation you will see how Dante wrestles with both Neoplatonic and Christian themes.

A third problem is that of reconciling the universal and material dimensions. The Christian doctrine of the Incarnation of God into a particular person and the promised resurrection of the physical body at the last judgment violate the Neoplatonic hierarchy of being.

From a Christian point of view, Neoplatonism did not provide the means for salvation through God's grace, but instead provided a contemplative journey that would be too difficult for most people. Christianity provided a more reasonable template for an ordinary person to live the good life and be saved at the end of it.

Yet the Christian tradition inherited much from Platonism and Neoplatonism, as they provided the philosophical environment of early Christianity. Recall the beginning of John's Gospel that correlated Christ to the 'Word' (*logos*) that is inseparable but derived from the first person God – just as the Intellectual Principle proceeds from the One. This will continue through the history of Christian doctrine as the doctrine of the Trinity was elaborated further and further.

Christianity inherited from Neoplatonism the notion that God is by nature a unity and simplicity, for if God were made of parts, he would be subject to change and would be modified from elsewhere. Since life down here is compounded and everything is subject to change, how do we account for both God's simplicity and our complexity and also maintain the Christian God's personal involvement in our world? Plotinus and others came to the rescue.

In the fourth century, Augustine of Hippo was inspired by Neoplatonism but was made uneasy by it. Augustine converted the Intellectual Principle to *Ideas in the mind of the Christian God*, partly to solve the problem of the sequence of creation in Genesis.

Through Divine Ideas the personal deity becomes the source of all created earthly things but in a secondary way, much like Dante's distinction between Adam and Christ who were created directly by God and the rest of us who are in-formed through the stars and planets and their angelic helmsmen.

Closer to Dante's time were contributions from Thomas and Bonaventure. Although we generally think of Thomas of Aquinas as a medieval Aristotelian, his depiction of divine Ideas (that the models for substances are eternally in the mind of God) was influenced by Neoplatonism and has its origin in Augustine.[21]

Bonaventure, who we met in *Paradiso* 12, was the Franciscan contemporary of the Dominican Thomas of Aquinas. Bonaventure took from Christian Neoplatonism and gave back the concept of *exemplarism*, whereby the things of the world are footprints of God and rational beings are his more direct images. Bonaventure's concern was the return trip to God from the particulars of our world.

Dante, following other traditions, brought Neoplatonic doctrine directly into the realm of cosmology. *Paradiso* 2 tells us of the dispersal of divine Unity from the *primum mobile* through the fixed stars and then through the planetary spheres, depicting Form becoming further and further differentiated and then ready to act upon the material principle on the level of Earth.

This is reinforced by the *Paradiso*'s emphasis on gradations of light – symbolic and also literal. We saw this as early as the first lines of the *Paradiso*; like rays from the Sun lighting up the heavenly and earthly cosmos, divine being (God's glory) diffuses through the universe in some parts more and in other parts less (*Paradiso* 1:1-3). Here is the metaphysics of creation and salvation expressing itself through the visible Heavens.

Greatly influential for Dante's cosmological synthesis were the Arab philosopher Avicenna and, closer to his own time, Thomas' own teacher Albertus Magnus. Here is a summary of Albert's teaching about the universe's hierarchy, what we nowadays call 'The Great Chain of Being'.

> The First Cause [understood] as God, is an absolutely transcendent reality. His uncreated light calls forth a hierarchically ordered universe in which each order of being reflects this light. God's giving existence to creatures is understood ... as their procession from him as from a first cause. At the top of this hierarchy of light are found the purely spiritual beings, the angelic orders and the intelligences. [Albert] carefully distinguishes these two kinds of beings. He basically accepts the analysis of the angelic orders as found in Pseudo-Dionysius' treatise of the celestial hierarchy. The intelligences move the cosmic spheres and illuminate the human soul. The intelligences, just as the order of angels, form a special hierarchy. The First Intelligence... contemplates the entire universe and uses the human soul, as illuminated by the lower intelligences, to draw all creatures into a unity.
>
> Beneath the angels and intelligences are the souls that possess intellects. They are joined to bodies but do not depend on bodies for their existence... Each human soul has its own intellect. But because the human soul uniquely stands on the horizon of both material and spiritual being it can operate as a microcosm and thus can serve the purpose of the First Intelligence, which is to bind all creatures into a universe.[22]

The poet Dante transformed this into cosmology and these lines could serve as a summary of much of the *Paradiso*. Today known mostly through his more famous student Thomas of Aquinas, Albert is an important source for Dante. He, more than his famous student, was a 'natural philosopher' interested in understanding the phenomena of this world and of the Heavens. Albert was far more accepting of both magic and astrology than was Thomas but he was less systematic and his writings are not as easily available to modern readers as those by his prized student.

All this may seem a far cry from contemporary thinking but is not far from those of many modern astrologers. As we have seen, Neoplatonism in its cosmological forms leaves room for a formal relationship between configurations of the Heavens and conditions on Earth, a step-down process whereby divinity diffuses through the configurations of the stars and planets to the changing circumstances on earth. By capturing the stellar configuration of the moment of an individual's birth one finds the person in the universe, the particular individual in-formed by the universal surrounding heavens.

There have been some modern astrological thinkers who have attempted to render astrology into a Neoplatonic format. One highly influential astrologer was Dane Rudhyar (1895-1985) whose Neoplatonism was more attitudinal than systematic. Rudhyar made several forays at a symbolic cosmology from a model influenced by Neoplatonism (and modern spiritual esotericism). A different attempt was made by Anthony Damiani (1922-1984) and his students, culminating in the publication of *Astronoesis* in 2000. Below is an excerpt from that book's introduction that is not only Neoplatonic in concept and language but also reads like a summary of the early cantos of the *Paradiso*. According to this formulation, the astrological signs correlate with Plotinus' Intellectual Principle or *Nous* or the Christian Ideas in the mind of God.

> "If we conceive of the universe as an Idea within the Self, we may be able to comprehend how various portions of that Idea were explored and described by these ancient seers, who then associated specific types of primal intelligence with the zodiacal signs. Each type of intelligence was pictorialized as an animal – as intelligence personified – which would ultimately be traced back to an Idea. Each of these intelligences is a universal substance correlated to a sign. These reason-principles – the signs – are the paradigms of all living forms or species symbolized by the archetypal zodiac.... In this sense the stars are a theophany of radiating intelligences, distributing their presence and informing the universe through patterns of intellectual energy... the Earth is also a recipient of the Ideas, and through the intermediary of the rational powers of the Sun gradually there is organized and manifested on Earth a variety of species that will partially and imperfectly reflect the Ideas or animal intelligences..." (pp.12, 14-15)

Astronoesis follows with a complex set of Neoplatonic concepts related to specific concepts of astrological symbolism. Although within a modern astrological framework, this work is inspired by some of the same philosophy as used in the *Divine Comedy*. In spite of its rather complicated architecture, I would like to see *Astronoesis* have greater prominence in today's world of astrology.

Far closer to modern astrology's current mainstream is the emphasis in some circles on 'archetypes' – 'first forms' or 'principal forms'. Although ultimately derived from Neoplatonism, the concept of archetypes has come to us from twentieth-century psychology. Today the word 'archetype' is commonly associated with Carl Jung. Influenced by developmental motifs fashioned by Sigmund Freud and inspired by a dynamic view of the human unconscious, Jung thought of archetypes as basic categories of human mind that reside in the collective unconsciousness. From these archetypes arise humanity's symbols and patterns of behavior in their great diversity, from trends in fashion, entertainment, and the arts, to mass movements to an individual's dreams and psychological conflicts. The concept of archetypes allows people to understand their lives in terms of universal human concerns.

In parallel with the relationship between Plato's Forms and the specific things in our world they embody, Jungian archetypes manifest in our personal and collective experiences but are themselves unconscious, impersonal, and unfathomable. While Neoplatonism employs the Intellectual Principle and its Forms to help shed light on the supposed darkness of our ordinary experience, Jungian archetypes bring the darkness of unconsciousness into the light of ordinary discourse.

It was natural that the Jungian depiction of archetypes would find its way into astrology, bringing together psychological motifs and astrological symbolism to create a template for a psychological application of astrology. With the addition to the astrological meanings attached to the modern planets Uranus, Neptune, and Pluto, this has helped open astrology to a portrait of human nature that has a depth and richness previously unavailable to the field. Many well-known astrologers such as Liz Greene have used astrological symbolism in an individual's astrological chart to comment on archetypal patterns in a person's psychological framework. Like Jungian psychology, psychological astrology can be a tool of personal growth toward individuation or a fully integrated personality.

Any new trend carries some problems, however. First, there seems to be some confusion about what an archetype is and what a symbol is and which symbols of astrology are archetypal. The second concern is danger of psychological reductionism. There are questions of an ultimate ground of an archetypal realm, the relationships between the physical planets in space and the human psyche, and the use of modern scientific paradigms to account for an archetypal approach to astrology.

Most astrologers use 'astrological archetype' to refer to the planets alone, but I have seen signs and elements also rendered as archetypal. How does an astrologer decide which of astrology's features (planets, signs, aspects, etc) are archetypes and which are symbols? What is the functional difference between archetype and symbol? The implication is that an archetype, as a 'first form', is a primary being from which a symbol is derived. But if we say that all of astrology's features have archetypal status or can be reduced to archetypes then the word becomes just a synonym of 'symbol' and we've gone from essences to words.

What is the relationship between archetype as a psychological matrix and a planet that may correspond to it? If my mother appears in a dream, what archetype is invoked, the Great Mother or the astrological Moon? Between Mother and Moon, which is the archetype and which the example, which is the stamp and which is the wax?

With an expansion of astrology into areas of psychology, there has been the inevitable danger of reducing the astrological to the psychological and an exclusive focus on personal growth.* Traditional astrologers like me criticize their archetypal-psychological comrades for transforming life's vicissitudes into internal issues, discounting the dumb realities of fortune's turnings: we get cancer and scholarships, lose weight and loved ones, survive earthquakes or, like the medieval poet, leave our home city never to return. Among modern astrologers there are different approaches to the application of astrological description and prediction.

Is it possible to use a broader range for archetypes and not overemphasize the realm of the psychological? In the next section we look at modern astrologer Dennis Elwell (1987) whose range of astrological symbolism

---

* This has been seen to manifest even in 'mundane' astrology or the astrology of world or political events: major astrological shifts (e.g. modern planets entering signs or phases between the modern planets) become markers of planetary shifts of consciousness, reducing astrological symbolism to psychological growth but on a global level.

is truly multivalent; he uses planets as first forms but calls them 'holons', not 'archetypes'. Ray Grasse (1996) also describes planetary archetypes in ways not exclusively psychological.

Is there a higher or deeper realm than the archetypal, what we might call the numinous or divine? Grasse (1996) provides an intriguing concept of 'Primary Archetype', an image of wholeness that is expressed through the image of the Sun, the number One, and primary principles of Egyptian and Chinese thinking.[23] Does a Primary Archetype have a greater ontological status than other planetary archetypes or is it the first among equals?

The Heaven of the *Divine Comedy* is centered on God, through which all created things – including the Divine Ideas, mediated through stars and angels – receive their existence and meaning. From modern archetypal astrologers I see vague references to Cosmic Being or Cosmic Intent, presented in a way that would survive about fifteen minutes in a medieval university classroom. If the modern astrological universe is also thought of as hierarchically arranged, much is missing in its depictions of its upper reaches.

This omission manifests as a rather narrow view of human potential. In *The Atman Project* and elsewhere, Ken Wilbur posits the peak of personal psychological growth as a 'centaur' stage, wherein one has attained an integration of body, emotion, and mind. This is not greatly different from the medieval 'rational soul' we discussed above or even the Jungian concept of 'individuation'. In the *Divine Comedy*, this was the attainment of the pilgrim Dante at the top of Purgatory – but he still had to go through Paradise. Modern archetypal astrologers, who too often focus solely on the psychological dimensions, are vague about more otherworldly or super-natural possibilities for astrology or for their clients. In my view a complete astrology would have to include dimensions of life beyond psychological individuation.

How do astrological archetypes or symbols express themselves through the physical planets as they move through the zodiac, through the signs of the zodiac or the circles of equator and ecliptic? Can modern archetypal astrologers account for a link, or to bridge the gap, between psyche and the visible and physical sky? Dante's hierarchical model of astrological effect has sophistication and subtlety although it will seem outdated to the modern mind. Here is one possible modern approach from Richard Tarnas in *An Introduction to Archetypal Astrology*.

> "I believe that a more plausible and comprehensive explanation [than the physical] is that the universe is informed and pervaded by a fundamental holistic patterning which extends through every level, so that a constant synchronicity or meaningful correlation exists between astronomical events and human events. This is represented in the basic esoteric axiom, 'as above, so below', which reflects a universe all of whose parts are integrated into an intelligible whole."[24]

To posit a philosophy whereby everything is interconnected, however, tells us nothing about astrology in its traditional and present forms. If there is a 'fundamental holistic patterning', how are astrology's symbols more fundamental than the major arcana of the tarot or the Chinese elements or the hexagrams of the *i ching*? These are also examples of holistic patterning.

Others look toward modern physics for answers and the same criticisms apply. Some cite the quantum principle of indeterminacy, dynamics of subatomic physics and action at a distance, or theories asserting that every part of the universe reflects its entirety.

To the extent that these ideas are valid and puncture the certainty of the mechanistic-materialistic model that is alien to astrology, they are a good thing. Again, these new discoveries of science do not account for astrology in its application of moving planetary bodies, astrological symbolism, and characters or events on earth. They merely provide a small opening.

Any current metaphysics of modern astrological archetypes is in its early stages and is more general and allusive than explanatory or comprehensive. Notions of holism and synchronicity are just beginning in their development, and changes in how wisdom expresses itself always happen slowly. They cannot yet approach the sophistication and depth of the cosmology we have seen in Dante who was heir to centuries of Neoplatonic, Aristotelian, and Christian inquiry into cosmology and metaphysics. Perhaps we modern people should proceed more self-critically, to let ourselves be humbled and to be challenged by, for example, the depth and reach of Dante's grand synthesis.

The Aristotelian Thread and Astrological Causes

Ancient and medieval thinkers have always found the legacy of Aristotle a good corrective for the idealistic or otherworldly tendencies of Neoplatonism. A Neoplatonic approach cannot fully account for the complex spirit of the *Divine Comedy*'s cosmology, nor can it fully account for the depth of the art of astrology as we practice it today. Here we look at the legacy of Aristotle not just as a set of doctrines but as (1) a vocabulary of matter and form, of movement, substance, actuality, contingency, and potentiality that pervades the *Divine Comedy*, and (2) as an attitude of a greater attentiveness to the details of nature and how ordinary things are. Aristotelian thinking, particularly the doctrine of the four causes, may be particularly useful for modern astrologers in understanding their own work.

Although most people place Europe's 'Scientific Revolution' centuries later, one could argue that it began with a new approach to reality from the transmission of Aristotle during the medieval era.* Although the Aristotelian approach to nature was largely conceptual, its focus on the material world set the stage for more empirical investigations centuries later.

In the *Divine Comedy* we meet The Philosopher himself early in the poem among the "virtuous pagans". Pilgrim and guide see Aristotle, surrounded by other philosophers attending to him, designated as '*l maestro di color che sanno*, "the master of those who know." (*Inferno* 4.131)

The structure of Hell is attributed to Aristotle: in *Inferno* 11, Virgil directly refers to Aristotle's *Nicomachean Ethics* in dividing Hell into the realms for incontinence, malice, and "mad bestiality".** This is Aristotle the ethicist. In the middle cantos of *Purgatorio* and of the entire poem, Virgil's exposition of the different kinds of love is derived from The Philosopher's division of the soul into sensitive and rational faculties. Previously Marco the Lombard, following Thomas of Aquinas, asserted that stellar causation applies to the sensitive and not the rational faculties. This is from Aristotle the biologically-based psychologist.

---

*   See Grant, Edward (1996)
** See *Nichomachean Ethics* Book Five and its depiction of justice and injustice.

From the *De Caelo* or 'On the Heavens' and from the last book of *The Metaphysics*, Aristotle the cosmologist influenced the medieval temperament and Dante's viewpoint. Like Plato, Aristotle argued for a radical distinction between Heaven and Earth. This is based on Heaven's unchanging and orderly nature and Earth's continual movement. We see this through the geometry of circles and lines: circles (in Heaven) have no opposites or points of termination. Earthly things, consisting of lines that go up, down, and sideways, have beginnings, ends, and opposites. We have seen abundant use of lines – with crosses – and circles in Dante's depiction of Paradise. The distinction between terrestrial and celestial nature is in close parallel to the medieval distinction between the natural and the supernatural.

> **Aristotle and Creation**
>
> According to the Christian doctrine of Creation, God brought into being the material substrate from which the things of our world consist. This is different from the Neoplatonic view of nature as a step-down process from God to Earth. Dante uses Aristotelian vocabulary to depict this.
>
> *"Forma e materia congiunte e purette*
> *Usciro ad esser che non avia fallo,*
> *Come d' arco tricordo tre saette."* (Paradiso 29:22-24)
>
> "Form and matter, conjoined and pure,
> came into being without flaw,
> like three arrows from a bow with three strings."
>
> Form without matter designates the angels; matter and form together are the planetary bodies, and the first matter that is informed from above is the Earth.
>
> Soon afterwards (lines 31-36) Beatrice says this in a different way: the angelic level is "pure act", *puro atto*, the Earth level is pure potentiality *pura potenza*, and in the middle are the stars and planets which combine the two.
>
> Beatrice's presentation assumes that the Earth level is matter seen as potentiality awaiting actualization from above – this doctrine is Neoplatonic. Yet the vocabulary is Aristotelian.

Let's first look at the vocabulary of necessity and contingency. Before giving his dark prophecy to the pilgrim, Cacciaguida first cites his ability to clearly see contingencies as necessities. To a Heavenly being all events of the past, present, and future are depicted in eternal sight, therefore all times are simultaneous in eternity and the future is as discernable as the past.

What is a 'contingency'? This term, designates events that are the result of circumstances, that could have been otherwise, that usually appear to us as 'chance'. If I get a flat tire on my next bicycle ride, or if a very large check unexpectedly comes to me, these contingent events will appear to be accidents of bad or good fortune respectively. Yet we can also think of contingency in terms of *probability*: if you learned that I was bicycling near a beach lined with shells or nearby a nail factory, or that a wealthy relative of mine had passed away and an estate lawyer was attempting to reach me, these events will seem like less of a surprise. The word 'accident' originally referred to a contingent event; today we think of accidents merely as arbitrary and surprising.*

Generally speaking, unanticipated events are the result of causes and conditions too complex to be understood directly but are not 'random'. According to Christian thinking even the smallest details of the world are spanned by God's omnipotence, and in the clear vision of *Paradiso* 17 Cacciaguida sees contingencies as necessities. The condition of randomness that is a prerequisite for something being ominous and subject to divination cannot happen in this universe: the divine has replaced the diviner.

We now turn our focus to the famous Aristotelian doctrine of the four causes, for this doctrine is relevant to many passages we have considered and because they apply to how traditional and modern astrologers think of their work. The main source of Aristotle's doctrine of causes is Book 2 of *The Physics*. One way to approach these causes is to return to *Purgatorio* 25 and its depiction of a human embryo and its development and then *Paradiso* 2. Instead of looking at early human development and

---

* Using these two situations, an astrologer may retrospectively see that these events may explain how Saturn transiting natal Mercury or Jupiter and Uranus transiting natal Sun had manifested for this person. If the accompanying facts are also known by an astrologer, it is more likely to be seen as a possible outcome in advance. This is in the realm of prediction based on following nature and making an interpretation on its account.

the progression of Being through Neoplatonic lenses we will see them as an Aristotelian might.

Purgatorio 25 contains an account for the origin of a human life. As we have previously seen, the process would begin when the *sangue perfetto*, the perfected blood, descends from a man's heart to become the in-forming principle, which, when it flows into the woman's material environment, gives rise to a new body, becoming the 'material cause'. Then from the fetus *la virtute attiva*, the 'active power', begins to develop the human soul, first like a plant and then changing in form and complexity. This is similar to the Aristotelian 'efficient cause'. What makes for life is the movement of the formative power acting upon matter to bring about a particular life that they would call a 'soul'. Yet this new being, through its generic nature, also has a purpose or *telos* that is flourishing as a human being. Here is a glimpse of Aristotle's famous four causes, or four accounts by which we can say we know something.*

This also allows us to see Beatrice's discourse in *Paradiso* 2 differently. When read in an Aristotelian style, she describes a dynamic process similar to the embryology of *Purgatorio* 25: from God and then through the stars and planets, the Earth's many compounded things receive certain movements (efficient causes), formal characteristics (formal causes) and accompanying purposes (final causes). The material is down here to be formed from above.

We can ask ourselves what something is made from (the 'material cause'), what activates motion or rest (the 'efficient' cause), the form or pattern of something by which we name it (the 'formal cause'), and its purpose or the sake of which something exists (the 'final' cause). Modern thinking tends to focus on material and efficient causes; Aristotle and his successors contend that it takes all four causes to account for something.

We now describe these causes in application to astrology using both divinatory and natural models. Many of astrology's skeptics consider astrology invalid because 'astrological effects' cannot be scientifically accounted for or statistically justified. This judgment seems inappropriate because its concept of cause is restricted to efficient cause only.

---

* Medieval writers, not The Philosopher (Aristotle) himself, first coined the terms 'material', 'efficient', 'formal', and 'final' to denote Aristotle's four causes.

The relationship of meaning between Heaven and Earth that is astrology is not based on material cause, that of which something is made. Modern cosmology tells us that the matter of our being, all the modern elements, have their ultimate origin in the early universe and the galaxies and stars that coalesced after the Big Bang. Ancient and medieval natural philosophers emphasized that Earth and the Heavens were different substances and obeyed different laws; modern cosmologists emphasize our physical ties to the stars and planets above us. This would be an example of material cause that is *simultaneous with its effect*.

An *efficient cause* comes from the outside and impels a body's motion, causing that body to change or continue in some way. Efficient cause implies activity already begun which, acting upon a substance, causes a specific change in that substance.

Efficient causes line up sequentially and the time of efficient cause is *linear from past to present to future*. I kick a ball toward the goal, the ball moves slowly, and the bored goalkeeper picks it up. It takes 8.3 seconds for a ray leaving from the Sun to arrive on Earth: the rays are the efficient causes for the Earth's heat and its outdoor light; therefore if the Sun went out as you read this sentence you would not know it for 8.3 seconds. The resulting movements from efficient cause often continue over time: when I begin the movement of a mechanical clock by winding it up or putting in a new battery, the mechanism is in place that will sustain the movements on the surface of the clock.

Clearly there is efficient causation between the heavens and Earth but it is not astrology. The Sun warms and gives daylight and the Moon affects tides and some cycles in nature, but no beams from Venus cause mad love (or zombie uprisings) on Earth and Mars may appear red in the sky but its rays do not make us hostile. Often our astrology seems to speak the language of efficient cause, especially when discussing one's natal chart being 'hit' by transiting planets or planets directed by solar arc.* Soon we will discuss astrology's predictive techniques as examples of *formal* causation.

Some aspects of efficient causation have influenced astrology in

---

* Although transits relate to current planetary movement onto zodiacal positions in a natal chart, 'solar arc directions' move all planets in a uniform way. This movement is the same as the natal Sun's movement of one day after birth corresponds to one year of a person's life.

the past. Ptolemy's *Tetrabiblos* was greatly influential and was a work with which Dante was familiar. In Book 1 Ptolemy based astrological influence upon the planets' physical effects on the Earth's atmospheric environment and then on us at the time of birth. (Ptolemy appeared to ignore these causal possibilities when he moved to astrological methodology later in the *Tetrabiblos*.)

Thomas of Aquinas taught that efficient cause was the only legitimate use of stellar causation: "if one were to apply the observation of the stars in order to foreknow those future things that are caused by heavenly bodies, for instance, drought or rain and so forth, it will be neither an unlawful nor a superstitious divination."[26] In *Purgatorio* 16 Marco the Lombard tells us that the stars "set us in our motions" but he does not explain how this occurs: he may be literal according to efficient cause or metaphorical by way of formal cause that we discuss below. If we think that the stars and planets are efficient causes only, we too may be subject to the "bad faith" – denial of personal responsibility – Marco counsels against.

A *formal cause* attempts to answer what something is and seems to be the most elusive of the four causes. Often it is approached through sense perception. A particular material object becomes an idea in somebody's mind through that object's *form*. In Virgil's depiction of how we invest objects of the mind with appetite or love, the form of the object of desire must be present in the mind so that desire continues when the object is absent. Traditional accounts of the relationship of sense perception to knowledge parallel the relationship between matter (sense experience) and form (our notion of a thing).

Form is the boat or mountain that a painting depicts: the colored canvas sheet is the *matter* upon which the form of boat or mountain appears. Form makes a human being or cat from a collection of flesh and bones; when the human being or cat dies, the material substance loses its form and it becomes something else – a corpse. Using an example we have seen often in the *Divine Comedy*, form is the impression made by a stamp on wax (the matter) to make a seal. (It is interesting that our word 'character' is based on the Greek word for the impression made upon wax.) A form may be generically originated but it comes into being *simultaneously* with the object that now becomes available to our senses.

You may be suspecting that there is some overlap between Aristotle's concept of formal cause and the Platonic notion of Forms of which material things partake. They are similar although their metaphysics differs. Remember that the Platonic Forms reside prior to and outside the particular object; the Aristotelian understanding is that the form resides with a particular object, as the soul as the form of the body is inseparable from the body. The second difference is that Plato's forms tend to be static, like geometrical shapes and concepts, and those of Aristotle would have growth and development constituting their nature. This reflects Aristotle's interest in living processes.

Let's bring these causes together and discuss astrology. We begin by looking at astrology as an *interpretative* art and a *divinatory* art as described earlier. Then we will reconsider astrology as *nature*.

Using concepts of material, efficient, and formal cause, what are the relationships between the configurations of the heavens, the astrological chart, the astrologer as artist, and the situations of life here on Earth?

If the purpose of the medical arts is health, the purpose of the astrological art is a greater understanding. This is accomplished through the interpretation of the astrologer, whose application of astrology is moved (efficient cause) by the client or 'objective' situation and also by the information provided by the astrological chart.*

What is the astrological chart? It supplies information about the configurations of the sky at a particular time and from a particular place, and becomes the *form* of which the sky's configurations are *the matter*.

How does the chart relate to the person or situation it depicts? The chart is also the form of the person or situation expressed as astrological symbolism. Mediated by the astrologer doing the interpreting, the astrological chart becomes the form of the individual or situation depicted. Therefore the chart is simultaneous with both the Heavens and the person depicted – if they are connected through the artist's interpretation. Otherwise we are in the oily wetlands of trying to apply efficient cause to a symbolic system.

---

* In the first of his famous 146 Considerations concerning judging a (horary) astrological chart, Guido Bonatti cites three motions that begin the process: (1) the motion of the soul of the person prompted to ask the question, (2), the motions of the planets themselves, and (3) the motion of the free will that prompts one to ask the question. Dykes (2007), p.264.

Importantly, when connections between a person or event and the planetary configurations do not occur the astrologer cannot do good interpretative work. In both cases matter and form have become disconnected.

It is difficult to engage with a natal or event chart (the form) without knowing something about the person or event (the matter). It is difficult to find an 'astrological signature' for a politician or a terrorist attack, a movie star or sociopath: the symbols of astrology do not explicitly yield these categories of information. However, knowing that I am looking at the chart of this particular person or that event or question, the chart begins to disclose itself to me. In this way the 'form', the chart, becomes alive when combined with the 'material' of what the chart is to be about. As soul is to body, the astrological chart is to the person or circumstance depicted.

It is the *astrologer* who informs the chart, who gives it meaning. If the astrologer is confronted with a chart that may not be accurate or reflect the condition of the heavens of the person's birth or an event or a question, the astrologer's confident interpretative mind usually vanishes. In the mind of the astrologer, a separation between the 'material' of the Heavens and the 'form' of the chart creates an impasse.

Then there is the opposite situation, familiar to astrologers but bewildering to everybody else, when 'the wrong chart works' – an astrologer accurately interprets a chart that is *later* proven factually incorrect. That these charts are 'valid' is one of the baffling implications of astrology as primarily a divinatory and interpretative art. For a compelling presentation of 'the wrong charts working' see Cornelius (2003) Chapter 12.

In all these cases the determining factor is the astrologer's confidence in or distrust of a chart's objective validity; the form of the chart in the astrologer's mind creates or destroys its interpretative possibilities. As a divinatory art, it is the mind of the astrologer, and not the 'objective' situation depicted in the astrological chart, that gives the chart its meaning. For that reason, an uncertain but accurate chart is difficult to read but one can arrive at a correct interpretation based on one that turns out to be objectively inaccurate. This model of astrology is based not on the natural philosophy of the ancient and medieval eras or the science of our times but on phenomenology, the study of how things *appear* to us and how this shapes the meanings things have for us. Again, Cornelius' *The Moment of Astrology* gives us the best account of this approach.

We now leave behind the divinatory nature of astrology and return to natural astrology. Here configurations of the heavens have their own effects on the Earth's circumstances and individuals whether or not an astrologer is around to record or interpret it.

Sometimes astrologers blend efficient with formal causes. They may hesitate to say that the Sun's changes in declination – its movement above and below the Earth's equator – would fall under the category of efficient causation and give astrological effects. Yet twentieth century astrologer Dane Rudhyar (1978) brings in a correspondence which verges on efficient cause to account for the natures of the twelve signs of the zodiac. He explains the astrological signs by means of the gradations of day and night of the Northern Hemisphere throughout the year, likening day and night to symbolic principles of human individuation and collectivity respectively, the astrological signs carrying the oscillations between day and night.

We return to astrological prediction, for it seems to imply – or perhaps mimic – efficient causation. Transits, the most common predictive indicator for modern astrologers, are based on the planets' ongoing motion: as transiting planets make contact through the zodiac with positions in someone's natal chart, he or she experiences conditions relating to the dynamic of the transiting planet affecting the natal position. In spite of appearing to be efficient cause, however, transits are an example of formal causation. *For the outcome is simultaneous with, and does not precede, its astrological indicator.* This is also the case for other predictive techniques such as eclipses and lunations, progressions, solar returns, directions, profections, and planetary period systems.[*] Astrologers look for correlations between the configurations of the sky with the astrological chart and specific events and circumstances in the life of the native. These correlations are formal, not efficient causes.

---

[*] Some astrologers label others 'deterministic' or 'fatalistic' because they look for specific events that correspond with predictive indicators. They appear to make the same error as their scientific critics mistaking efficient cause for formal cause.

In the work of English astrologer Dennis Elwell we find a depiction of astrology that distinguishes between efficient and formal causes. Although he leans toward a Neoplatonic attitude toward astrology and its relationship to higher Being or Divine Intent, his approach seems also Aristotelian.

Elwell uses a metaphor that is also the title of his book *The Cosmic Loom* (1987). But first he writes that there are two ways of dividing an orange. We could cut the orange horizontally, crosswise into slices. Each slice would cut through the different segments of the orange. The other way is to divide an orange vertically into its natural segments. In the case of weaving, the crosswise strands are called the *weft* and Elwell calls these 'horizontal'. The 'vertical dimension' is lengthwise and in weaving is called the *warp*. According to Elwell, this is how is the cloth of our world is woven.[27]

Our normal 'scientific' understanding that incorporates efficient cause corresponds to Elwell's horizontal *weft* dimension. For a human being this may be the 'objective' dimension of his or her life – heredity and environment, health and circumstances. In the world this dimension conforms to discrete events that constitute the daily news around us.

All these occasions and individuals also operate on the vertical or *warp* dimension. Astrology's domain is this vertical dimension. Events may appear coincidental when looking at them horizontally from the weft dimension, but are actually connected on the vertical warp dimension. From weft to warp and from efficient to formal cause, horizontal contingency has become vertical meaningfulness.

To illustrate astrology's warp or vertical dimension, Elwell relies on the basic planetary symbols but extends them across many areas: the elemental, mineral, and bodily, natural and historical events, psychological attitudes and spiritual aptitudes. Happily he does not reduce the range of astrological symbolism to the psychological, the mundane, or the spiritual but includes them all.

Following Elwell's template here's my own example using Mars. This red planet appears to move around the Earth and has physical characteristics but also has a spiritual essence. Mars events, however, include sudden outbursts, fevers, athletics and warfare, cooking and surgery. Mars gives angry people, animals, and muscular bodies, heroes and spiritual crusaders. Anything with the color red has attributes of

Mars, including rashes and metals that rust like iron. The influence of Mars or any other planet does not discriminate between external and internal manifestations. (As mentioned earlier, Elwell calls collections of qualities that adhere in an astrological planet not archetypes but "holons".)

Recently one of my clients had a terrible day and later gave me permission to write about it. Earlier that day her ex-boyfriend showed up at her workplace; he was enraged and verbally abused her in public. On her way to see me for an astrological update her brakes suddenly failed in her car and she had an automobile accident. By this time my client was quite agitated. (I do not know if she was wearing red that day.) A Mars transit was strongly affecting her natal chart (transiting Mars in Virgo forming a 90° square to her natal Sun and Mercury in Gemini), and the result applied both to her behavior and also to her environment. Did her ex-boyfriend suddenly show up at her job and did her car's brakes decide to stop working, resulting in a highway accident, all because of *her* transit?

The horizontal or *weft* dimension, which is that of *efficient cause*, is one way of seeing my client's terrible day – as a co-incidence of random events. Her ex-boyfriend was not exactly peaceable to begin with, and he had just moved out of her apartment. The mechanic who was working on my client's car had questioned the brakes before returning the car, but the then-boyfriend who got the car and talked with the mechanic didn't share that part of the conversation with my client. She had had a difficult day at work for other reasons, she was very irritable and maybe impulsive, and the Friday afternoon traffic was slow and the other drivers were also impatient. Different causal streams came together, yet we know her accident was not chance; instead it was Mars in its *formal* influence on my client and her world.

Dennis Elwell's weaving metaphor gives us perspective on the relationship between efficient and formal cause in astrology. In *The Cosmic Loom* Elwell uses examples equally between mundane and natal astrology and shows natural astrology at its most compelling.

So far we have looked at material, efficient, and formal causes, only three out of four. In our last pages we examine 'final' cause. Does astrology have a teleological dimension? Or, put differently, does astrology express a cosmic nature that is purposive?

Conclusion: What are the stars and planets for?

The familiar examples of Aristotle's final causes are in nature. The final cause of a seed is the plant's development; our teeth are for the purpose of helping us ingest food by biting and chewing; the final cause (or 'end') of any living thing is its full life and overlaps with its formal cause. If efficient cause is from past to present and present to future and formal causes arise simultaneously with their objects, we can think of final causes from potential to actual and from future to present.

In Statius' commentary on the origins of the human being in *Purgatorio* 25, he depicted the embryo changing from the appearance of one life form to another until its human body was complete, possessed of a human soul, and constituting one particular human being. The full human being would be the final cause for this process that began as a fetus.

For Aristotle, the purpose or final cause of human beings is their physical and mental thriving, rational 'happiness' or *eudemonia* being most conducive to our formal nature as rational animals. Although he frequently expressed the belief that our social connections are important to our thriving as human beings, Book 10 of the *Nichomachean Ethics* posits that the contemplative life is the happiest and most flourishing life available to us. Taking from Aristotle and others, the medieval viewpoint was that our greatest activity possible was the contemplation of divinity that anticipates the direct vision of God when we are in Paradise. This viewpoint forms the final ten cantos of *Paradiso*.

Neither *Purgatorio* 25 nor *Paradiso* 2 seem to relate directly to final causes; both are concerned with activation from above and not with corresponding motions that would arise from below. Recall *Paradiso* 1 when Beatrice and her student have begun to ascend bodily through the element fire toward the Sphere of the Moon (Lines 103-142). Within the divinely ordained order, all beings have their different outcomes ("ends") according to their own natures. Our familiar four elements, seeking their natural places, have their own destinations but humans and angels may strive consciously toward God. All this is managed by providence (*la provedenza*) from Heaven to the swift *Primum Mobile* to the stars and planets below. Beatrice concludes: because you (the pilgrim Dante) have been liberated from your faults, physically ascending toward God is your natural inclination and purpose.

Western science and philosophy is uncomfortable with the idea of final cause because it implies that nature is purposive, and to many this comes close to the universe being conscious. Consider, however, the seemingly miraculous parts and functions of humans and other living creatures; modern science accounts for this through a process of natural selection that requires the accretion of millions of random events occurring over a very long time without an endpoint. Others, mostly religious thinkers, think that the universe has a purposeful trajectory and even a final condition in the distant future. This view is best articulated by mid-twentieth century paleontologist and theologian Teilhard de Chardin whose *Phenomenon of Man* (1955) depicted the entire planet evolving toward an "Omega Point" that is God.

Most astrologers, modern or traditional, are comfortable with a universe containing conscious intent that may invest being with purpose.* Dennis Elwell has given us a rather circular description of final cause: "the result may itself be the cause of whatever it takes to achieve the result."[28] According to him, each planet appears to have its own intention; together planets manifest a higher will that operates and manifests through their configurations and how they manifest in our worlds. This brings Elwell rather close to Dante's viewpoint.

Elwell discusses an "event level" that is perceptible by the senses, being the weft dimension conforming to efficient cause; the vertical warp dimension is the "meaning level" that signifies what an event is about, the dimension that astrology articulates. Additionally he also posits an "intent level" – the purpose of person or event from a cosmic viewpoint.[29] He asserts that the meaning or vertical dimension also operates from the material to the spiritual. Ultimately astrology is a language of the "higher self", that universe of which human consciousness is an active participant. Yet astrology also operates on the level of the everyday.

As with the archetypal astrology previously discussed, Elwell's

---

* There is one major difference between Aristotelian and these astrological suppositions: Aristotle's teleological approach extended mostly to individuals as members of species or classes of beings, but to the modern astrologer a natal chart is a blueprint for one person only. For many astrologers, each person has an individual providential calling that can be gathered from the natal chart, and its timing for development gathered through astrology's predictive indicators.

metaphysics raises more questions than it provides confident answers. Some of the limitations of archetypal astrology are also his. His view of astrology, however, includes and values a more complete range of experience than do his archetypal peers who tend to over-focus on the psychological dimensions of experience.

I conclude by commenting on a current bifurcation of the astrological community with different models of the astrologer's calling. They reflect fundamental differences on what it is to be a human.

In one corner are 'event-oriented' astrologers who use both traditional and modern techniques. Their work is concerned with prediction and appears to rely on efficient cause but, as we have seen, it is actually formal cause. Their focus is on matters of fortune, a concern with their clients' happiness and success.

In the other corner are the 'humanistic' astrologers whose work is characterized by strict loyalty to a teleological focus: the natal chart itself discloses the life purposes of the individual and the means to attain them. This is allied with the psychological and archetypal viewpoint cited above, whereby difficult situations are to be overcome through insight and focused activity. I include among them astrologers who interpret the astrological chart with reference to clients' multiple lifetimes. They discuss features of the natal chart that may help accomplish this lifetime's 'soul's purposes' and what spiritual obstacles are most important to counter.

Many in this group sense that they are practicing the astrology of a more advanced era when people's attention is toward issues of personal and spiritual growth, instead of the vicissitudes of outer circumstance. In this way they are acknowledging the higher purposes of their clients, not just telling them how to get by in a difficult world.

They contrast their style with more traditional approaches they deem 'deterministic', an astrology that purportedly lives off of the fear of a universe that will turn Fortune's Wheel arbitrarily. Instead of fear, they foster in their clients a sense of personal empowerment and spiritual or psychological purpose. They feel that it is all too easy for 'event-related' astrologers to be oracular, in a negative way, and thus create dependency in the client.

Event-inclined astrologers have a different point of view, of course. Often they feel that modern psychological teleological approaches result in conceptual fuzziness, new age pedantry and sanctimony. They submit that modern astrologers give short shrift to life concerns that have not changed over the millennia: fame and career, family, love, health, and happiness – the areas of life most subject to the ups and downs of fortune. It is very easy, they say, for a modern astrologer to set up him or herself a new-age guru. The fourth *bolgia* beckons.

From the early fourteenth century, Dante's *Divine Comedy* provides a template through which we can reconcile these differences by understanding that fortune and providence are complementary and both express who we are; both are creatively explored through the symbols of astrology.

In the context of the evil events that will eventually befall the pilgrim, the *Divine Comedy* puts the question of fortune front and center. We have seen several of the inmates and citizens of the afterlife relate prophecies of Dante's personal catastrophe to come. Additionally there is concern for a cultural milieu that had declined considerably in moral effectiveness and value. Bad fortune has beset the pilgrim and his world together.

This culminates in Cacciaguida's prophecy in *Paradiso* 17. Indeed personal calamity awaits his descendant and Cacciaguida goes into detail about this. Connecting the personal with the historical, his personal prophecy to the pilgrim occurs only after depicting the social and moral decline of Florence. Although Dante's exile is a terrible personal event during a time of social decline, God's plan – providence – is also fully at work, but one has to see it. The role of Cacciaguida's prophecy is to disclose to the pilgrim how his bad fortune can become service of God and nourishment for others. Fortune – or we might just call it fate – has not been replaced or even transcended but *included* within a larger range of meaning. *Nowhere in the poem does Dante pretend that his upcoming personal catastrophe doesn't matter.*

The poet of The *Divine Comedy* may find much to admire in modern psychological and spiritual astrology. Its art can illuminate the different harbors or ports we are inclined to and tell us the planetary movements that provide opportunities for us. He might also find it bloodless and prone to bullshit, especially in its dismissive stance toward Lady Fortune and her place in the scheme of things. He might consider this dismissal of fortune to be impious.

The great poet would also have had difficulties with astrology focused mostly on fortune that is dismissive of any attempts to find higher meaning in the vicissitudes of human circumstance. When we look to those in the *Inferno* whose main concern is fortune, from Brunetto Latini to the diviners in the Fourth *bolgia* and the "evil counselors" below, we find that it was not their predictions or advice that were problematic but the narrow context in which they occurred. For all their emphasis on fortune there was no sense that there was a larger field involved – except maybe as something to be bargained with to better one's chances.

At its best astrology allows our individual concern with fortune to drive us upwards toward a larger view, so that what happens to us is not just about us but the entire world. In their movements and their relationships to the Earth, astrology's stars and planets reveal to us an essential meaningfulness we can understand and apply to our own lives. We can apply astrology to the turnings of our Wheel of Fortune, but with a view toward the eternal.

We return to our early discussion of Boethius' *Consolation of Philosophy*. Think back to heartbroken Boethius in his prison cell as he receives a visitation by Lady Philosophy. She tried to cheer up the despairing philosopher with her admonishments and theoretical constructs, all of which were valid. However, like Dante contemplating his upcoming exile, Boethius missed his wife and children and his advantages in life. Try as she might, Lady Philosophy could never quite change the prisoner's mind. Maybe the wrong Lady showed up.

Notes

1. Durling/Martinez (1996) p.407
2. Barolini, Thordolinda, "Canto XX: True and False Seers". From Mandlebaum et al (1998)
3. Statius Thebiad, 7.690-823
4. See Alison Cornish, "The Harvest of Reading". She stresses the contrast Dante makes between Arruns divining in his cave above and the peasants below doing honest work.
5. Adapted from Getty, R.L. p.17-18
6. *Convivio* IV. xvi.6. Referenced by Hollander (2000), p.378
7. Cornelius (2003), pp.197-198
8. Greene, Liz (2010). p.20.
9. Campion, N. (2008), p.196
10. Liddell and Scott, *Intermediate Greek-English Lexicon* (1972), Oxford University Press. p.704
11. Cassata, L. "The Hard Begin" from Mandlebaum, A. (1998)
12. Hollander (2003), p.754
13. Thorndike, L. pp.556-557, 607-610
14. Kaske, C. and Clark, J. (1989) p.45
15. Campion, N. (2009) p.67
16. Thorndike (1929), p.828
17. Crane, J. "The Peculiar Development of the Modern Astrologer" (2000) http://www.astrologyinstitute.com/Articles/article_modern.htm
18. Martinez, "Canto XXV: Statius's Marvelous Connectionof Things". In *Lectura Dantis: Purgatorio* (2008) Ed. Madelbaum. Berkeley and Los Angeles: University of California Press.
19. Hollander (2007), pp.52-53
20. Durling (2010), p.62
21. *Summa Theologica* 1, question 15.
22. Führer, Markus, "Albert the Great", *The Stanford Encyclopedia of Philosophy* (Spring 2011 Edition), Edward N. Zalta (ed.), forthcoming URL = <http://plato.stanford.edu/archives/spr2011/entries/albert-great/>
23. Grasse, Ray (1996), *The Waking Dream: Unlocking the Symbolic Language of our Lives* (Quest Publications), *The Mountain Astrologer* #155, February/March 2011.
24. Tarnas, Richard. "An Introduction to Archetypal Astrology" http://www.cosmosandpsyche.com/pdf/IntroductiontoAstrology.pdf (June 2010) p.2
25. Perry, Glenn, "The Emerging Field of Archetypal Cosmology", *The Mountain Astrologer* #155, February/March 2011.
26. Summa I, qu.15
27. Elwell (1987), pp.24-25
28. Elwell (1987), p.126
29. Elwell (1987), p.133

Appendix 1: The Divine Comedy as Poetry

The *Divine Comedy* is a poem of over fourteen thousand lines of rhymed verse. Not acknowledging its poetry is like discussing the ceiling of the Sistine Chapel without letting on that there is a large painting within it.

One outstanding feature of Dante's poetry is its stylistic variety. Its poetic voice changes considerably through Hell, Purgatory, and Heaven to reflect the different people and settings that the pilgrim encounters. The *Divine Comedy* moves through satire, diatribe, philosophical and theological argumentation, contemplative ecstasy, and some of the sweetest lyrics written.

There are many different ways to translate The *Divine Comedy* into English. To briefly illustrate Dante's poetry and some possible English renderings I take as example two passages from the *Purgatorio*. The first is at the beginning of *Purgatorio*'s first canto and signals an important turning point in the poem. The second example is further along in *Purgatorio* 8 and I include it for its sound qualities and ways of reproducing them in English.

Planet in Sky

Dante and Virgil have just emerged from Hell and have climbed back onto the surface of the Earth. In Hell we find no Sun, no stars and no planets. Now, at the very beginning of the *Purgatorio*, after the invocation, Dante finds a sky full of beauty and symbolism. First let's just look at the Italian alone.

> "*Dolce color d'oriental zaffiro,*
> *che s'accoglieva nel sereno aspetto*
> *del mezzo, puro infino al primo giro,*
>
> *a li occhi miei ricominciò diletto,*
> *tosto ch'io usci' fuor de l'aura morta*
> *che m'avea contristati li occhi e 'l petto.*

Lo bel pianeto che d'amar conforta
faceva tutto rider l'orïente,
velando i Pesci ch'erano in sua scorta." (*Purgatorio* 1:13-21)

Each line is about the same length – eleven syllables. Together with its tight rhyme scheme and the even stress patterns of Italian it makes for a steady rhythm throughout the poem.

The first tercet rhymes the end of lines one and three (*zaffiro* and *giro*). If you look at the second tercet, you see that the words *diletto* and *petto* rhyme with *aspetto* in the first. This continues further: *morta* ends the second tercet's second line and rhymes with *conforta* and *scorta* which end lines one and three of the third tercet. The formal pattern is: ABA – BCB – CDC – DED, etc. This rhyme scheme links together all the lines in an elaborate chain of end sounds. This is called *terza rima* and Dante developed it specifically for the *Divine Comedy*. Some English poets have attempted to imitate this difficult pattern as, for example, in Shelley's 'Ode to the West Wind'. Although the Italian language is richer in rhyme than English, for Dante to have sustained this for over 14,000 lines of very good poetry is close to miraculous.

"*Dolce color d'orïental zaffiro,*"
The sweet color of oriental saffire

"*che s'accoglieva nel sereno aspetto*"
gathering the serene countenance

"*del mezzo, puro infino al primo giro,*"
of the air, pure to the first circle

The first line *Dolce color d'orïental zaffiro* almost doesn't need a translation. Most straightforward would be "The sweet color of oriental sapphire", and Longfellow, Durling, and Hollander give us just that. Yet there are other possibilities for this line.

"Dolce" is commonly translated as 'sweet', and the word appears in the *Inferno* to refer nostalgically to the life and the sky above. However, Mark Musa and W. S. Merwin give us 'tender' for *dolce*. Moving to the second word of the first line, Charles Singleton translates *color* as 'hue', Musa as 'tint', and Ciardi as 'azure'.

I prefer the direct 'sweet color'. 'Sweet' is one of the finer words of the English language and well-conveys the contrast between the hopelessness of Hell and the better things ahead. 'Color' contrasts with the pallor of Hell, and then seems more realistic to the act of perception. Beyond Hell we would first notice color itself, then what color it is – in this case the azure or blue of sapphire.

Now we arrive at the sapphire. Is it better to translate *d'oriëntal* as 'oriental' or 'east'? The origin of the sapphire, the east, is also the direction in which the pilgrim will see Venus. The fair planet is rising ahead of the Sun and therefore is oriental. This not only makes Venus beautiful to behold in the pre-dawn sky but auspicious as the escort of the Sun that is about to rise. We could say that Venus heralds the Sun. We see the coupling of 'east' and 'ascending' elsewhere in the *Divine Comedy*. 'East' and 'ascending' also refer to Christ. Although *d'oriëntal* is used twice in these three tercets, many translators call the first 'oriental' and the second one 'east'.

Now we take on the last line's *primo giro*, for which the English is simply 'first circle'. What, in the context of just landing on the outskirts of Purgatory, is the 'first circle'? It makes no sense for it to be the circle of Moon, the closest planetary rung in Paradise. Instead most commentators see *primo giro* as the horizon. Hollander, Musa, Ciardi, and Merwin all give us 'horizon'. Longfellow and the prose translations of Singleton and Durling retain 'first circle'.

I prefer the more literal 'first circle'. This foreshadows the structure of what is to come, the terraces of the mountain of Purgatory and the perfect circles of the realms of Paradise. We tend to think of the horizon as a flat plane but it's also a circle, measured across in degrees of azimuth. (Up-down is 'altitude'.) The first circle of the horizon is the first rung of all the circles from the Earth's surface and is immediately *here*. As we have seen in the first line of *Purgatorio* 2, Dante is quite capable of using the word *l'orizzonte* if that's all he wanted to say.

> "*a li occhi miei ricominciò diletto,*
> *tosto ch'io usci' fuor de l'aura morta*
> *che m'avea contristati li occhi e 'l petto.*"

> renewed my eyes' delight
> having become free of the dead air
> That weighed heavily on my eyes and chest

The last line here has the word *petto*, which can mean either 'breast' or 'chest'. Ciardi renders it 'soul' and Musa 'heart', words that are emotionally evocative but often specifically psychological or spiritual. Most translators render *petto* as 'breast', but Hollander gives us *petto* as the more unpoetic 'chest'. I prefer the Hollander version: in addition to articulating the psychic burdens of Hell, Dante is also trying to express Hell's physical effect: dead air impedes eyesight and makes it difficult to breathe – these let us in on Hell's pervasively suffocating nature.

> *"Lo bel pianeto che d'amar conforta*
> *faceva tutto rider l'oriente,*
> *velando i Pesci ch'erano in sua scorta."*

> The beautiful planet that strengthens love
> made all the orient smile
> veiling the Fish that are her escort (13-21)

The third tercet finally presents its object Venus, planet of beauty and, in the context of *Purgatorio* 1, a symbol of hope. The planet of love depicted here is the first object sighted after the narrow egotism of Hell. This planet of love prefigures God's love that is present among Purgatory's suffering and that pervades heaven and the grand conclusion of the poem.

Lo bel pianeto – the 'fair or beautiful planet' – that *d'amar conforta*. Hollander gives us 'emboldens love'; to Singleton it 'prompts' love; to Merwin Venus 'inclines us to love'; for Ciardi and Durling it 'strengthens love'. This last one seems to be the most direct rendering of *conforta*. Longfellow gives this line as 'The beauteous planet, that to love incites'. The causal relationship between Venus and love is left vague. Following Dante, all tread lightly here. In *Inferno* 5 we learn about how easy it is to use love as an excuse for wrongdoing. In *Paradiso* 8 we are told that the world once believed that the Cyprian (Venus the goddess) 'beamed rays of maddened love' (Hollander). The best rendering of *conforta* in this context is not entirely clear.

What is the relationship between Venus and the stars of Pisces? Bright Venus hides or veils (*velando*) the dim stars of Pisces. Many translators render the last word *scorta* as 'train', although I do not think that is the best selection. 'Train' implies that the stars follow the planet Venus; the word itself is of course close to our word 'escort' and simply means to accompany and perhaps guide Venus. I would imagine that Dante would have Venus amidst the stars of Pisces and veiling them by its brightness – not leading them. Venus in the *tropical sign* Pisces could have been leading the stars in the *constellation* Pisces, due to the very slow apparent movement of the fixed stars we call the 'precession of the equinox' (which Dante was well aware of). But then how could a planet both lead and veil the stars in its vicinity? I will have to go along with rendering *scorta* as 'escort'.

There are other translation issues in these three tercets but I leave them now. We move to a totally different passage in the *Purgatorio*.

Snake in Grass

Our second example is from *Purgatorio* Canto 8, and I include it for its specific qualities of expressive sound in poetry.

Up to this time, Dante and Virgil have been moving toward the ledge of the mountain of Purgatory, encountering people, who, for one reason or another, need to wait until they can begin the process of purification. Dante and Virgil are just below the ridge that will later carry them to the mountain. They are near the Valley of the Kings, a beautiful landscape containing once-distracted nobility who had delayed their own spiritual progress. As night arrives there's an element of danger. Two angels had arrived to protect the pilgrims' nighttime. Sordello, another poet who at this time accompanies pilgrim and guide, points out the snake in the grass. I urge the reader simply to attend to the sounds of this verse.

> "Tra l'erba e' fior ven'ia la mala striscia,
> volgendo ad ora ad or la testa, e 'l dosso
> leccando come bestia che si liscia." (*Purgatorio* 8.100-103)

The reader may notice that the last syllables of the first and third lines rhyme and in the third line there is an internal semi-rhyme: *bestia* (beast) and *liscia* (to smooth or preen) carry much the same sound.

The snake is referred to as a *striscia* – a streak or stripe. Note how, beginning midway in the second line, hard consonants keep company with many s sounds – sibilants – giving our ears the sound this snake makes: Dante does not say what one hears but sounds it out instead. Through the poet's choice of words we hear the sliding and maybe the hissing of the creature and its proud preening attitude.

Now we look at the different possibilities for translations. I begin with John Ciardi. It was his version that I first read over thirty years ago when I was first introduced to Dante. Ciardi rhymes the end of the first and third lines throughout his rendering of the poem.

> Through the sweet grass and flowers the long snake drew,
> turning its head around from time to time
> to lick itself as preening beasts will do.

Throughout his well-known and poetically beautiful translation, Ciardi makes many sacrifices to the pattern of rhyme he uses. In this stanza there are no sounds of hissing and slithering; instead Ciardi attends more to the snake's preening style. Note that the sibilants that appear in the 'sweet grass and flowers' are within pleasant words that fail to communicate any threat from the snake.

Now we look at Henry W. Longfellow's rendering from the nineteenth century. He follows the conventions of formal style of which he was a master.

> 'Twixt grass and flowers came on the evil streak,
> Turning at times its head about, and licking
> Its back like to a beast that smooths itself.

Longfellow also loses much of the hissing sound but makes up for it by using a lot of hard consonants, in contrast to the use of the word 'smooths' toward the end of the third line. Although some readers may find his English to be artificial, these lines give us a sense of him as a fine American poet.

Like Longfellow, Mark Musa writes in blank verse – mostly ten syllables per line, unrhymed, stressing every second syllable. Here is Musa's version of these lines.

> Through grass and flowers slid the viscous streak,
> stopping from time to time to turn its head
> and lick its back to make its body sleek.

Musa certainly attends to sound effects in his first line. His choice of 'slid' to move the snake seems quite good. Instead of the usual 'evil' for *mala*, he gives us 'vicious' – this word changes the meaning slightly but is a word that sounds like a snake moving in the grass. Like Ciardi and

Longfellow, Musa uses hard syllables to convey the malice of the snake, but also hits on 'sleek' at the end to return us to the sound of the snake moving in the grass.*

Here's one by Jean Hollander from her more recent *Purgatorio*. Her style has more the spontaneous feel of much contemporary poetry.

> Through grass and flowers slid the evil streak,
> turning its head from time to time to lick its back
> like a beast that sleeks itself.

She also finds much in the sliding snake that 'sleeks', and brings together 'streak' and 'sleek'. Note also the many hard consonant endings in this tercet that give the words some ugliness – a fine contrast to the fine colors and scents of the valley they are in.

I end this discussion by mentioning translations in prose that allow greater flexibility in rendering the original more faithfully into English. In past decades, John Sinclair and Charles Singleton have produced the best-known prose versions. We now have a more recent version of the *Divine Comedy* by Robert Durling that translates into prose but with line breaks similar to verse. Here is from his translation of the *Purgatorio* (2003).

> Among the grass and the flowers came the evil slither, now and again turning its head and licking its back like a beast that smooths itself.

I particularly like the 'evil slither' of the snake; these words contain a lovely oily feel.

In general, which translations do I recommend to the reader? I recommend many of them at once, for there is much to learn from them all. And there are many more versions that I do not mention here, because I am less familiar with them. I do have a few opinions, though.

John Ciardi, Henry Longfellow and Dorothy Sayers have much to commend them, although the modern reader may find their formal styles a bit old-fashioned. It is hard not to like Mark Musa's verse translations and I often recommend them to somebody who is new to the material.

---

* Although here Musa rhymes the first and third lines, his rendering of the Divine Comedy does not generally employ rhyme.

For a more contemporary feel, I have enjoyed and recommend the translations of Robert Pinksy for the *Inferno* (that is wonderful to read aloud), M. S. Merwin for the *Purgatorio*, and Jean Hollander for all three canticles. To help the reader follow Dante's Italian and for their own stylistic merits I recommend the prose translations from Charles Singleton, John Sinclair, and in particular the more recent work of Robert Durling.

Appendix 2: An Astrological Chart for Dante

In some alternate universe there is a piece of parchment somewhere that tells the day and time that Dante was born. Even a documented birthday would be an improvement over our lack of reliable information about Dante's birth. I would even settle for finding a statement to a third party that says, for example, "Dante told his friend Forese that he was born on…" Because Dante was such an important historical figure and an interesting personality, and because his life had such oscillations of circumstance, I should at least attempt to construct a usable astrological chart for him.

There is some circumstantial evidence that Dante knew his astrological chart. Dante knew astronomy and astrology during a time in which astrology was practiced. He was also consummately interested in himself and used both numerological and astrological symbolism in his work. As discussed previously, we can surmise from *Inferno* 15 that Dante's youthful mentor Brunetto Latini had known Dante's astrological chart well enough to assert that the poet would be successful in life and also predict that he could be undone by powerful enemies.

It is possible that the poet's understanding of his own birth chart was incorrect; he may also have taken 'poetic license' and presented things differently from his own better knowledge. Nonetheless, I feel obliged to use what information we have from the poet to assign him a natal chart, with the understanding that a trustworthy documented chart would replace my best efforts here.

The task is to come up with an astrological chart that would (1) conform to various passages in the poet's work, (2) contain features that a medieval astrologer could use meaningfully, and (3) satisfy the modern astrologer's desire to understand the person and account for major events in his life.

The normal procedure for 'rectification' – determining a plausible chart for somebody – is to first narrow down a natal chart from more general indicators, e.g. one's Sun sign or month of birth, to those that would be specific, such as Moon and especially the Ascendant sign. The next step may be to narrow things down further by considering a person's physical and psychological characteristics and then using 'the accidents of the native' – the important events in his life – that could determine predictive indicators that correspond to specific life events. By using the scant documentary evidence that exists, citing indications from Dante's poetical work, and looking at the year preceding his exile from Florence, I have arrived at a plausible birth chart for the poet. Here are the steps I took to arrive at the chart given on page 271.

Dante thought his natal Sun was in Gemini; he states this clearly in *Paradiso* 22.112-120. Previously Dante and Beatrice have ascended all seven planetary spheres, and are now on the band of the fixed stars and the zodiac. The pilgrim finds himself on the constellation of Gemini and praises the stars where the Sun resided when he drew his first breath. (According to the astrology of Dante's lifetime, Gemini would do so through its affinity with the planet Mercury who governs Gemini. Dante mentions not Mercury but Sun here, in keeping with his emphasis on the realm of the fixed stars and the zodiac and on the Sun's light.)

Dante once said that he was born in May 1265.[1] According to the Julian calendar used during his lifetime, we can surmise that Dante was born sometime in the second half of that month, when the Sun was in Gemini. (Remember that in Dante's time this calendar was about nine days behind the modern Gregorian calendar that dates from the late sixteenth century.)

Another clue is given in the *Paradiso*. I return to Cacciaguida's conversation with the pilgrim upon the sphere of Mars. Dante's admiration for and identification with Cacciaguida is also apparent throughout their conversation. In *Paradiso* 16.37-39 Dante's ancestor alludes to the year of his birth: the time between "Ave" (the Annunciation) and his birth was 580 ingresses of Mars into Leo. Dante probably thinks (or wanted to think) that he has Mars in Leo. It would strengthen his identification with Cacciaguida as if they were connected by the stars as well as by blood. Mars entered Leo shortly after 6 AM on May 26 1265.

Where might Dante's Moon have been? When Mars entered Leo the Moon was in the last degrees of Libra; for the rest of May the Moon was in Scorpio and in Sagittarius. An astrologer would have to weigh the very different qualities of these Moon placements. I will discard Libra as a possibility, for there is a far smaller chance of the Moon being in

Libra during this time, nor does Moon in Libra quite sound like Dante. A different possibility is Moon in Sagittarius that has visionary buoyant qualities.

One may consider the often-tortured emotional intensity that commonly accompanies Moon in Scorpio. Malefic Mars in Leo would be the dispositor for Moon in Scorpio; on the other hand, the benefic Jupiter in Taurus would be the dispositor for a Sagittarius Moon. My sense of Dante inclines me toward Moon in Scorpio.* Therefore we are looking for an astrological chart for the last days of May 1265 and with Moon in Scorpio.

Now we need to arrive at a time of day. Usually this is a more difficult step but here we have some help, at least speculatively.

Sometime in the middle 1290s Dante wrote a set of poems called the *Rime Petrose* that depicts Dante's attraction to a woman "of stone". Robert M. Durling and Ronald Martinez have presented a close examination of these poems in *Time and the Crystal* (2000) and I have found their presentation very helpful here. One of the four poems of particular interest begins with the line *Io son venuto al punto de la rota*. The poem presents coldness through the different realms of nature, beginning with the heavens themselves then descending in to the climate, birds, animals, and the earth itself – in contrast to the poet's warm and ultimately hopeful heart. Its first stanza may contain an inversion of the poet's astrological chart.

Let's look over this first stanza which depicts the cold sky. It begins with the line "*Io son venuto al punto de la rota*," "I've come to the point of the wheel". Durling and Martinez note that it is not the Sun that has come to the wheel but the poet himself. This may tip us off that what the sky depicted, symbolizing the woman and his futile longings, contrasts with Dante's own chart.

---

* If Dante does have Moon in Scorpio – or thought he did – this supplies a personal layer of meaning to the ominous and enigmatic opening of *Purgatorio* 9 in which the pilgrim sees "Tithonis' concubine" in the East. It is commonly interpreted that these lines refer to the Moon rising in the East with gems on her forehead in the shape of a scorpion. Replacing the Sun of day in Purgatory, Scorpio Moon rising at night forms a background for the pilgrim as a fallible and spiritually regressive person who cannot advance on his own.

Here are the first lines in Italian and a prose translation by Durling.

"Io son venuto al punto de la rota
che l'orizzonte, quando il sol si corca,
ci partorisce il geminato cielo,"

I've come to the point of the wheel where the Horizon gives birth
at sunset to the twinned heaven...

Dante begins with a discussion of the *Descendant* – where the Sun goes down – opposing an Ascendant governed by the twins – Gemini. This is a symbolic depiction of thwarted romantic connection: Dante is the Gemini Ascendant (and astrological First House) and this stony cold woman the Descendant (and Seventh House). In the astrology of Dante's time and afterwards, the First House represents oneself (or the initiator of an action or a question) and the Seventh represents the marriage or romantic partner (or adversary). This opening also suggests a Gemini Ascendant in the poet's astrological chart that would give him a birth time of near sunrise.

Then the poem continues by describing positions of planets. Let's follow it awhile.

"e la stella d'amor ci sta remota
per lo raggio lucente che la 'nforca
sí di traverso, che le si fa velo;"

and the star of love is kept from us by the sun's ray that
straddles her so transversely that she is veiled;

"Love's own star" is obviously Venus; she is away because the Sun, the beams of the 'bright ray', intercedes and hides her from sight. Because Venus is hidden, she is limited in her abilities, and by implication she would be less able to return his love.

"e quel pianeta che conforta il gelo
si mostra tutto a noi per lo grand'arco
nel qual ciascun di sette fa poca ombra:"

and that planet that strengthens the frost shows itself to us entirely,
along the great arc where each of the seven casts a shadow,

Saturn and no other planet can (or would want to) strengthen frost.

During the daytime the path of planets in northern lattitudes close to the Tropic of Cancer trace a wide arc, a *grand 'arco*. Saturn is depicted in Gemini or Cancer. (In May 1265 Saturn was retrograde, moving from the early degrees of Cancer to the late degrees of Gemini, near the Tropic of Cancer.)

Is there an astrological configuration with Gemini rising and Sagittarius Sun setting with Venus and Saturn close to the Tropic of Cancer and Venus hidden by the Sun? Here's one possibility (below).*

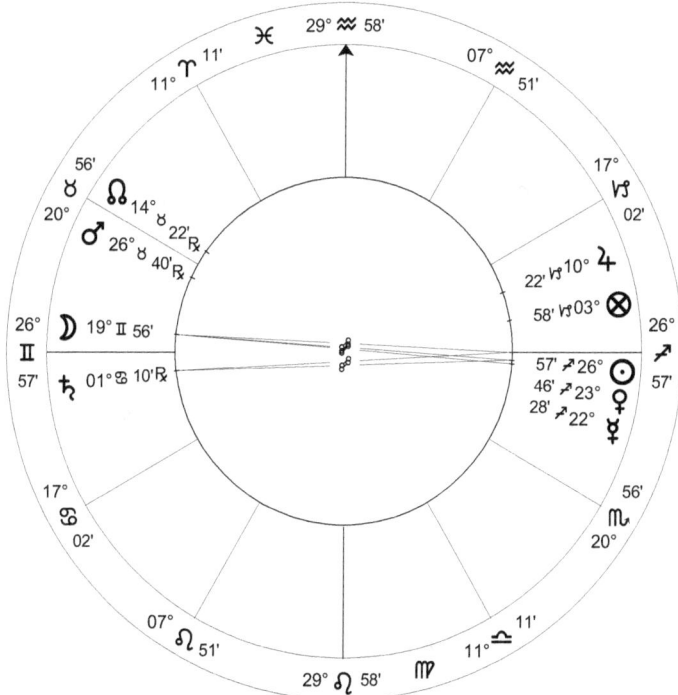

Dante's *Rime Petrose*: 10 December 1296, 4.20 PM LMT -0:45, Florence, Italy. 43N46, 11E15

---

* Martinez and Durling (1990) p.81 supply a different astrological chart for this poem: December 24, 1296 at 5:30 PM for Florence. Their chart for two weeks later features Sun conjunct Venus but Cancer rising and a Capricorn Sun. They were looking for a conjunction of Sun and Venus; since in the poem Venus is hidden by the Sun's rays and not the Sun's body, a close conjunction does not seem to be necessary. However the Martinez/Durling chart has the advantage of Saturn having retrograded back into Gemini where it was when Dante was born.

> **This Chart's Symbolism**
>
> We could treat this chart (shown on previous page) like an astrological depiction of thwarted love. The Ascendant represents the ambitious lover, the Descendent his object of affection. The Moon – the general significator of the event or situation – is near the Ascendant in Gemini, opposing the many planets in Sagittarius in the Seventh, indicating a possible meeting of the hearts but with great difficulty. Mercury, governing this Ascendant, is close to the Descendant (representing the woman), and is closely conjunct Venus that could indicate her attractiveness. Both Mercury and Venus are close to the Sun – 'combust' – and would be weakened. Mercury (the would-be lover) is governed by Jupiter that is also in the Seventh House, the place of the lady; she is clearly in charge of the situation. Saturn is in the First House, even further indicating romantic futility.

If this chart was a deliberate inversion of Dante's own natal chart, the poet would have a Gemini Ascendant and Gemini Sun. In late May 1265 Sun and Mercury were in Gemini. In late May 1265 Venus was in mid-Cancer and bright as an evening star, inverting the fair planet's position in the chart above. Saturn is the exception: in late May 1265 Saturn was in early Gemini and also on the largest part of the arc of the zodiac.

Here is a possible chart for the poet: May 28 1265 at 4:40 AM in Florence, Italy. (Facing page)

This and the chart that follows it use the Alcabitius quadrant house system that was used during Dante's lifetime. For now I have omitted the modern planets. In this way the chart resembles one that the poet may have thought to be his own.

Does this chart describe the poet? Does it conform to the *Divine Comedy*'s frequent assertion of Dante's fortunate stars but also difficulties that may arise? Let's first focus on Mercury and Saturn.

Mercury having recently escaped from combustion with the Sun, is retrograde but in its own sign Gemini and in its own terms. Mercury is also oriental, a visible morning star, and fulfills the medieval conditions

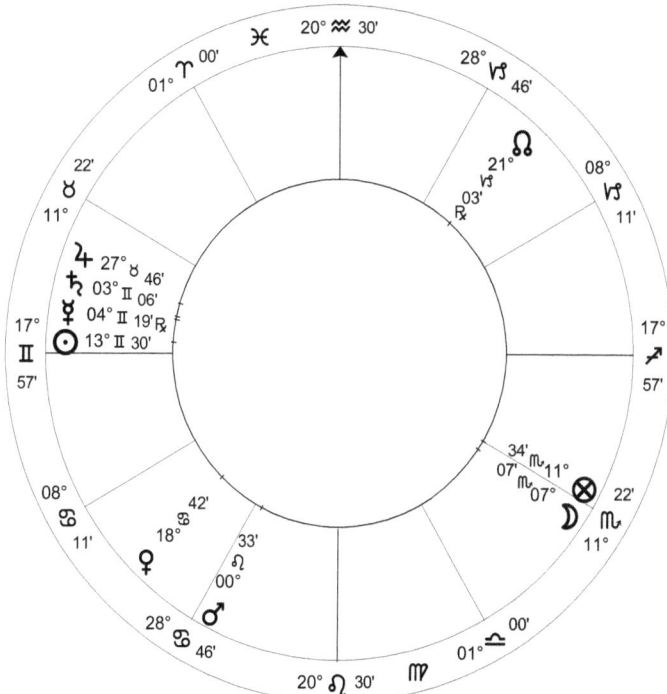

Dante – rectified. 28 May 1265, 4.40 AM LMT -0:45, Florence, Italy. 43N46, 11E15

for planetary sect. This is a mostly fortunate planet with one huge difficulty that we will consider shortly.

Saturn is in its own triplicity and, with Mercury, fulfills the conditions of the medieval doctrine of planetary sect. These are all conditions of strength in matters governed by Mercury, the dispositor of planets and an Ascendant in Gemini. Additionally Mercury joins Saturn and these two planets are strongly tied together.

Together with Jupiter, Mercury and Saturn are oriental and can be indicators of worldly success. Mercury conjunct Saturn may present itself in the variability and the detailed architecture of the *Divine Comedy*, its many worlds and poetic styles, its sensuality and its theology, that all come together in its organization. Jupiter, in a different sign from Mercury and Saturn, has a different agenda.

All astrologers reading this would quickly note that Mercury, Saturn, and Jupiter are all in the twelfth house, a place of planetary debility.

One concern of the cadent twelfth house, among other things, is *secret enemies*. It is difficult for me to look at Jupiter in Taurus in the place of secret enemies and not think of Pope Boniface VIII. Considering Dante's placements in the difficult twelfth house, Brunetto Latini's concern about those who do not wish the poet well seems quite appropriate.

The Moon is in fall in Scorpio and is close to the cadent sixth house (another planetary debility) and the Moon's square from Mars (Moon's dispositor) only increases Moon's emotional intensity. Both Moon and Mars are in fixed signs that may indicate emotional perseverance and uncompromising activity. On the happier side, Moon is joining Venus by trine in the Moon's domicile Cancer and indicates confidence and success in artistic or romantic endeavors.

I now add another chart on the outside to create a biwheel. The chart inside is that of Dante but with the modern planets also appearing. The

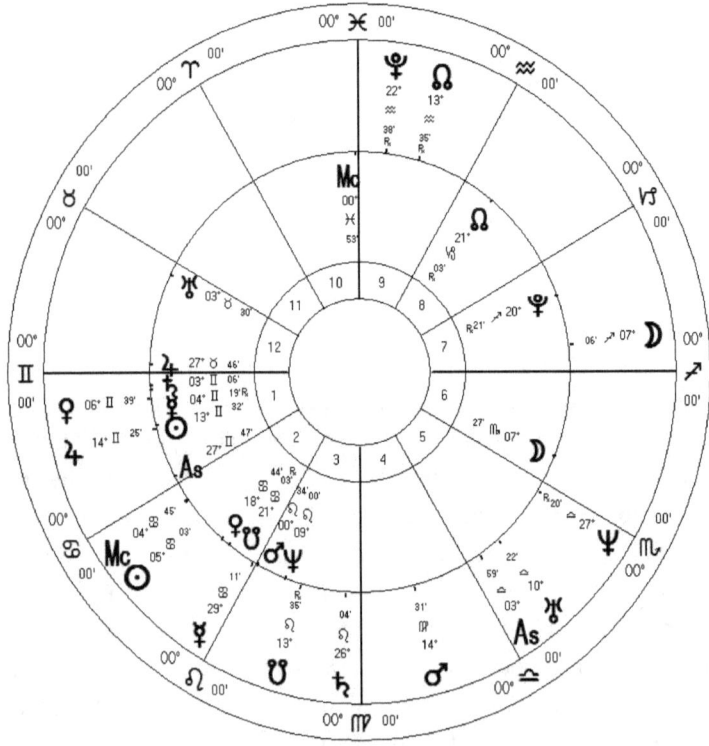

Inner wheel: Dante natal
Outer wheel: Opposes Pope Boniface 19 June 1301 12.00 PM 43N46
011E15 Florence, Italy

chart on the outside is for the day in 1301 when Dante gave a speech to oppose Pope Boniface's request for allied forces from Florence. This biwheel allows us to note the effect of the modern planets on this birth chart, and also help determine what planets were transiting his natal chart during this critical time in the poet's life, what began a chain of events culminating in his exile from Florence.

First let's ponder his natal chart on the inner wheel that shows the modern planets Uranus, Neptune, and Pluto. We see Pluto in the Seventh House that traditionally gives indications of marriage and also open enemies. Uranus has a combustible – and very stubborn – square with Mars that only amplifies the intensity of the Moon-Mars connection mentioned above. To bring a quality of spiritual yearning and occasional emotional cluelessness, Moon is in square with Neptune.

To assess this difficult year for Dante, we first look at medieval predictive indicators. For the year of Dante's exile, the *profection* (advance) of the Ascendant was to the Twelfth House. This would make Venus, ruler of Taurus, the 'Lord of the Year' after his birthday in 1301. In Dante's solar return Venus was in opposition to the Midheaven that signifies career and leadership, and was in an applying square to a difficult Saturn in the Eighth House: this compromises Venus' otherwise positive qualities during the year.

By *direction* Sun had moved to a conjunction with Venus: although this would ordinarily be a very positive development, the fair planet's rulership over the twelfth house, and its compromised status in that year's solar return, further focuses our attention to matters of the Twelfth House of undoings and secret enemies. Under these circumstances it would have been far better for him to utilize Venus by finding a good woman or strengthening his marriage.

Modern astrology's predictive indicators emphasize planetary *transits* that connect moving planets with natal positions. When we look at Dante's transits for the time before Dante's exile we see him in a mixed situation. The positive side is represented by transiting Jupiter: during this time the poet assumed political leadership and controversy, becoming associated with the cause of Florence's independence from Papal hegemony. This increased public role is indicated by Jupiter transiting Dante's Saturn/Mercury conjunction. Transiting Jupiter was coming close to the Sun and would shortly afterwards cross his Ascendant. All this should have been good news for him.

At the same time, though, transiting Mars had approached a square to all of his Gemini planets and his Ascendant, signifying intense political combat with a strong adversary. Dante's medieval contemporaries might have noticed these transits, although transits were not emphasized in medieval astrology as they are today.

Making matters more difficult for Dante and a red flag for modern astrologers was transiting Pluto that was moving retrograde toward a station upon his Midheaven degree. This was a time of great potential for Dante's participation in the larger scene of Italian politics but accompanying great risk. Later in the summer there was a total solar eclipse at 19° Leo near transiting Pluto and also opposing his Midheaven. All of this is ominous.

Here is how things developed. During the summer of 1301 transiting Saturn was moving to a square to Dante's natal Jupiter in the Twelfth – this would not be a great time to go into conflict with the head of a religion. Over the next several months Saturn entered Virgo: when the French captured and the Black Guelfs occupied Florence late in 1301, transiting Saturn was at station close to a square to Dante's Sun. Additionally, in the early summer of 1301 transiting Neptune was retrograde in the late degrees of Libra; later Neptune the planet would go direct and in October it would enter Scorpio. In early November 1301, during the same week that the French entered Florence, transiting Neptune went into a square to Dante's natal Mars. This rendered the poet and presumed political leader powerless and helpless.

If we move to the early days of 1302, when Dante's exile from Florence became formal, transiting Jupiter in Gemini moved toward an opposition to Dante's natal Pluto: it was his enemies and not him that benefited from Jupiter (Dante's natal Pluto is in his Seventh House of open enemies). Although transiting Pluto had moved away from Dante's Midheaven degree, there was a solar eclipse on January 29 at 17° Aquarius, two degrees from his Midheaven and this sealed the poet's fate: during this week that the leadership of Florence leveled trumped-up charges against the poet, resulting in his official exile, later in a sentence of death *in absentia* and the confiscation of his property.

The reader may note the coincidence between the strength of this chart to account for Dante's exile and the main theme of our larger enterprise. The chart could be replaced by reliable historical documentation of Dante's birth day and time and by a chart that could better account for other events in this man's notable life. Until a better one comes along, however, I stand by this one.

Notes

1. Durling M. and Martinez, R. (1990) p.84

Bibliography

Dante: Translations and Commentary

Ciardi, John *The Divine Comedy* (1954/1970) New York: New American Library

Durling, Robert and Martinez, Ronald, L. *Purgatorio* (2003) New York/London: Oxford University Press

_____ *Inferno* (1996) New York: Oxford University Press

_____ *Time and the Crystal: Studies in Dante Rime Petrose* (1990) Berkeley: University of California Press. Available online from http://www.escholarship.org/editions/view?docId=ft8s200961&brand=ucpress

Hollander, Robert and Jean *Paradiso* (2007) New York: Doubleday

_____ *The Inferno* (2000) New York: Anchor Books

Lancing, Richard *The Convivio, by Dante Alighieri* (2008) http://dante.ilt.columbia.edu/books/convivi/convivio.html

Longfellow, Henry Wadsworth *The Divine Comedy of Dante* (2007) Nu Visions Publications, www.nuvisionpublications.com

Merwin, M. S. *Purgatorio* (2000) New York: Alfred A Knopf

Musa, Mark *The Divine Comedy Vol. I: Inferno* (1986) New York: Penguin

_____ *The Divine Comedy Vol. III: Paradise* (1986) New York: Penguin

Pinsky, Robert *Inferno of Dante* (1994) New York: Farrar, Straus and Giroux

Rossetti, Dante Gabriel *The New Life* (2002) New York: New York Review of Books

Sinclair, John *Dante's Paradiso* (1961) New York: Oxford University Press

Singleton, Charles *Divine Comedy Paradiso II: Commentry* (1973) Princeton NJ: Princeton University Press

_____ *Divine Comedy Purgatorio II: Commentary* (1973) Princeton NJ: Princeton University Press

_____ *Divine Comedy Purgatorio I: Text* (1973) Princeton NJ: Princeton University Press

Primary Works: Other

Al-Kindi, *On the Stellar Rays* (1993) translated by Zoller, R. Berkeley Springs WV: Golden Hind Press

Aristotle, *A New Aristotle Reader* (1987) Ackrill, J. (ed.) Princeton NJ: Princeton University Press

Boethius, *The Consolation of Philosophy* (2008) translated by Slavitt, D. Cambridge MA: Harvard University Press

Bonatti, Guido, *Book of Astronomy* (2007) translated by Dykes, B. Golden Valley MN: Cazimi Press

Cicero, *The Nature of the Gods and On Divination* (1997) translated by Yonge, C. D. Amherst NY: Prometheus Books

Ficino, Marsilo *Three Books On Life* (1998) translated by Kaske, C. and Clark, J. Binghamton NY: Center for Medieval and Early Renaissance Studies

Ibn Ezra, Abraham *The Beginning of Wisdom* (1998) translated by Epstein, M. Reston VA: Arhat Publications

Lucan, *Civil War* (1992) translated by Braund, S.H. Oxford: Clarendon Press

Plotinus, *The Enneads* (1992) translated by MacKenna, S. Burdett NY: Larsen Publications

Ptolemy, *Tetrabiblos* (1994) translated by Robbins, F. E. Cambridge MA: Harvard University Press

Statius, *Thebiad* (1922) translated Calder, G. London: Cambridge University Press

Virgil, *The Aeneid* (2006) translated by Fagles, Robert. New York: Penguin Books

Internet on the *Commedia*

Catholic Encyclopedia (including Thomas of Aquinas, *Summa Theologica*), online edition copyright 2006 by Kevin Knight http://www.newadvent.org/cathen/

Dante Dartmouth Project – http://dante.dartmouth.edu/

The World of Dante – http://www.worldofdante.org/

Danteworlds – http://danteworlds.laits.utexas.edu/

Secondary and Modern Astrology

Auerbach, Erich *Dante: Poet of the Secular World* (2001) New York: New York Review of Books

Aveni, Anthony *Conversing with the Planets* (1992) New York: Random House

Boitani, Piero "The Sibyl's leaves: Reading *Paradiso*" *The Tragic and the Sublime in Medieval Literature* (1989) Cambridge, New York: Cambridge University Press, pp.143-180

Campion, Nicholas *A History of Modern Astrology Volume 2: The Medieval and Modern Worlds* (2009) London: Continuum Books

───── *The Dawn of Astrology* (2008) London: Continuum Books

Cantor, Norman *Civilization of the Middle Ages* (1994) New York NY: Harper Collins

Clements, Robert (ed) *American Critical Essays on* The Divine Comedy (1967) New York: New York University Press

Copelston, Frederick *A History of Philosophy Vol. II: The Medieval Era* (1993) New York: Image Books

Cornelius, Geoffrey *The Moment of Astrology* (2003 2nd edition) Bournemouth: Wessex Astrologer

Cornish, Alison *Reading Dante's Stars* (2000) New Haven: Yale University Press

Damiani, Anthony *Astronoesis* (2000) Burdett NY: Larsen Publications

Edinger, Edward *Anatomy of the Psyche* (1985) Peru IL: Open Court Publishing

Elwell, Dennis *Cosmic Loom: The New Science of Astrology* (1987) London: Unwin Hyman

Fergusson, Francis, *Dante* (1966) New York: Macmillan

Freccero, John *Dante: The Poetics of Conversion* (1986) Cambridge MA: Harvard University Press

Ganiban, Ronald T. *Statius and Virgil* (2007) New York: Cambridge University Press

Gilson, Simon *Medieval Optics and Theories of Light in the Works of Dante* (2000) Lewiston NY: Edward Mellen Press

Grandgent, C.H. *Dante* (1916) New York: Duffield and Company

Grant, Edward *The Foundations of Modern Science in the Middle Ages* (1996) Cambridge: Cambridge University Press.

Hawkin, Peter S. and Jacoff, Rachel (eds) *The Poets' Dante* (2001) New York: Farrar, Straus, and Giroux

Hyman, Arthur and Walsh J. (ed.) *Philosophy in the Middle Ages* (1977) Indianapolis IN: Hackett Publishing

Kay, Richard *Dante's Christian Astrology* (1994) Philadelphia: Pennsylvania University Press

Lewis, C. S. *The Discarded Image* (1964) London: Cambridge University Press

Lewis, R. W. B. *Dante* (2001) New York: Viking

Luke, Helen *Dark Wood to White Rose* (1989) New York: Parabola Books, MacMillan

Moore, Edward "Dante's Astronomy" *Studies in Dante: Third Series* (1903) Oxford: Clarendon Press

Tierney, Brian and Painter, Sidney *Western Europe in the Middle Ages, 300-1475* (1970) New York NY: Alfred A. Knopf

Patch, Howard *The Goddess Fortuna in Medieval Literature* (1927/1967) New York: Octagon Books

Pertile, Lino "*Paradiso*: A Drama of Desire" from Barnes, J and Petrie, J. (eds) *Word and Drama in Dante: Essays on the* Divina Commedia. (1993)

Reynolds, Barbara *Dante: The Poet the Political Thinker, The Man* (2006) London: Shoemaker and Hoard

Ross, David *Aristotle* (reprint 1964) London: Methuen

Rudhyar, Dane *An Astrological Tryptich* (1978) New York NY: Aurora Press

_____ *Astrological Signs: The Pulse of Life* (1978) Boulder CO: Shambhala Publications

_____ *The Astrology of Transformation* (1984) Wheaton IL: Theosophical Publishing House

_____ *The Galactic Dimension of Astrology* (1975) New York NY: Aurora Press

Singleton, Charles *Journey to Beatrice* (1967) Cambridge MA: Harvard University Press

_____ *Studies in Medieval and Renaissance Literature* (1966) London: Cambridge University Press

Tester, S. J. *History of Western Astrology* (1987) New York: Ballentine Books

Thorndike, Lynn *A History of Magic and Experimental Science Volume 2* (1929) New York: Macmillan

Zoller, Robert *The Lost Key to Prediction: The Arabic Parts in Astrology* (1980) New York: Inner Traditions

Articles

Bloomfield, M. "The Origin of the Concept of the Seven Deadly Sins" *The Harvard Theological Review*, Vol.34 no.2 (April 1941) pp.121-128

Getty, R.J. "The Astrology of Nigidius Figulus (Lucan I, 649-65)" *The Classical Quarterly* Vol.35 nos.1/2 (Jan-April 1941), pp.17-22

Greene, L. "Is Astrology a Divinatory System?" *Culture and Cosmos* Vol.12 no.1 (Spring/Summer) pp.3-33

Gross, K. "Infernal Metamorphoses; An Interpretation of Dante's Counterpass", *MLN* Vol.100 no.1 Italian issue (Jan. 1985) pp.42-69

Kay, Richard "Unwintering January" ("Paradiso" 27.142-143) *MLN* Vol.118 no.1 Italian issue (Jan. 2003) pp.237-244

Kieckhefer, R. "The Specific Rationality of Medieval Magic" *The American Historical Review* Vol.99 no.3 (June 1994) pp.813-836

Sweeney, L. "*Idealis* in the Terminology of Thomas Aquinas" *Speculum* Vol 33 no.4 (Oct. 1958) pp.497-507

Toomer, G.J. "Prophatius Judaeus and the Toledan Tables" *Isis* Vol.64 no.3 (Sept. 1971) pp.351-355

Index of Proper Names

A

Adam *xxivn*, 12, 71, 89, 105, 106, 115, 133, 138, 167, 228, 233
Adrian V, Pope 61
Alberigo, Fra 18, 189n
Albertus Magnus 113, 198, 199, 214, 227n, 234
Amphiaraus 176, 202
Argenti, Fillipo 15-16
Aristotle *x, xxv*, 19, 90-91, 147, 159, 182, 208, 212, 213, 220-221, 229-230, 240-241, 242, 243n, 246, 251, 252n
Arnaut, Daniel 31, 68
Arruns 177-178
Asclepius 197
Asdente 183
Atlas, Charles 51
Augustine of Hippo *xiii*, 155, 227n, 230, 233
Avicenna 230, 233

B

Belacqua 31, 33, 38, 39, 57, 84
Benedict 128-129, 155
Bernard of Clarivaux 100, 129, 154-158
Bocca delgi Abati 17-18
Boethius 19-21, 23-24, 113, 255
Boitani 179n
Bonagiunta of Lucca 64, 68, 191
Bonatti, Guido *xiii, xvi*, 23, 102, 108-109, 112, 122, 182-183, 186, 201, 204, 246n
Bonaventure 35, 113, 115, 233
Boniface VIII, Pope 17, 61, 138, 153, 205, 272-273
Boorstin, Daniel 117
Borgese, Giuseppe 15n
Buonconte da Montefeltro 32, 39-40, 198n

C

Cacciaguida 89, 99, 119-121, 124, 128, 163, 193-195, 209, 228, 242, 254, 266, 274
Calchus 180, 181, 184
Calvacanti, Guido 16, 109, 204
Campion, Nicholas 200
Capet, Hugh 61
Cappocio 206, 206n
Carroll, John 107, 127n
Casella 31
Cato 29, 31, 33
Charles I of Anjou 61
Charles II of Anjou 107
Charles of Valois 61
Charon 3
Chaucer, Geoffrey 206
Ciacco 189
Ciardi, John 98, 259, 260, 262, 263
Cicero 96, 185-186
Clement V, Pope 153
Congrande della Scalla 192
Conradin 61
Constance 102, 104, 105n
Cornelius, Geoffrey 186, 207n, 247-248
Cornish, Alison *xi*, 43n, 94n, 146n

D

Damiani, Anthony 235-236
Damian, Peter 127-128
Diomedes 103, 202
Dionysus (Pseudo-) the Areopagate 146, 230, 234
Dominic 12, 35-36, 113-115, 129, 145, 167, 228
Donati, Corso 102, 191
Donati, Forese 31, 64, 64n, 101, 191
Dostoyevsky, Fyodor 224
Duns Scotus 233-235

Index   283

Durling, Robert xi, 28, 38, 57, 79-80n, 88, 92, 95, 161, 164, 175, 226, 227n, 258, 263, 264, 267-269, 269n, 275n

E
Elwell, Dennis 237-238, 249-251, 252-253
Epictetus 21
Euryplyus 179-180, 202
Ezra, Ibn 7, 9
Ezzelino da Romana 109, 182

F
Farinata 7, 16, 26, 109, 189
Ficino, Marsilio 200
Figulus 178, 181, 186
Fillipo Argenti 15-16
Folquet of Marseilles (Folco di Marsiglia) 109
Francesca di Rimini (and Paulo) 13, 14-15, 103, 106
Francis of Assisi 12, 35-36, 113-115, 129, 145, 155, 167, 205, 228, 233
Frankfurt, Harry 181n
Freccero, John xi, xxivn, xxvin, 43n 164-165
Frederick II 31, 102, 105n, 182
Freud, Sigmund 222, 236

G
Geryon 8, 174
Grandgent, Charles 141
Grant, Edward 240n
Grasse, Ray 238
Greene, Liz xv, xxvin, 185, 236
Gregory, Pope (the Great) 125
Gregory, Pope VIII 79, 128
Griffolino 206, 206n
Guido da Montefeltro 182n, 201, 204-204
Guido del Duca 12
Guinizelli, Guido 31, 64, 68

H
Henry VII of Luxemburg 153
Hippocrates 197

Hollander, Robert and Jean xi, xxvin, 19n, 39, 78, 100, 103, 107, 116, 127n, 141, 158, 161, 163, 259, 260, 264
Homer 14, 188, 204

J
James, apostle 133, 134, 135, 136
Joachim of Fiore 115, 116
John, apostle 133, 134, 135, 137-138, 152
Joyce, James 204
Jung, Carl 46n, 236
Justinian 98, 105, 105n, 111

K
Kant, Immanuel 224
Kay, Richard xi, 141
Kieckefer, Robert 197

L
Latini, Brunetto 13, 16-17, 17n, 22, 64n, 171-172, 189-190, 255, 265, 272
Leah 70, 78
Lilly, William 186
Longfellow, H.W. 40-41, 258, 259, 260, 262, 263
Lucan 177-178, 184, 186, 188
Lucifer 4, 10-11, 18-19, 26, 30, 32, 70, 99, 148, 150n, 198, 198n,
Luke, Helen 46

M
Macrobius 93, 96, 97
Manfred 31-32, 33, 37, 40
Manto 178-178
Marco the Lombard 54-55, 108, 120, 208-210, 213, 216, 240, 245
Martel, Charles 107-109, 208, 215-216, 221
Martinez, Ronald xi, xii, 267-269, 269n
Mary 98, 133-135, 145, 154-155, 156, 157-158

Matelda 71, 78-80, 106
Merton, Thomas 32n
Merwin, M.S. 41, 80, 173, 258, 259, 260, 264
Mill, John Stuart 222
Moore, Edward xi, xxvin, 43n
Musa, Mark 14, 15, 78, 85, 140-141, 258, 259, 260, 262-263, 264

N
Nicholas, Pope III 17, 61
Nino, Judge 31
Nohrnberg, James 8

O
Oderisi 48, 190-191
Ovid 66, 139, 159, 177

P
Pertile, Lino 162n
Peter, apostle 133, 134, 135, 136, 137-139
Phillip IV of France 61
Phlegyas 6, 15
Piccarda 98, 101-105, 105n, 155, 163
Pier della Vigne 13, 19n
Pinsky, Robert 264
Plato (and author of the *Timeaus*) 19, 57 97, 97n, 110, 122, 147, 164, 167, 219, 220, 229-230, 231, 236, 246
Plotinus 230-231, 233, 235, 253,
Ptolemy, Claudius xxii, 5-6, 107, 219, 245

R
Rachel 70, 78
Rahab 109
Reynolds, Barbara 149
Richard of St. Victor 127n
Ripheus 125
Romeo 19n, 105
Rudhyar, Dane xiv, xxvin, 36-37, 130, 235, 248
Ruggieri, Archbishop 18, 103

S
Sapia 49
Sayers, Dorothy 263
Schicchi, Gianni 206n
Schnapp, Jeffrey 42
Scot, Michael xiii, xvi, 182, 183
Servius 82
Shantideva 51n
Shelley, Percy 258
Siger of Brabant 113, 115
Sinclair, John 111, 263, 264
Singleton, Charles viii, xi, 76, 78, 136, 258, 260, 263, 264
Sinon 180
Solomon 115-116
Sordello 31, 39, 40, 41, 261
Spinoza, Baruch 222
Statius 31, 61-63, 66, 66n, 68, 69, 71, 176, 177, 179, 188, 208, 213-215, 251

T
Tarnas, Richard 239
Teilhard de Chardin 252
Tennyson, Alfred Lord 204
Thomas of Aquinas (character in *Paradiso*) 35, 113, 114, 115, 145, 228
Thomas of Aquinas (medieval philosopher) 61, 167, 198, 199, 212, 214, 217, 218-220, 224, 227n, 233, 234, 240 245
Thorndike, Lynn 197, 201
Tiresias 176-177, 179, 184, 188, 202
Trajan 48, 125, 125n

U
Ugolino 18, 19n, 31, 155, 202
Ulysses 13, 103, 139-140, 173, 188, 189n, 193, 202-204

V
Vanni Fucci 190

Virgil (poet of *The Aeneid*) *xviii-xix,*
xxi, xxv-xxvi, 21, 73, 82, 91, 106,
119, 125, 134, 145, 150n, 158, 187,
189n, 194

W
Wilbur, Ken 238
Wilde, Oscar 109
William of Ockham 224

Y
Yeats, W.B. *vi*

References to Specific Cantos

Inferno 1   xxii-xxiii, 191-192
Inferno 3   3, 4, 91
Inferno 4   4, 14, 240
Inferno 5   14-15, 67, 106, 107, 260
Inferno 6   189
Inferno 7   22-24, 25, 53, 120
Inferno 8   15
Inferno 9   144, 188n
Inferno 10   7, 26, 189
Inferno 11   25, 240
Inferno 12   7, 182
Inferno 13   49n
Inferno 14   11-12
Inferno 15   xvii, 16-17, 22, 64n, 171-172, 188-189, 265
Inferno 16   xvii, xxiv
Inferno 17   174
Inferno 18   8, 67
Inferno 19   17, 153
Inferno 20   ix, xxi, 10, 12, 13,25, 58, 108, 171, 174-183, 193, 195, 198, 199, 202, 207, 225
Inferno 24   111, 190
Inferno 26   10, 35, 173, 189n, 202-203
Inferno 27   182, 198n, 202, 204-205
Inferno 29   25, 206-207
Inferno 30   207
Inferno 31   150n
Inferno 32   10, 17-18
Inferno 33   18, 155, 198n
Inferno 34   18-19, 26

Purgatorio 1   xxi, 28-29, 42, 107, 151, 257-261
Purgatorio 2   31, 33, 34-35, 139n, 145
Purgatorio 3   31, 33, 37, 38, 39
Purgatorio 4   31, 32, 33, 37-38, 84
Purgatorio 5   24, 32, 39, 198n
Purgatorio 8   31, 40-42, 96, 190-191, 260, 261-263
Purgatorio 9   xxii, 42-45, 57, 75, 267n
Purgatorio 10   7, 45-47, 191
Purgatorio 11   48, 190
Purgatorio 13   48, 49-50
Purgatorio 14   12, 49-50
Purgatorio 15   25, 51-54
Purgatorio 16   54-55, 108, 120, 208-210, 245
Purgatorio 17   47, 55, 210-211
Purgatorio 18   55, 56-57
Purgatorio 19   57-61, 127n
Purgatorio 20   61
Purgatorio 21   62
Purgatorio 22   62-63, 179
Purgatorio 24   64, 191
Purgatorio 25   65-66, 213-215, 242, 243, 251
Purgatorio 26   xvii, 67-68
Purgatorio 27   35, 68-70, 106, 145
Purgatorio 29   42, 71-73
Purgatorio 30   73-74, 150, 173
Purgatorio 31   74-76
Purgatorio 32   77
Purgatorio 33   78-80, 92, 192-193

Paradiso 1   90-96, 136, 224, 227-228, 233, 251
Paradiso 2   100-101, 147, 224-227, 233, 242, 251
Paradiso 3   101-103, 155, 163
Paradiso 4   97, 104, 162
Paradiso 5   104
Paradiso 6   xvii, 19n, 105, 111
Paradiso 7   xvii, 105
Paradiso 8   79, 106-108, 215-217, 260, 264
Paradiso 9   109-110, 145
Paradiso 10   7, 12, 94, 110-113, 116, 135, 163, 164
Paradiso 11   12, 36, 113-114, 145, 228
Paradiso 12   36, 113, 114-115, 228
Paradiso 13   115, 151, 167, 224, 228
Paradiso 14   12, 115-116, 118
Paradiso 15   119, 162-163
Paradiso 16   119, 120, 245, 266
Paradiso 17   121, 193-195, 210-211, 242

Paradiso 18   121, 123, 211-213, 254
Paradiso 19   124-125
Paradiso 20   125
Paradiso 21   126-128, 164
Paradiso 22   xix, 128-132, 174, 266
Paradiso 23   133-135
Paradiso 24   135, 163, 164
Paradiso 25   136
Paradiso 26   137-138
Paradiso 27   131-132, 138-141, 193
Paradiso 28   90, 141-147, 164, 166
Paradiso 29   94, 146-149, 156, 166, 181, 232, 241
Paradiso 30   12, 115, 150-153
Paradiso 31   154-155
Paradiso 32   155-157
Paradiso 33   xv, 136, 157-168

Also by The Wessex Astrologer - www.wessexastrologer.com

Patterns of the Past
Karmic Connections
Good Vibrations
The Soulmate Myth: A Dream Come True or Your Worst Nightmare?
The Book of Why
Judy Hall

The Essentials of Vedic Astrology
Lunar Nodes - Crisis and Redemption
Personal Panchanga and the Five Sources of Light
Komilla Sutton

Astrolocality Astrology
From Here to There
Martin Davis

The Consultation Chart
Introduction to Medical Astrology
Wanda Sellar

The Betz Placidus Table of Houses
Martha Betz

Astrology and Meditation
Greg Bogart

The Book of World Horoscopes
Nicholas Campion

Life After Grief : An Astrological Guide to Dealing with Loss
AstroGraphology: The Hidden Link between your Horoscope and your Handwriting
Darrelyn Gunzburg

The Houses: Temples of the Sky
Deborah Houlding

Through the Looking Glass
The Magic Thread
Richard Idemon

Temperament: Astrology's Forgotten Key
Dorian Geiseler Greenbaum

Nativity of the Late King Charles
John Gadbury

Declination - The Steps of the Sun
Luna - The Book of the Moon
Paul F. Newman

Tapestry of Planetary Phases:
Weaving the Threads of Purpose and Meaning in Your Life
Christina Rose

Astrology, A Place in Chaos
Star and Planet Combinations
Bernadette Brady

Astrology and the Causes of War
Jamie Macphail

Flirting with the Zodiac
Kim Farnell

The Gods of Change
Howard Sasportas

Astrological Roots: The Hellenistic Legacy
Joseph Crane

The Art of Forecasting using Solar Returns
Anthony Louis

Horary Astrology Re-Examined
Barbara Dunn

Living Lilith
M. Kelley Hunter

The Spirit of Numbers: A New Exploration of Harmonic Astrology
David Hamblin

Primary Directions
Martin Gansten

Classical Medical Astrology
Oscar Hofman

The Door Unlocked: An Astrological Insight into Initiation
*Dolores Ashcroft Nowicki and
Stephanie V. Norris*

Understanding Karmic Complexes
Patricia L. Walsh

Pluto Volumes 1 & 2
Jeff Green

Essays on Evolutionary Astrology
Jeff Green Edited by Deva Green

Planetary Strength
Bob Makransky

All the Sun Goes Round
Reina James

The Moment of Astrology
Geoffrey Cornelius

www.ingramcontent.com/pod-product-compliance
Lightning Source LLC
Chambersburg PA
CBHW051110230426
43667CB00014B/2512